# Growing Penstemons:

## Species, Cultivars, and Hybrids

**American Penstemon Society**

**Compiled by Dale Lindgren and Ellen Wilde**

Botanical Drawing by Rhonda Nass
Diagrams by Ellen Wilde

**ISBN 0-7414-1529-1**

**Published by:**

PUBLISHING.COM

**519 West Lancaster Avenue**
**Haverford, PA 19041-1413**
**Info@buybooksontheweb.com**
**www.buybooksontheweb.com**
**Toll-free (877) BUY BOOK**
**Local Phone (610) 520-2500**
**Fax (610) 519-0261**

*Printed in the United States of America*

*Printed on Recycled Paper*

*Published June 2003*

## Picture Credits

Front cover from upper right, clockwise:
1. *Penstemon triflorus*, Tucson Botanical Garden, Tucson AZ, by Al Guhl
2. *Penstemon secundiflorus*, garden, Pojoaque, NM by Barbara Weintraub
3. Large - flowered Penstemon Hybrid Seed Mix, garden, Schoneiche, Germany, by T. Unsner
4. *Penstemon cobaea*, National Wildflower Research Center, Austin TX, by Ellen Wilde
5. *Penstemon arenicola*, garden, Pojoaque, NM by Barbara Weintraub
6. *Penstemon jamesii*, garden, Santa Fe, NM by Ellen Wilde
7. *Penstemon baccharifolius*, garden, Tucson AZ, by Al Guhl
8. *Penstemon albertinus*, Gibbonsville, ID, by Dr. Dee Strickler
9. *Penstemon digitalis* cv. 'Husker Red' garden, Schoneiche, Germany, by Thea Unsner
10. *Penstemon ovatus*, garden, Santa Fe, NM by Ellen Wilde
11. *Penstemon rupicola*, Larch Mt., OR, by Dr. Dee Strickler
12. *Penstemon ellipticus*, Glacier National Park, MT, by Dr. Dee Strickler

Back cover from left to right
1. *Penstemon petiolatus,* High Country Gardens Nursery, Santa Fe, NM by Ellen Wilde
2. *Penstemon smallii*, Blowing Rock, NC by Julia Way
3. *Penstemon tubaeflorus*, Caney, KS, by Ralph Bennett
4. *Penstemon cardwellii* cv. 'Roseus', garden, Lakewood, CO by Ann Bartlett
5. *Penstemon heterophyllus* cv.'Catherine de la Mare', garden, England by Dr. Dale Lindgren
6. *Penstemon rydbergii*, Cedar Breaks National Monument, UT by Ellen Wilde
7. *Penstemon palmeri*, Albuquerque Botanical Garden, Albuquerque, NM by Ellen Wilde
8. *Penstemon teucrioides*, High Country Gardens Nursery, Santa Fe, NM by Ellen Wilde
9. *Penstemon strictus*, Agua Fria Nursery, Santa Fe, NM by Ellen Wilde
10. *Penstemon venustus*, eastern WA by Ellen Wilde
11. *Penstemon nitidus*, garden, Santa Fe, NM by Ellen Wilde
12. *Penstemon grandiflorus* cv.'Prairie Snow', North Platte, NE by Dr. Dale Lindgren
13. Penstemon x 'Breitenbush Blue', garden, Lakewood, CO by Ann Bartlett
14. *Penstemon clutei*, Sunset Crater National Monument, AZ by Ellen Wilde
15. *Penstemon linarioides*, garden, Santa Fe, NM by Ellen Wilde
16. *Penstemon glandulosus*, garden, Santa Fe, NM by Ellen Wilde
17. Penstemon x 'Wine Kissed', garden, OR, by Christine Ebrahimi
18. *Penstemon barbatus* cv. 'Schooley's Yellow', North Platte, NE by Dr. Dale Lindgren
19. Penstemon x 'Ruby Glow', garden, England, Jean Witt

### The Authors

Dr. Dale Lindgren is Professor of Horticulture at the University of Nebraska West Central Research and Extension Center at North Platte, Nebraska. His work includes the selection, development and release of native plants for ornamental use. He has released several named selections of penstemons. He has served the American Penstemon Society as president and is currently editor of its Bulletin.

Ellen Wilde has gardened for more than 60 years and is a native plant enthusiast. She considers all penstemon species native! She is a past director of the seed exchange and currently custodian of the APS library and slide collection.

# Dedication and Acknowledgements

This book is dedicated to Robin and Kenneth Lodewick, longtime members of the American Penstemon Society, who have devoted countless hours for many years to researching and publishing information about penstemons. They have been unfailingly generous in sharing the results of their efforts.

It is also dedicated to all the botanists and field workers who have collected data for many herbaria and published it in local, state and regional floras.

Over the more than 50 years of the existence of the American Penstemon Society, many members have contributed notes to the <u>Bulletins</u> of the Society on their experiences in growing and propagating penstemons, and much other information that would help gardeners enjoy them. We are grateful for all their notes.

We would particularly like to thank the following members and others who have encouraged, read, criticized, added to our information and proofed some chapters of this publication over the last few years. It is better for all your contributions!

Robin and Kenneth Lodewick, Dr. Noel Holmgren, Dr. Roger Peterson, Donald Humphrey, James Swayne, Louise Parsons, Virginia Maffitt, Robert McFarlane, Laurin Wheeler, Thea Unsner, Jack Ferreri, Ann Bartlett, Dr. Dee Strickler, Polly and Mike Stone, Michael Evans, Christine Ebrahimi, Jean and Bill Heflin, Peter James, David Way, Robert Nold, Gail Haggard, Sally Walker, Dr. Andrea Wolfe, Jeni and Bob Pennington and Ron Ratko.

Special thanks for computer help to Dale Wilde from his wife, Ellen

What would a book on flowers be without photographs?! We are most grateful to all those who have contributed pictures for the book. The names of those used on the covers are on the previous page. Since we sought an inexpensive way to get this material out to a wide audience, we were unable to use in it all the colored pictures we would have liked. **However, APS member William Gray has volunteered his services to prepare a Computer Disc of over 500 penstemon photographs that will be available from the Society later in 2003.** This is a service of inestimable value that everyone will benefit from and appreciate! We thank him from the bottom of our hearts!

There is a huge amount of information about penstemons to be found in many sources. This book is an attempt to bring together that which will be most helpful to beginners interested in growing penstemons. Changes may occur in classification and as more penstemons are available to gardeners, there will be better information on germination times and methods and on the range over which they can be grown. Errors may also be found in this publication. We look at this as a work-in-progress and hope our audience will respond with additions and corrections that can be incorporated into future editions. Please send your comments to and request information about the picture CD from Ellen Wilde <ellenw@ swcp.com>. Profits from the sale of this book will go to the APS and the library of the Santa Fe Botanical Garden which will house the library and slide collection.

# Contents

**Picture and Author Credits**

**Dedication and Acknowledgments**

# Chapter 1

## An Introduction:

## Background and History of Penstemons and the American Penstemon Society

Because you picked up this book, you probably know and have grown a few penstemons and appreciated their beautiful colors, drought tolerance and disease resistance. You may know that there are quite a few, but have no idea of the amazing variety of colors, shapes and sizes that are available for you to grow. There are penstemons for almost every type of climate and garden. This guide will introduce them to you.

Penstemon plants may be anything from low-growing mats to small bushes or tall spires. Penstemon flowers may look quite different from each other but all are tubes that widen before dividing into two lips that have two lobes on the upper lip and three on the lower lip. To distinguish them from other tubular flowers, look into the tube. If there are four fertile stamens with anthers and one stamen without anthers, called a staminode ("Beardtongue"), the flower is probably a penstemon. (There are four closely related genera that were previously included in the genus but were reclassified after additional study as *Keckiella, Chionophila, Nothochelone* and *Pennellianthus*).

Their bewildering names and the great number of penstemons have made it difficult to choose the ones best for a particular gardening situation. Members of the American Penstemon Society have been growing them and collecting information about them from many sources for over fifty years. The more they have learned, the more enthusiastic they have become. We have tried to present this information in an easily readable form. We hope you too will become addicted and want to try many more species, cultivars and hybrids.

Many different species in the genus *Penstemon* occur in the wild in each of the states of the US (except Hawaii) and in Canada, Mexico and Guatemala. The ones occurring naturally in each state and province are listed in Appendix 2. Penstemons have been in cultivation in many other countries. Cultivars have been selected and propagated and hybrids created in North America, New Zealand, Great Britain and Europe and are very popular. These as well as the natural species are described and growing information provided.

**Species** are the variations of the genus. Each has been written up in a recognized botanical journal, and named and described in Latin for universality. A "type specimen," deposited in a recognized herbarium, serves to establish its characteristics. Names of species or their status as species or variety or subspecies may change as specialists learn more about them. The name of a species consists of the capitalized and italicized genus name (*Penstemon*) and the uncapitalized, italicized specific epithet *(secundiflorus)*. The species name may be descriptive of the plant or the location where it was first found, or the name of a person the taxonomist wanted to honor, in a Latin form *(jamesii)*. Variety or subspecies may be added, also in Latin and italics.

**Cultivars** (cultivated varieties) are forms of species that are outstanding for color, size or performance. Hybrids are also cultivars but will be treated in this guide as a separate category. Cultivars should be reproduced by cuttings or divisions to maintain the characteristics for which they have been selected. Cultivar names are usually the genus and specific epithet in italics followed by the chosen capitalized name enclosed in single quotation marks and not in italics.

Sometimes only the genus and cultivar names are used, with or without the abbreviation cv. (*Penstemon cardwellii* cv. 'John Bacher' or Penstemon cv. 'John Bacher' or Penstemon 'John Bacher').

**Hybrids** are created by pollinating one species with the pollen of another species to produce seeds from which will grow new plants that have characteristics of both parents. Sometimes hybrids are the result of a single pollination or they may be the result of many generations of crosses. Most successful hybrids are the result of a series of crosses. They are propagated by cuttings and division or they may be developed through seed selection into strains that maintain the desired characteristics but have some variation. Anyone can create a hybrid. A later chapter will tell you the mechanics. It is fun and rewarding for anyone with patience! Many come from the gardens of home gardeners, although the majority of those that are widely distributed have been produced by seed companies, nurseries and university agricultural research centers. Names of hybrids are usually the capitalized genus name, followed by a times sign (x), read as "hybrid", and the assigned name which is capitalized, not italicized and enclosed in single quotation marks (Penstemon x 'Elfin Pink').

## Pronunciation

Botanical names are one of the big problems in popularizing wildflower species, but they are necessary for proper identification. The following observations from William T. Stearn's *Botanical Latin* apply:

"Pronunciation varies strikingly among professional botanists."

"Individual botanists rarely use any rule of pronunciation consistently."

Botanical names are commonly pronounced as if they were English words but differences do occur. Most people will pronounce names as they have heard mentors pronounce them and no one can say another's pronunciation is wrong. Just as some say "to-may-to", others say "to-mah-to", and neither is wrong. Usually every vowel is pronounced. Very long names have a secondary accent (*pseud'-o-spec-ta'-bi-lis*). Species names that are derived from a person's name should be accented where it would be in the name, such as the first syllable in "*eatonii*". For most people it is easier to use the possessive form of the person's name and many people do (Eaton's Penstemon).

## History

The first scientific description of a penstemon was made by Dr. John Mitchell of Virginia in the American Colonies in 1748. He named the genus *Penstemon*. The name is believed derived from the Latin words "*paene*" meaning "almost" and "*stemon*" referring to the threadlike sterile stamen of the flower.

At that time, plants were most important as sources for medical treatments. Physicians studied botany and were constantly on the lookout for new plants. Over the next century many penstemon species were identified, frequently by physicians on surveying expeditions of this new land. Sixty-three species of penstemons had been identified and named in the United States and Mexico by 1850.

In the early nineteenth century, several penstemon species collected in Mexico were sent to Europe, where the first European hybrids were developed. Cross-breeding produced many beautiful varieties with larger bells and unusual markings. New varieties are registered every year. These large-flowered hybrids are popular in mild climates but have not been widely grown in the more severe climates of North America because they do not survive outdoors and must be wintered over in a greenhouse.

In the early twentieth century, penstemons were still relatively unknown to most gardeners in the United States although the number of species described by professional botanists had grown to over 150. Botanists were beginning to work on classifying them. Seed and plant catalogues were listing a few penstemons. Western-American gardeners were trying to learn to grow penstemon species because so many of the cultivated flowers which had come from more benevolent climates would not stand up to the harsh climate, poor soil and limited water available in the western states.

"Round Robins", or correspondence circles, for gardeners became popular in the 1930s and 1940s in the United States, especially among people on isolated farms. Myrtle Hebert of Denton, Montana, participated in several robins and wrote about the wildflowers that she succeeded in growing. Penstemons were among her favorites. Flower Grower Magazine offered to match people with special gardening interests who would write to them. An avid gardener in a suburb of Washington D.C., who was attracted to penstemons but had no luck in growing them, sought the names of others interested in corresponding about penstemons and received several, including Mrs. Hebert. After a few rounds of letters, this gardener, Ralph Bennett, suggested that a society be formed to publish articles containing information from the letters on growing penstemons, and to facilitate a wider distribution of penstemon seeds from all across the country. Thus, the American Penstemon Society (APS) was formed in December 1945. Members were required to grow penstemons and report to the corresponding secretary twice yearly on their progress. Mrs. Hebert's personal interest in each member, warmth and cheery personality made the American Penstemon Society a very popular organization. Publicity on a daily radio program about gardening subjects that was broadcast from Shenandoah, Iowa and sponsored by Henry Field Seed Company, brought many new mid-western members. Articles about the Society in the magazines Flower Grower and Horticulture and the Bulletin of the American Rock Garden Society brought in enthusiastic and hard working members from other parts of the country and so the Society grew. The Bulletin of the American Penstemon Society was produced on a mimeograph machine, assembled by hand and mailed to ninety members by the second issue in May 1946.

Dr. Francis Pennell, curator of botany at the Academy of Natural Sciences of Philadelphia, maintained the best herbarium collection of pressed penstemon specimens anywhere at that time and was the author of "The Scrophulariaceae of Eastern Temperate North America" and other publications describing penstemons among other native plants. He was very helpful to the new society in verifying the identities of the species they had been growing. These numbered about 100 by the beginning of 1947.

Glenn Viehmeyer, principle hybridizer at the North Platte Experiment Station in Nebraska, his interest piqued by a gift of penstemon seeds from a member of the society in the early 1950's, was one of the first to create North American hybrids from penstemon species.

Ralph Bennett was a court reporter and had no botanical training before the Society was formed, but he became a dedicated student of penstemons. He served as the first president of the Society and read everything published about penstemons. He wrote many papers on the species and summarized reports from robin letters for the Bulletin of the American Penstemon Society.

In the 1950's, with help from Dr. David Keck at the New York Botanical Garden and later from Dr. Richard M. Straw of Los Angeles State College, he wrote technical booklets on several subdivisions of the genus and a Manual for Beginners with Penstemons. In 1960 he published Penstemon Nomenclature, a summary of all the names ever given to penstemon species, that clarified much of the confusion over species names. It was distributed with the APS bulletin of that year. He also started the APS slide collection and the library.

The Society continued to grow and in 1979 the mimeographed 8 ½ by 11 inch Bulletin became a 5 ½ by 8 ½ printed volume, which was much easier on those who had done the mimeographing, compilation and mailing of the larger Bulletin, and also on the postage account. Soon thereafter colored photographs replaced drawings for the covers.

Many changes in penstemon species names were made during the last third of the 20th century, as well as discoveries of new species. A few species were moved to other genera. A new and expanded Penstemon Nomenclature, based on Bennett's work, was compiled by Ken and Robin Lodewick in 1988. They have also published Field Identifiers and Keys to the many species of penstemons. A new Key to the Genus Penstemon became available in 1999 and their new edition of Penstemon Nomenclature became available in 2002 to bring them up to date for the 21st century. This guide is based on their work, except that some species names which not all authorities recognize have been added to help the gardener who comes across them on seed lists.

Material used here is from articles published in the Bulletin of the American Penstemon Society and information from many other books and articles, regional floras, seed catalogues and members' experience in growing penstemons. There is still much to be learned about this fascinating and variable genus and it is hoped that this book will stimulate additional research and reporting about penstemons by gardeners as well as the wider use of these wonderful plants.

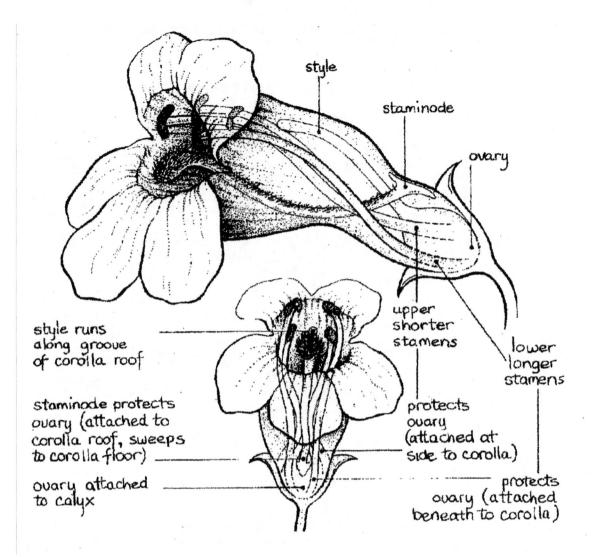

style

staminode

ovary

style runs
along groove
of corolla roof

staminode protects
ovary (attached to
corolla roof, sweeps
to corolla floor)

ovary attached
to calyx

upper
shorter
stamens

lower
longer
stamens

protects
ovary
(attached at
side to corolla)

protects
ovary (attached
beneath to corolla)

Enlargements of anthers after opening:

anthers parallel,
opening from distal
end

anthers diverging,
opening from distal end
with S-shaped twist

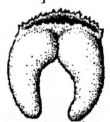

anthers parallel,
sac-like, opening across
top; toothed opening

anthers opposite,
opening along one side,
forming pockets; may or may
not open across connection

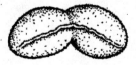

anthers opposite,
opening flat (explanate)

# Chapter 2

## The Descriptions of Penstemon Species and their Cultivars

Penstemon is one of the two or three largest genera of North American wildflowers. Botanically, penstemons are in the Scrophulariaceae or Figwort family, along with snapdragon, foxglove, paintbrush, veronica, monkey flower, lousewort, owl-clover, and other less well-known wildflowers.

Penstemons can be found from alpine areas to low desert. Some are dryland species; others occur in mountain meadows, rocky cliffs, gravelly roadsides and woodlands. They grow in sand, gravel, ash, oil shale, gumbo clay, alkaline soils, and acidic soils. Some are easy to grow and some quite challenging. Many of them are adaptable to a great variety of growing conditions and will be hardy over a wide climate range. **Only a few tolerate only very specific growing conditions, but are untried in a variety of different conditions and may prove to be more tolerant than expected. Experimentation is needed.**

Some penstemons are herbaceous but most form a woody base to maintain themselves in dry conditions and have basal leaves that are persistent. They can form sub-shrubs or shrubs but never become trees. They are generally considered perennials, some being short lived, almost biennial, but most live many years if given appropriate conditions.

Penstemon species have been named by many people over the years and botanists have tried to bring some order to their separation and classification, but it should be remembered by gardeners that species are extremely variable and are still evolving, so that one species may have many variants, some that have been named and some not. Natural evolution results over eons as species experience different conditions. It should not be expected that the plants within a species renewing themselves by seed always look exactly alike. Think of the variation within the species *Homo sapiens!*

## The Flower

The penstemon flower consists of five **sepals,** which together make up the **calyx,** and the **corolla** which is primarily tubular and more or less flared outward to form the throat that then divides into two lips, the upper one with two lobes and the lower one with three lobes. Sometimes the division into two lips (**bilabiate**) is very noticeable and at other times barely discernible (**regular**). The flower may have **glandular hairs** (a hair with a minute bead of clear liquid at its apex) and/or (non-glandular) hairs. Two pairs of **stamens,** each with two pollen-filled **anther cells** may or may not be exserted beyond the throat. Anthers should be observed **after they open** to record their characteristics, which are very useful in identifying and classifying the species. Common shapes after opening are shown in the diagram on page 7. The point where the anther cells join is called the **connective.** The line where the anther cells split open is called the **suture.** It may or may not have fine hairs or teeth along it and may or may not cross the connective. The **staminode,** a stamen without anthers, can be smooth (**glabrous**) or bearded. Sometimes staminodes are broadened at the tip (**dilated**) and sometimes **recurved** or **notched**. Staminode characteristics are also useful in identification. Other features of the flower to be noted are the presence or absence of hair on the lower lip, presence or absence of guidelines from the lobes into the throat and whether the anthers and staminode are **exserted**

# Flower Shapes

Lobes
extended
forward,
bilabiate

Lobes
extended
vertically,
bilabiate

Regular
not
bilabiate

Lobes
flared,
bilabiate

Lobes
reflexed,
bilabiate

Shark's head shape

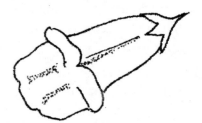
Campanulate with keel on upper lip,
ridges on lower lip

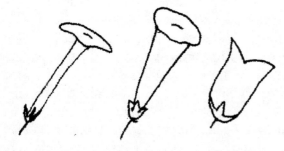
Salverform        Funnelform        Campanulate

Ampliate

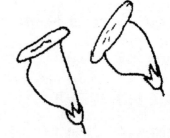
Ventricose        Ventricose-
ampliate

(extend beyond the throat) or **included** (remain within the throat), or just reach the opening of the throat. Most anthers are included and this will generally not be mentioned unless they are otherwise. The **ovary**, **style** and **stigma** make up the **pistil** which is usually not visible until the corolla disappears or is removed. The **style** lies along the roof of the corolla. Use of a small magnifier or 10 power lens to observe these details will increase your knowledge and pleasure in becoming acquainted with all flowers!

## Flower Shapes

Some species have a ridge or "**keel**" the length of the upper, or dorsal side of the throat. Some have ridges on the lower, or ventral side. The throat may enlarge gradually or abruptly. Those that expand somewhat abruptly on both sides are called **ampliate** or **inflated** and those that are greatly expanded on the lower side are described as **ventricose**. A few are both (**ventricose-ampliate**). Some remain tubular with very slight expansion. Those that remain a tube until the lobes abruptly flatten out are called **salverform**. Those that expand evenly from the base of the flower are called **funnel-form** and those that are bell-shaped are called **campanulate**. The lobes may **flare** in all directions, **extend forward**, **extend up and down vertically** or be **reflexed**. Flowers that have extended upper lobes and reflexed lower lobes are often described as a **shark's head**. A few have a palate on the lower lip that extends upward to close the throat. You will find many flowers that are "in-between" and don't exactly fit any of these types!

# Leaf Shapes and Types

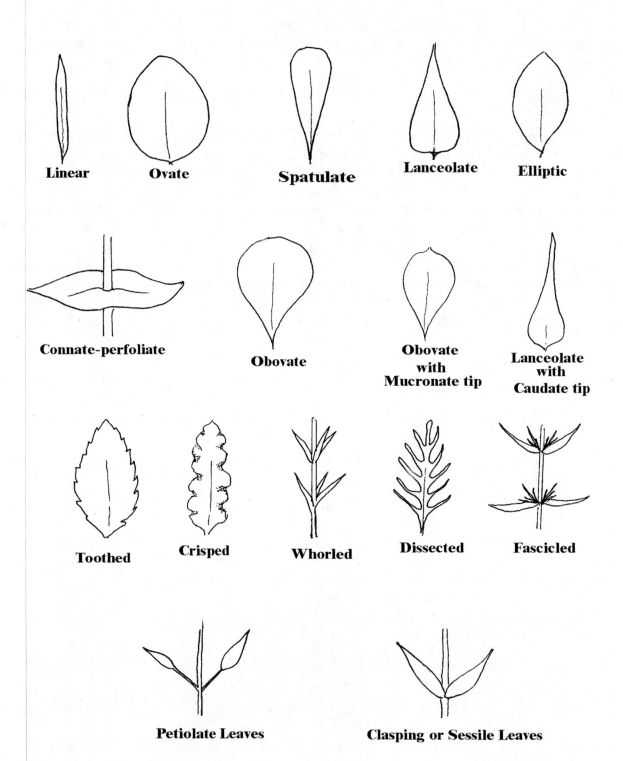

Linear    Ovate    Spatulate    Lanceolate    Elliptic

Connate-perfoliate    Obovate    Obovate with Mucronate tip    Lanceolate with Caudate tip

Toothed    Crisped    Whorled    Dissected    Fascicled

Petiolate Leaves    Clasping or Sessile Leaves

## Leaves

Penstemons have variable leaf forms and often there are many shapes and sizes of leaves on the same plant. Leaves may be anything from needle-like (*Penstemon pinifolius*) to thick and broad (*Penstemon pachyphyllus*). They may be smooth-edged (**entire**), wavy-edged (**crisped**), finely or sharply **toothed,** or **almost dissected**. Usually, those species of wetter climates have thin green leaves. Leaves without hair are described as **glabrous.** Many dryland species have foliage and stems that appear whitish, gray-green or gray-blue because of a waxy coating that reduces transpiration and are described as **glaucous**. Other species have a coat of fine hairs on the leaves, and possibly also on the stems, that cause them to appear pale gray or almost white and may be described as **canescent**. Leaves of some species have fine hairs that are topped with a clear secretion and are described as **glandular.**

Most species form **basal rosettes** of leaves. Stem or **cauline** leaves are opposite in all but a few species and often each pair will be at a ninety degree angle to the pair above it. A few species have leaves in threes and are said to be **whorled.** Stem or **cauline** leaves frequently differ in shape from the basal leaves. Most plants have leaves that grow at the base of and within the **inflorescence (**a term for all the flowers on a main stem) that are called **bracts** and are usually smaller. A few species have leaves that are fused around the stem. These are described as **connate-perfoliate**. Sometimes the basal leaves disappear at the time of bloom and start to grow again later in the summer to build up energy for the next year's flowers. Usually basal leaves persist through the winter and on many species they turn a deep maroon in cold weather.

# Types of Inflorescence

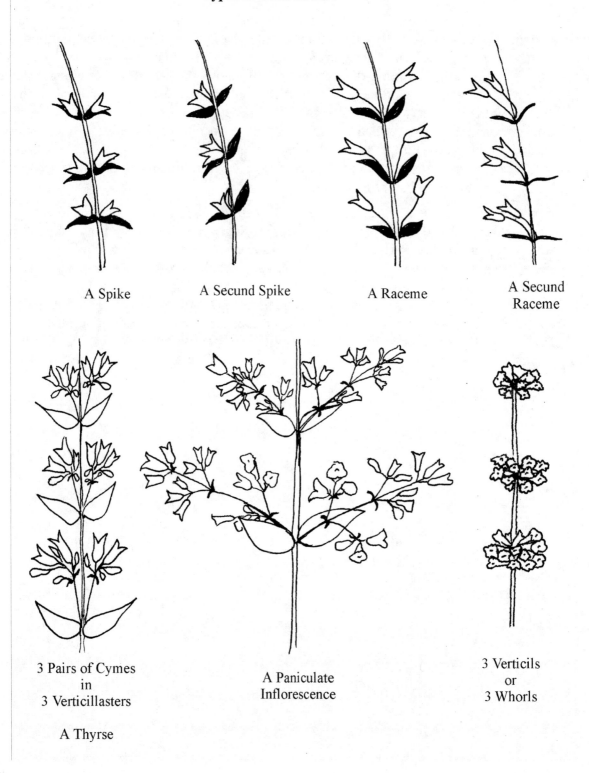

A Spike

A Secund Spike

A Raceme

A Secund Raceme

3 Pairs of Cymes
in
3 Verticillasters

A Thyrse

A Paniculate
Inflorescence

3 Verticils
or
3 Whorls

## The Inflorescence

The flowers may be arranged in different ways on the stem. A **spike** has flowers arising directly from the main stem, or on extremely short **pedicels** (flower bearing stems), forming a very narrow inflorescence. A **raceme** has flowers on longer pedicels usually arising in pairs from the stem. It may be narrow or open. A **thyrse,** the most common arrangement, has two secondary stems called **cymes** at each node of the main stem of the inflorescence. A **cyme** has few to several flowers on pedicels in a cluster, of which the terminal flower blooms first. The two clusters may form a ring around the main stem called a **verticillaster,** or false whorl. Sometimes side stems that bear flowers may continue to extend and may be quite open. They are described as **paniculate.** The flowers in each of these arrangements may face all directions or may be **secund**, all facing the same direction, or **subsecund**, where they face halfway around the stem. **Verticils** are clusters of flowers arising at nodes spaced along the stem. They are also called **whorls.** When verticils and verticillasters are close they can form a continuous inflorescence. When separated or interrupted they are often described as a candelabra arrangement.

Since flowers vary infinitely, they may also fall somewhere in between these categories!

Using the above terminology, the following descriptions are intended to help non-botanists and gardeners visualize the plants and how they could fit into a garden. They are not intended to be used for identification, because much more detailed descriptions from botanical floras are needed for positive identification. Often closely related and similar species are mentioned to help the beginner who might know some of them. Species descriptions are arranged alphabetically to aid the gardener just beginning to be interested in penstemons who is not familiar with their classification into subgenera, sections and subsections. The classification system used by members of the American Penstemon Society and all the species which are currently placed in each of the divisions are found in the appendices. The classification into these groups will help the gardener locate other species with similarities. Following the descriptions of the species and cultivars is a short section giving a few generalities about the larger groups in the classification.

Cultivars are given with the species because they generally grow in the same conditions and require the same care. There are always new cultivars, but the ones given are those distributed by large nurseries. Some gardeners may choose the cultivar over the species. If a species name is found that is not given here, it may be a new species or a name placed in synonymy. The most recent edition of **Penstemon Nomenclature** should be checked. It must always be remembered that plants vary infinitely and the descriptions in this book give only limited information to help a gardener decide if the plant is of interest and worth further investigation and trial.

Elevations are only approximate to give an idea of the variety of conditions the species encounters in it natural habitats. Species may also enlarge their range.

Notes on cultivation and germination of seeds have come from letters and articles in the APS Bulletin, the writers' and other members' experiences. The times listed for germination after stratification are for gardeners who do not have greenhouse facilities with controlled temperature, humidity and air flow, but want to start their plants outdoors or in a cool basement, garage or porch. For those fortunate enough to have a greenhouse where ideal conditions can be maintained, stratification times may be much less.  Please write about or report your experiences in growing penstemons to other members and the American Penstemon Society, the Bulletin editor or to the e-mail address on the dedication page.  Information about individual species' needs and ease of cultivation will increase their use and popularity.  Much more information is needed and this book can be easily produced as a second edition with new information as it comes in.

Descriptions of the anthers and staminode will help with checking the identity of a species, especially if it has been misidentified, as happens often in nurseries and in seed exchanges.

The origins of names of species are given to help the gardener remember them and as a matter of interest.

Sizes of flowers in the wild can vary within a small range, so rather than give the range in each case they have been grouped as follows:

**Tiny = less than 12 mm or ½" in length**

**Small = 12 to 20 mm or about ¾" in length**

**Small to medium = 20 to 30 mm or about 1" in length**

**Medium to large = 30 to 38 mm or about 1 ½" in length**

**Large = over 38 mm or over 1 ½" in length**

## Descriptions of Species and Cultivars

*Penstemon abietinus* is an evergreen, creeping sub-shrub with bright to dark green, narrowly linear leaves less than an inch long on 3 - 10″ stems rising from older, sprawling, mat-forming stems. Its native habitats are low-rainfall pinyon/juniper, oak and sagebrush communities with gravelly limestone soil in central Utah at elevations of 5700 - 7600′. There the spikes of small, light to bright blue flowers appear in June and early July. It is related and similar to *P. linarioides.* Growers in MT, MI, NY and Cornwall, England report that it is easy to grow from seeds or cuttings, best in light or part-day shade, delicate and beautiful for a rock garden, although not showy. Seed germinates after about 12 weeks of cold **stratification**. (See chapter on Growing)

Anthers: blue-black, divaricate, open across the connective with toothed sutures; staminode golden-orange bearded, both more or less exserted

Name: Firleaf Penstemon

Subgenus Penstemon, section Ericopsis, subsection Caespitosi

*P. absarokensis* is usually less than 7″ tall with small to medium-sized bright blue flowers densely clustered and facing one direction above rich green, slightly glossy, oval leaves. Flowers are like those of *P. glaber.* Its creeping habit can create large patches of color. It is found on nw. WY scree slopes between 6200 and 8800′. It has been grown in western Scotland successfully for years. It may be deciduous in some areas. Give cold moist stratification for 8 weeks, then move to 60°.

Anthers: narrowly divaricate, not open across the connective and having a few short hairs, forward pair projecting slightly; staminode usually smooth, white, included

Name: from the Absaroka Mts.

Subgenus Habroanthus, section Glabri

*P. acaulis* is a very small plant with tufts of erect, ½ to 1″ narrow, linear gray-green leaves. The small blue flowers nestle in the leaves. It grows in dry sandstone and clay at about 6000′ where WY, CO and UT meet, blooming there in June. Cultivation is not easy. Give seeds cold moist conditions for 12 wks. and move to 60°. May require 16 wks or more of varying temperatures for germination. It is most appropriately used in troughs or atop a wall where it can be appreciated at close range. *P. yampaensis* is sometimes listed as *P. acaulis* ssp. *yampaensis.* It is slightly larger. *P. acaulis* is limited to a very narrow range and may be considered a threatened or endangered species.

Anthers: blue-black and widely divaricate with toothed sutures; staminode large, golden bearded, exserted

Name: acaulis = stemless

Subgenus Penstemon, section Caespitosi

*P. acuminatus* has numerous small, pale to bright blue-purple flowers in 5 – 15 verticillasters on 6 - 18″ stout, nearly erect stems above thick, glabrous and glaucous, gray-green leaves which are attractive all year. It blooms in late April and early May. It occurs between 2100 and 4600' in se. WA, ID, nw. NV and e. OR. Variety *latebracteatus* has smaller flowers and wide bracts. The species is garden adaptable in sandy or gravelly soils in full sun. Gardeners in OR, WA, MT, NY have praised its color and sturdiness. It is related and similar to *P. nitidus*. Both are very early bloomers. Germinates after 4 – 12 wks. cold moist conditions followed by warmer temperatures.

Anthers: opposite and fully open but not explanate; staminode broadens at tip with short golden hairs; both barely exserted

Name: acuminate = tapering to a long point

Subgenus Penstemon, section Coerulei


***P. alamosensis*** shows its 1″ long, beautiful coral-red tubes with flaring, rounded lobes on stems up to 30″ high in late April and early May in its native canyons in sc. NM at about 5000'. The thin, blue-green basal leaves with crisped edges are exceptionally attractive even when the plant is not in bloom. It has been cultivated in many southwestern states in recent years and is easy in CO and NM. A nurseryman in southern France reports it is easy also. It seems to do best in moderately improved soil on slopes with good spring moisture. It has survived below 0°F temperatures and produces several stems of flowers that bloom over a long period. It germinates after 12 weeks of cold, moist stratification.

Anthers: wide-open and explanate; staminode smooth and bare

Name: from Alamo Canyon

Subgenus Penstemon, section Peltanthera, subsection Centranthifolii


***P. albertinus*** is a choice rock garden plant and a favorite in open wooded areas. It is usually 6 – 14″ tall with a basal mat of rich green, slightly toothed leaves. The many small blue flowers ring the erect stems in 4 - 8 verticillasters. It is easy to propagate from divisions or seed in lean, gravelly neutral to alkaline soils and is usually long-lived. It germinates after about 8 weeks of cold moist stratification or may be sown outside in moist, cold climates. It is found from sw. Alberta and se. British Columbia, to w. MT and se. ID between 2600 and 8000', where it may bloom from June until midsummer, and is reported to grow well in the Rocky Mt. States, IA, OH, NE, Newfoundland and Great Britain. It is similar to *P. humilis* and crosses with it and *P. wilcoxii.*

Anthers: open wide, not explanate; staminode densely yellow-bearded, included

Name: from Alberta, Canada

Subgenus Penstemon, section Penstemon, subsection Humiles


***P. albidus*** is the white penstemon of the prairies. It is common from s. Alberta, and Manitoba south to NM and TX on open high plains, where it blooms from May through June.. Sometimes the flowers are tinged pink or lavender. In cultivation it produces many stems to 16″ with a long inflorescence of up to 10 verticillasters of small flowers with flaring lobes that glisten in the sun because of their glandular hairs. Narrow gray-green leaves persist all year but are hardly noticeable. Give seed cold moist conditions for 8 weeks or sow outside in clay, sand or gravel alkaline soil and water generously in spring. This species is long-lived and survives summer drought conditions.

Anthers: black, opening widely, explanate, included; staminode has twisted golden hairs, included

Name: albidus = white

Subgenus Penstemon, section Cristati


*P. albomarginatus* is a very rare desert species from elevations between 2300 and 3000' in se. CA, s. NV and w. AZ, where it blooms from late March into April. The flowers are small to medium sized, pale pink to lavender with only a few open at a time on stems to 8". Pale green leaves with white margins crowd the stems. Many stems form an open, low bowl, broader than tall. It may be deciduous. It was grown in se. WA for 3 years.

Anthers, wide open, explanate; staminode usually glabrous

Name: albomarginatus = white-margined

Subgenus Penstemon, section Penstemon, subsection Arenarii


*P. alluviorum* is quite similar to *P. digitalis* except that the flowers are smaller but very plentiful. They are white with a tinge of pink or purple and occur in open panicles on 2 - 4' stems, blooming in May and early June. This plant is found in open, damp woodlands in neutral soil in OH, KY, MO, MS, AR, and IN. It has seldom been reported in cultivation but does well in moist, rich soil in full sun and survives 5°F. Seeds germinate after 8 weeks of cold, moist stratification.

Anthers: gray, widely divaricate and finely hairy; staminode golden bearded, slightly exserted.

Name: alluviorum = found in alluvial soils

Subgenus Penstemon, section Penstemon, subsection Penstemon


*P. alpinus* occurs south of the North Platte River in WY to central CO between 6,000 and 8,000'. It is similar to *P. glaber* and sometimes considered a subspecies of it. *P. brandegeei (P. brandegei)* is sometimes listed as a subspecies of *P. alpinus*. All have a crowded, secund inflorescence of medium to large flowers on stems from 4 - 32" tall with broadly lanceolate leaves that are glossy dark green. *P. alpinus* is a plant of the foothills, high plains and lower mountainsides, with rich blue flowers, medium to dark, and likes loose, gritty soil. The plant form may be erect or bowl-shaped. Look for it in bloom in June and July. Seed germinates after 2 mo. of cold moist stratification at 40° and at 70°F also. It has been reported successfully grown in MA, MI, Scotland and the Rocky Mountain States and is long-lived.

Anthers: divergent, dehiscing nearly to outer ends but not across the connective, suture finely toothed, slightly hairy sometimes; staminode usually broadened, slightly notched and barely exserted

Names: Mountain Penstemon, Pike's Peak Penstemon

Subgenus Habroanthus, section Glabri

*P. ambiguus* is one of the more unusual species, having salverform flowers in open panicles and a bush-like growth habit with very slender, almost unnoticeable leaves. The buds and outside of the flowers are usually rose-pink but the open face appears white, giving a pale pink effect to the whole plant. It is found at about 2500 - 6400′ from NV, UT, CO and KS, south to AZ, NM, TX and n. Chihuahua. Height may be from 8″ to 20″ tall and older plants spread widely. It blooms for a long period beginning in May at low elevations and often reblooms after summer rains. It has been successfully grown in WA, OR, IA, MI, PA and ME in sand and gravel beds in full sun. Propagation can be achieved by separating rooted side stems in late August or September and growing them on in sand. Fresh seed germinates readily at 70°F and plants self-sow in many locations; older seed requires stratification. In the southwest, unimproved sandy loam soil and full sun will grow *P. ambiguus* to perfection with occasional watering.

Anthers: black, opening full length and explanate; staminode: red, smooth, included

Names: Sand Penstemon, Bush Penstemon, Moth Penstemon

Subgenus Penstemon, section Ambigui


*P. ammophilus* is a rare species of the sand dune region of sw. Utah between 5,050 and 7,216′, being considered for listing as a threatened species. Flowers are blue-lavender, small, in few-flowered, close clusters in May and June on stems to 6″; leaves are gray and crisped. The entire plant is so sticky that sand grains adhere. It has not been reported in cultivation.

Anthers: somewhat divergent, opening narrowly; staminode white with dark hair, barely reaching the opening.

Name: ammophilus = sand-loving

Subgenus Habroanthus, section Glabri


*P. amphorellae* comes from the central Mexican highlands at 7000 - 8000′ from Coahuila to Guanajuato. It has numerous stems 12 - 16″ tall with sparse, medium-sized ventricose pale blue to lavender flowers, linear stem leaves with axillary bundles and no basal mat at blooming time.

Anthers: boat-shaped; staminode has a tuft of short yellow hair at apex.

Name: amphorellae = little pitcher-shaped flowers

Subgenus Penstemon, section Fasciculus, subsection Racemosi


*P. angelicus*, formerly listed as a subspecies of *P. clevelandii,* is up to 4 ½′ tall and has clear scarlet ventricose flowers in a narrow inflorescence. It is found only on an island off the coast of Baja California in the Gulf of California and has not been reported in cultivation.

Anthers: explanate and glabrous; staminode smooth, bare, slightly broadened at tip, both included.

Name: from location Isla Angel de la Guarda, Baja California, Mexico

Subgenus Penstemon, section Peltanthera, subsection Peltanthera


*P. anguineus*, from sw. OR and n. CA woodlands between 4000 and 6000′, has an open, spreading thyrse of pale to deep blue-purple, glandular hairy small flowers on several stems 1 -

3' tall in May and June. It is similar to *P. rattanii* and rarely cultivated but said to be easy. Allow 16 wks. at 40°F for seed germination.

Anthers: barely spreading, opening narrowly; staminode sparsely bearded and exserted

Name: Siskyou Penstemon; anguineus = like a snake

Subgenus Penstemon, section Penstemon, subsection Humiles


*P. angustifolius* has beautiful glaucous, gray-green lanceolate leaves and one to several stout, erect stems of small blue, pink or lavender flowers in 5 – 20 few to several-flowered whorls. It blooms from April to June in the high plains from NM and AZ north to MT and ND between 3900 and 7500'. The type variety in the northern part of the range has azure to deep blue flowers and is usually 8 - 12" tall. Variety *caudatus* is up to 24" tall and has longer leaves and paler flowers: it is found in s. UT, nw. NM and c. to s. CO. Very similar is the variety *venosus,* with veined leaves and bracts, found in UT, AZ and NM. Variety *vernalensis* with very narrow leaves and bracts is found in ne. UT. Variety *dulcis* with pink to rose flowers and narrow, linear basal leaves is found in wc. UT. All require sandy or gravelly neutral to alkaline soil, full sun and good drainage. Seed should be stratified in cold, moist conditions for 8 weeks and germinated at cool temperatures. Plants should be set out while the temperature is cool. Plants are not long-lived but will usually give a good show for 3 years. The species has been successfully grown in Great Britain, NY, MI, WI, and MN as well as in the Rocky Mt. Region.

Anthers: open full length but not explanate; staminode bearded with short golden hairs at the apex, recurved, just reaching the orifice

Names: Taperleaf Penstemon, Narrowleaf Penstemon

Subgenus Penstemon section Coerulei


*P. apateticus* see *P. miniatus*


*P. arenarius* is found in the sand dunes of w. NV between 4000 and 5900'. It has small, white to flesh-colored or pale lavender flowers on stems to 1' tall, appearing in May and June. Foliage is glaucous, toothed, sticky, with sand grains adhering. Not reported in cultivation.

Anthers: open wide, glabrous, not explanate; staminode golden-tufted at apex, included

Name: Nevada Sand Dune Penstemon

Subgenus Penstemon, section Penstemon, subsection Arenarii


*P. arenicola* is a compact plant with smooth, fleshy, glaucous blue-green leaves, usually 6 - 8" tall, with several stems and small bright blue flowers in a continuous cylindrical thyrse that begins blooming in April. The flowers have red-violet guidelines. It is found in sand and shale in sw. WY and adjacent UT and CO between 5900 and 7400'. It does well in the Rocky Mts. and NM and has been successful in e. WA and on the east coast in sand and gravel beds in full sun in rock gardens. Cold, moist stratification for 8 weeks followed by alternating cold and warm temperatures are needed for germination.

Anthers: opposite, not explanate, dehiscing full length; staminode densely golden-bearded, slightly exserted

Name: arenicola = living in sand; Red Desert Penstemon
Subgenus Penstemon, section Coerulei


**P. aridus** is most appropriately used in troughs because it needs to be seen at close range. It can be overlooked in a rock garden. The flowers are small and intensely blue on 4 - 8″ stems, and foliage is 1″ high in clumps of linear or slender spatulate leaves. It is found blooming in MT, ID and WY in sagebrush and grasslands on hillsides and in scree around 7300′ in late spring and early summer. It germinates in less than 2 wks. at 70°F. Gardeners have reported it easy in sand beds and long-lived and drought and cold tolerant in the Rocky Mt. States and MI, MN, IL, Newfoundland and Scotland.
Anthers: open wide; staminode golden bearded, included
Name: aridus = dry
Subgenus Penstemon, section Penstemon, subsection Humiles


**P. arkansanus** grows best without competition in open areas on shale and sandstone soils in AR, sw. MO, and e. OK, where it begins blooming in mid-May. It has broadly flattened, small, white or pale violet flowers, with violet guidelines in the throat, carried in an open panicle on stems 15 - 20″ tall. Midwestern and Eastern growers report it easy, dainty, long-blooming and reliable in almost any soil.
Anthers: widely divaricate, opening narrowly, staminode golden-bearded, both included
Name: arkansanus = from Arkansas
Subgenus Penstemon, section Penstemon, subsection Penstemon


**P. attenuatus** may grow from 4 - 27″ tall and is variable in form, some being quite slender and delicate and others sturdier. It is found from central WA to e. OR, ID, w. WY and MT from 5200 – 8200′, blooming from May to July. The typical species has small blue to blue violet flowers, but occasionally white, pale blue, yellow and cream-colored forms are found. Flowers are arranged in three to seven verticillasters about the main stem. Leaves are oval and rich green, entire to slightly toothed, and form a basal mat. Variety *militaris* is smaller with more densely clustered flowers; variety *pseudoprocerus* is short with smaller flowers. Variety *palustris* is reported to grow in marshy areas. Sometimes the yellow form is called variety *nelsoniae*. It is found in pine woods and rocky slopes in gravelly soils. Growers in regions of adequate moisture report it easy in alkaline, acid or neutral soils. It blooms from 4 – 6 weeks and makes a good garden display. Plants are long-lived. Seed germinates after 3 – 4 weeks at 70°F.
Anthers: widely divaricate, open narrowly, staminode golden yellow-bearded, both just reaching the opening
Name; attenuate = thin, slender
Subgenus Penstemon, section Penstemon, subsection Proceri


**P. atwoodii** has one to a few stems, is 5 – 16″ tall with slender leaves and distinct clusters of tiny, hairy and glandular, ventricose-ampliate lavender flowers with red-violet guidelines. It is a leafy plant, and occurs only in s. UT between 5400 and 8900'. It is considered a rare and threatened species and has not been reported in cultivation.

Anthers: widely divaricate, opening slightly, staminode golden-bearded, exserted

Name: honors Utah botanist N. Duane Atwood; Kaiparowits Penstemon

Subgenus Penstemon, section Cristati


*P. auriberbis* is a 4 - 12″ compact species from roadsides and plains in se. CO and ne. NM around 5400 to 9000'. Look for the upward-facing, small to medium-sized broadly open flowers that are pale orchid to lilac with a brilliant orange staminode in late May and June. The flowers are clustered in 3 - 8 close, few-flowered rings that are not distinct and are subsecund. This is a choice plant for the dry rock garden. Leaves are very narrow and gray-green, forming several clumps and often three to a node on the stems. It grows in sandy or loamy alkaline soils in the foothills, germinates best outdoors in sand and transplants easily while small. It is generally long-lived and hardy in USDA zone 5.

Anthers: widely divaricate, barely opening; staminode densely golden-orange bearded, exserted

Name: from auric, related to gold; Golden-bearded Penstemon

Subgenus Penstemon, section Cristati


*P. australis* comes from the southeastern states from se. VA to AL and is found in sandy coastal pine barrens. It grows from 15 – 30″ tall with small to medium-sized pink to violet flowers in narrow panicles above slender, toothed leaves. Look for the flowers in April and May. The flower is tubular with small lips, the lower lip white, projecting and marked with guidelines. Growers report it is easy and a profuse bloomer, somewhere between *P. hirsutus* and *P. arkansanus* in appearance. Plants have up to a dozen stems and bloom from one to two months. It has survived 10°F.

Anthers: widely divaricate, opening narrowly; staminode golden-bearded, both barely exserted

Name: austral = southern

Subgenus Penstemon, section Penstemon, subsection Penstemon


*P. azureus* is a n. CA and sw. OR species found between 1000 and 3300'. It is described as a sub-shrub, 12 - 18″ tall, but often trailing, with bluish-glaucous foliage and wide-throated, brilliant blue medium to large flowers, marked with white lines in the throat, and brownish-gold buds in a short open, secund inflorescence. It tolerates many soil types in full sun in low, moist climates with occasional watering and protection during the winter. It blooms from late May through August. In dry climates, part–day shade is recommended. Leaves are glaucous and almost blue-green. This is a difficult species, but the subspecies, *angustissimus,* with narrower leaves is said to be easier in cultivation. Germination percentage is usually low.

Anthers: sac-like with toothed sutures; staminode bare, included

Name: azure = sky blue

Subgenus Saccanthera, section Saccanthera, subsection Heterophylli

*P. baccharifolius* is a rare species from s. TX and Mexico, where it is found growing on limestone cliffs. It is somewhat shrubby with small oval, leathery leaves with toothed edges (sometimes not toothed or only at apex) on stems to 24″. Flowers are described as crimson to rose-scarlet with a white throat. The 1″ flowers are intensely glandular, forming a short inflorescence at the tip of each stem. It is reported to be long blooming. Very good drainage is required and it is a most desirable plant where temperatures do not drop much below freezing. It has been grown in VA, AZ, TX, WA, NM and CA.

Anthers: sac-like, opening close to the connective, barely exserted; staminode smooth, included

Names: Cut-Leaf Penstemon, Rock Penstemon; baccharifolius = leaves like Baccharis

Subgenus Penstemon, section Baccharifolii


*P. barbatus* occurs naturally in s. CO and UT, w. TX, NM, AZ and n. Mexico in the dry montane zone between 4450 and 8700′, but can be found in gardens from OR and Canada to ME, NC, Great Britain and Scandinavia. It grows anywhere from 15″ to 5′ tall with one to a dozen or more stems bearing slightly pendant, slender, medium to large scarlet tubes with a shark's head shape. Hummingbirds are attracted to it. Broad, crisped leaves identify the type species found in Mexico; more northerly varieties have narrow leaves. Sometimes the main stem branches. It is easily grown from seed in many different soils and blooms from early summer into fall. Planting 2 or 3 seedlings together gives a fuller appearance to the plant. Full sun and excellent drainage are necessary for upright stems where rainfall is heavy. In the west, part sun is satisfactory. It does well with richer soil and more moisture than most southwestern species and tolerates temperatures below 0° F. Germination occurs between 50 and 70°F. Occasional yellow, orange or pink forms appear. It hybridizes readily. Purple-shaded flowers are the result of hybridization. The type species has a densely yellow-bearded lower lip. In variety *trichander,* the anthers have hair and the palate is hairless; variety *torreyi* usually has a smooth lower throat, occasionally with long white hairs.


Cultivar:

'Schooley's Yellow' a floriferous and multi-stemmed plant with lemon-yellow flowers, to 2′ tall


Anthers: pale yellow, smooth, sutures toothed, projecting under the extended upper lip; staminode pale yellow or white, glabrous, included

Names: barbate = bearded or tufted with long hair; Scarlet Bugler, Southwestern Penstemon

Subgenus Habroanthus, section Elmigera


*P. barnebyi* is less than 8″ tall with gray-green leaves and a dense cluster of ½″ blue to violet or lavender ventricose-ampliate flowers with white throats, vertical lobes and prominent orange-bearded staminodes, in 3 to 6 verticils in late May and June. It occurs in limestone gravel and silt in NV and e. CA at 5000 - 8300′ and has not been reported in cultivation. It is closely related to *P. janishiae.*

Anthers: open opposite, explanate; staminode recurved and bright orange bearded, exserted

Name: Barneby's Penstemon, honoring Rupert Barneby (1911 - ) botanist

Subgenus Penstemon, section Cristati

**P. barrettiae** is a low, wide, spreading shrub that has beautiful foliage year-round if given protection from winter-burn and is an ideal plant for rock gardens in appropriate climates. Medium to large rose-lavender or lilac flowers rise above the foliage on short, slender, subsecund leafless spikes, up to 16″ tall, for two to five weeks, beginning in late spring. The foliage is leathery, glaucous, almost succulent, taking on a maroon cast in cold weather. It can be grown in acid, neutral or alkaline soils in full sun in some regions; in others part-day shade or a northern exposure may be better. It may take up to 3 years to bloom from seed. It is easily propagated from soft-wood cuttings in early summer. Growers suggest top-dressing with compost after blooming. It is a threatened native of the Columbia River Gorge near the Hood River at 1300′, but seed and plants are available and it has been reported to grow well beyond its region in MI, NE, ME, Newfoundland, Great Britain, Denmark and Germany. Seed germinates with 8 wks. cold, moist stratification.

Cultivar:
'Gina', has rose-pink flowers and silvery foliage, is very floriferous and may be a natural hybrid

Anthers: densely woolly, explanate; staminode bare, both included
Name: Mrs. Barrett's Penstemon, honoring Almeta Hodge Barrett (1833 - 1924) native plant enthusiast and collector
Subgenus Dasanthera

**P. bicolor** is a rare species from e. CA and w. NV at 2300 - 5000′, related and somewhat similar to *P. palmeri*. The serrate leaves are glaucous blue-green and the upper ones are perfoliate. The blooms are small to medium with moderately expanded throats and form a long spike on 2 - 4′ stems in the Spring. Some are white to cream with a little pink and subspecies *roseus* is rose-pink. It is found in gravelly or rocky desert soils at about 5600′ and has not been reported in cultivation.
Anthers: opening flat; staminode short, densely golden-bearded
Name: bicolor = having two colors
Subgenus Penstemon, section Peltanthera, subsection Peltanthera

**P. bolanius** is a rare Mexican species from the state of Jalisco, similar to *P. campanulatus*, but with broad, serrated leaves, found in dry uplands and not known to be in cultivation. It may reach 2′ and has stems densely covered with white hair.
Anthers: widely divaricate and open across the connective; staminode broadened at the tip, with a few short hairs or bare
Name: from Bolanos, Mexico
Subgenus Penstemon, section Fasciculus, subsection Campanulati

***P. bracteatus*** is a low plant related to *P. nitidus*, rarely reaching a height of 6″, with thick, glabrous and glaucous leaves and small blue to blue-violet flowers with spreading lobes in a congested inflorescence in June. It is found only in a small area of sc. Utah between 6900 and 8300′ and is considered a threatened species. It has been successfully grown in se. WA, blooming in the third year, and is reported a most desireable rock garden plant. Cold, moist stratification for 12 weeks is necessary to germinate the seed. It survives 0° F.

Anthers: opening narrowly, opposite; staminode with a dark gold-bearded tuft at the apex, included

Name: bracteate = having bracts

Subgenus Penstemon, section Coerulei

***P. brandegeei* or *brandegei*** is related to *P. glaber* and *P. alpinus* and is sometimes listed as *P. glaber* var. *brandegeei* or *P. alpinus* var. *brandegeei*. It occurs in n. NM and adjacent CO on plains and slopes at about 7000′ and is seen blooming in roadcuts at Raton Pass, NM from mid-June through July. With stout stems to 2′, topped with a dense, secund inflorescence of large blue to blue-violet flowers with bracts reaching beyond the inflorescence and large green leaves, it is quite showy. Cream-colored forms are occasionally found. It has performed well in western gardens, forming a multi-stemmed large bowl rather than the 1 – 3 stemmed plant seen in the wild. It is generally long-lived. It germinates after 8 wks. in cold, moist conditions and tolerates below freezing temperatures to 0° F.

Anthers: divaricate, not open across the connective; staminode distinctly broadened and notched, white, just reaching the lip.

Name: Brandegeei's Penstemon, honoring Townshend Stith Brandegee (1843 – 1925), collector

Subgenus Habroanthus, section Glabri

***P. breviculus*** comes from the Four Corners Region and grows in sandy, gravelly and clay soils among sagebrush and pinyon at 5300 - 6700′, where it blooms in May and June. It is related to *P. jamesii,* but the flowers are deeper in color, sometimes blue, not as inflated and with smaller, almost vertical lobes and a narrow mouth. Height may vary from 4 - 12″. The flowers, in a short, not congested inflorescence, are blue to purple, less than an inch long, glandular-hairy, with violet guidelines and pale hairs on the throat. Give seeds 5 weeks cold, moist stratification. It has been reported long-lived and excellent in a dry garden in Denver.

Anthers: opposite and explanate; staminode just reaching the opening with long, loose golden hairs

Name: brevis = somewhat short

Subgenus Penstemon, section Cristati

***P. brevisepalus*** has stems from 16 - 33″ tall and small to medium-sized pale lavender flowers with pale throats and purple guidelines in open panicles. The stem leaves are narrowly lanceolate and toothed. It is found in woodlands and on limestone cliffs from VA to OH, KY and TN, blooming in May and June.

Anthers: dark purple, widely divaricate and open across the connective; staminode barely exserted and bearded with yellow hair at the tip

Name: Short-Sepal Penstemon

Subgenus Penstemon, section Penstemon, subsection Penstemon


***P. bridgesii*** see ***P. rostriflorus***


***P. buckleyi*** is similar to *P. angustifolius* but with stout, erect stems, and is found in the Great Plains from KS to TX and NM between 3500 and 6000′, beginning to bloom in May. The small flowers can be pink, pale blue or lavender with dark guidelines in a narrow thyrse with 4 – 20 or more interrupted verticillasters. The leaves and bracts are glabrous and glaucous, broad and prominent. Stems are from 18 – 36″ tall. It germinates at cool temperatures after stratification and is long-lived. Growers from NE to CA have found it pleasing.

Anthers: narrow, open across the connective; staminode moderately bearded with golden hair, both included

Name: honoring Samuel Buckley (1809 – 1884), state geologist of TX and plant collector.

Subgenus Penstemon, section Coerulei


***P. caesius*** grows on the dry forest floor and rocky slopes of the southern Sierra Nevada and east of Los Angeles in CA in decomposed granite between 6500 and 9800′. Small, attractive, rounded blue-gray glaucous leaves form a basal mat from which 12 - 18″ stems with open panicles of red-violet to blue, small to medium-sized flowers with white lines in the throat arise. Look for it in flower in July and August. It germinates after 8 weeks of cold, moist conditions.

Anthers: sac-like, pale with fine teeth along opening; staminode smooth, included

Name: caesius = blue-gray

Subgenus Saccanthera, section Saccanthera, subsection Heterophylli


***P. caespitosus*** is generally a creeping mat or low mound of tiny gray leaves with small blue to lavender flowers, one or two at each node. Older plants spread to 1′ or more in diameter. It usually has a flush of flowers in May and June and occasional blooms throughout the summer. It is a native of dry southwestern plateaus in s. WY, nw. CO, c. UT, and n. AZ between 6000 and 10,660′. It seems to do best in rock gardens in hot sun areas with some protection part of the day and soil that is a mixture of clay and gravel. Allow 12 wks. for cold, moist stratification and bring to 70°F. It is easily propagated by cuttings or divisions. Two varieties, *desertipicti* and *perbrevis,* are distinguished from the type mostly by the shape of their leaves and locations where found. Variety *suffruticosus,* sometimes identified as *P. tusharensis,* has more erect flowering stems from a mat-like base. Gardeners in NM, CO, ND, PA and Ontario have reported that this species does very well and is most pleasing.

Anthers: sacs open widely, opposite; staminode orange-yellow bearded, both just reaching the opening or barely exserted

Name: caespitose = growing in tufts or clumps; Mat penstemon

Subgenus Penstemon, section Ericopsis, subsection Caespitosi

***P. calcareus*** is a low species of the California deserts with gray-green leaves having a frosted appearance and several stems of small, deep pink to rose-purple flowers in 2 to 6 tight clusters. The stems are from 4 - 10″ tall. It is rare and found only on limestone cliffs between 3600 and 6400′. Only one grower in VA has reported success with it.

Anthers: open wide and explanate; staminode densely bearded with golden hair

Name: calcareous = of limestone; Limestone Beardtongue

Subgenus Penstemon, section Cristati


***P. californicus*** forms a low mound of almost silvery canescent narrowly elliptic leaves. The flowers are a deep red-violet or blue-violet on stems above the clump to 6″. It has been successfully grown in VA and se. WA as well as CA, NM and CO. It blooms in May and June in stony and sandy soils among chapparal and pinyon/juniper communities from 4000 - 7500′ in s. CA and Baja CA, Mexico. Give cold, moist conditions for 8 weeks to germinate. It is reported to be long-blooming and self-sowing and will rebloom after shearing.

Anthers: wide open, opposite; staminode yellow-bearded, barely exserted

Name: California Penstemon

Subgenus Penstemon, section Ericopsis, subsection Linarioides


***P. calycosus*** is a plant of the eastern woodlands from MI to MO and ME to n. AL. It grows 2 - 3′ tall and bears erect panicles of almost white to pink, rose, or rosy-purple, medium to large flowers with long sepals. It is easy to grow in sun or light shade and long-lived. Allow 12 wks. of cold moist stratification with light for germination. Stem leaves are a rich green, broader than similar species and finely toothed. Eastern growers report that it makes an excellent border plant and stems remain upright even in heavy rain.

Anthers: opposite, barely opening, brown; staminode yellow-bearded at apex

Names: calycosus = with prominent calyx; Pink Digitalis

Subgenus Penstemon, section Penstemon, subsection Penstemon


***P. campanulatus*** is a beautiful Mexican species from the north-central part of the country and as far south as Puebla, that has been widely grown in North America and Europe. It grows to 3′ and has many stems with large campanulate flowers in shades from pale pink to red-violet and purple with an open white throat. The broadly lanceolate leaves are finely toothed and glossy green and have bundles of small leaves in their axils so that a dense, bushy effect is created. It blooms over a long season in its native habitat, from late April to October. Stems have a tendency to sprawl. It has been reported to survive temperatures below zero F, but generally performs better in milder climates. It is said to readily self-sow and can be easily propagated from cuttings. Many named hybrids are available and since it easily hybridizes, many unnamed varieties are also called *Penstemon campanulatus.* It is widely grown on the west coast where it is said to bloom as long as 6 months. It has also performed well in CO, NM, PA and VA with a shorter bloom season, and has persisted for several years.

Anthers: opposite, opening across the connective but not explanate; staminode golden bearded, barely exserted

Name: campanulate = bell-shaped

Subgenus Penstemon, section Fasiculus, subsection Campanulati


***P. canescens*** grows in mountain woodlands from IN, OH, and PA, to w. VA and as far south as n. AL, where it blooms April through June. It produces erect stems of medium to large pink to old rose or lavender to plum-colored flowers, with sharply defined violet guidelines within the pale throat, in open panicles that may reach 24″. The whole plant is finely hairy. Gardeners report it performs best in well-drained, slightly enriched soils with part-day shade in hotter parts of the country and in the open in more moist climates. Seed germinates in 8 weeks in cool conditions with natural or artificial light.

Anthers: widely divaricate, moderately open; staminode densely yellow-bearded, exserted

Name: canescent = white or hoary

Subgenus Penstemon, section Penstemon, subsection Penstemon


***P. cardinalis*** is among the hardiest of the southwestern species. It has broad, dull green leaves and narrow racemes of 1″, pendant crimson flowers on stems to 28″ tall. The flowers are tubular, slightly ampliate, somewhat constricted behind the small lobes, of which the lower ones are darkly bearded. This species is native to the canyons of s. NM and TX at elevations from 4500 - 6000′, where it blooms in May, but has been cultivated in a variety of soils from NV and CA to ME and VA. It is easy to grow in well-drained sunny spots and is a late and long bloomer. It germinates at both 40° and 70° F. Subspecies *regalis* has longer sepals than the type and broader stem leaves.

Anthers: divaricate, opening only at the distal ends with toothed sutures; staminode bearded at apex, included

Name: cardinal = important, of a deep scarlet color

Subgenus Habroanthus, section Elmigera


***P. cardwellii*** is a beautiful, shrubby evergreen ground-hugging plant from WA, OR and n. CA. Its brilliant colors can be seen spreading through many cut-over areas and gravelly roadsides in the mountains, between 1300 to 6300′ from early May through July. Woody stems form a clump 8 - 10″ high that may be several feet wide in the wild but is usually less than 2′ in cultivation. The numerous bright pink to purple flowers rise on 4″ stems above the foliage clump. The flowers are medium to large with a prominent keel on the dorsal side and bloom for 3 – 5 weeks. Leaves can be light to dark green, broadly elliptic and finely toothed, turning deep purple in winter. It is grown successfully in most northern states, Long Island, southern and eastern Canada, Great Britain, Scandinavia and Europe. It should be cut back after bloom for compactness and given protection in snowless areas. If the plant has suffered heavy winter damage it should not be pruned until mid-May when new growth has started so that healthy stems are not removed. Propagation from cuttings in late spring and early fall is easy in a sand and peat mix. Germinates best after 8 wks. of cold moist stratification.

Cultivars:

'Albus' large form with white flowers

'Blue Skies' light bluish flowers and medium green leaves

'Cheri' pink and red forms

'Floyd McMullan' dark wine-red flowers above low compact mound of foliage

'John Bacher' vigorous white-flowered form with dense light green foliage to 12″ tall

'Roseus' has abundant deep pink flowers

'Thurman's Form' robust form with blue-purple flowers


Anthers; widely divaricate, explanate, woolly, included; staminode slender, yellow-bearded, included

Name: honors Dr. James Robert Cardwell (1830 – 1916), dentist, horticulturalist and founder of Oregon Horticultural Society

Subgenus Dasanthera


*P. carnosus* grows 6 - 14″ tall and has oblong, thick, glaucous and glabrous leaves and small, moderately ampliate lavender-pink to blue-violet flowers in 5 – 10 verticillasters, about half the length of the stem. It is found in c. and ne. UT at 4900 – 8500′, blooming from May to July. Allow 12 wks. cold moist stratification for germination of seeds. May be long-lived or not, depending on site.

Anthers: open opposite and full length; staminode yellow-orange bearded, both included

Name: carnus = fleshy

Subgenus Penstemon, section Coerulei


*P. caryi* blooms in the Bighorn Mountains of WY and the Pryor Mountains of MT between 6500 and 7500′ in June. It is variable in height from 3 – 16″, the more compact form being very desirable for rock gardens. The flowers are medium to large, blue to blue-violet, somewhat secund, in a narrow open raceme. The leaves are slender and rich green, forming a mat over several years. It has been successfully cultivated in mountainous regions of the US, in the Midwest and in Europe in sandy, gravelly soils. Generous moisture in early spring is necessary for good bloom. Seed germinates after 6 weeks of cold, moist stratification.

Anthers: moderately divaricate with loose white hair, staminode lightly bearded, both included

Name: Cary's Penstemon, honoring Merritt Cary, collector in 1910

Subgenus Habroanthus, section Glabri


*P. centranthifolius* is fairly common from almost sea level to 6000′ in the deserts and foothills of s. CA and Baja CA from March through June. The flowers are slender scarlet tubes, more than an inch long with small, barely flared lobes, pendant from the upper half of stems that may be up to 4′ long. The lower portions of the stems have glaucous and glabrous, entire gray-green leaves. It does well in cultivation in mild climates, probably not much below 15°F, but has lived

5 years in Denver, CO, with sandy or porous rocky soil and does not need cold stratification for seed germination.

Anthers: divaricate and explanate; staminode bare, both included

Name: centranthifolius = leaves like the plant Centranthus

Subgenus Penstemon, section Peltanthera, subsection Centranthifolii


***P. cerrosensis*** is an 18" multi-stemmed plant with scarlet flowers found only in canyons of a small island, Cedros, off the coast of Baja CA and not known in cultivation.

Anthers: divaricate and explanate; staminode bare

Name: cerro = hill

Subgenus Penstemon, section Peltanthera, subsection Centranthifolii


***P. cinicola*** is usually 6 - 10″ tall in June and July with tiny dark blue flowers clustered in 2 – 5 rings and is similar to *P. peckii*, but smaller. Cauline leaves are slender and curve downward. It occurs in dry volcanic soils in n. CA and OR between 4000 and 7400′ and has been successfully cultivated in many areas. Allow 8 wks. of cold moist conditions for germination. It is very well liked, producing lots of flowers, and will rebloom if cut back after the first flush of bloom.

Anthers: divaricate and explanate; staminode dilated, tufted with short yellow hairs at apex, included

Name: cinicola = growing in ash; Ash Beardtongue

Subgenus Penstemon, Section Penstemon, Subsection Proceri


***P. cleburnei*** see ***P. eriantherus***


***P. clevelandii*** blooms in the arid deserts and canyons of s. CA and Sonora, Mex. at elevations from 1300 - 4500′ from March to May. Fuschia pink to red-purple 1″ long, funnel-form flowers with small flaring lips cover the upper half of 2′ tall stems from March to May in their native habitat. Leaves of the typical species are slightly toothed and deep green, not perfoliate. Leaves of subspecies *connatus* are blue-green and sharply toothed, upper ones connate-perfoliate; the flowers have barely opened anthers. Leaves of subspecies *mohavensis* are coarsely toothed, not perfoliate and bright green and the flowers narrower and constricted before flaring and with a densely hairy staminode. This species is hardy to some degree of frost and ssp. *connatus* has been grown in se. WA. The type species was successfully grown in VA but only bloomed one year. Otherwise it has only been reported from CA and AZ.


Cultivar:

'Santa Catarina' 36", magenta-pink flowers with dark stems; recurrent flowering after cutting back


Anthers: opposite and varying in opening; staminode bare or as described above

Name: honors Daniel Cleveland (1838 – 1929) lawyer; Santa Rosa Penstemon

Subgenus Penstemon, section Peltanthera, subsection Peltanthera

*P. clutei* is a lovely pink-flowered species from the volcanic soils in and around Sunset Crater in n. AZ at about 7000′, blooming in June. Several stems to 40″ have medium to large, broadly ampliate flowers with abruptly flaring lobes above broad, blue-green, glaucous, toothed leaves. It is easy, hardy, drought tolerant, thrives in many types of soil, and is long-lived. Growers from WA, NM, CO, NE, NJ, NY, and Manitoba have raved about it. It self-sows in many gardens. Allow 8 weeks cold moist conditions for germination.

Anthers: divaricate and explanate, staminode bare or only slightly hairy, both included

Names: Clute's Penstemon, honoring collector, William N. Clute (1865 – 1950); Sunset Penstemon

Subgenus Penstemon, section Peltanthera, subsection Peltanthera

*P. cobaea* is the largest-flowered penstemon species occurring in the United States and is found blooming from late April in TX to August in OK, AK, MO, KS, NM and s. NE. Flower color varies from white to pink, pale purple and deep purple (the deep purple sometimes listed as var. *purpureus*), usually with prominent guidelines in the widely expanded throat. Flowers may be almost 2″ long in cultivation and make a pleasing contrast with other smaller flowered plants. The leaves are large, dark green, entire to toothed, sometimes glabrous and glossy and sometimes downy. Stems are stiffly erect, 1 to 2′ tall. *Penstemon cobaea* has been in cultivation for many years; has been grown from NM and CO to Michigan and VA and has been used in many hybrids. It is very hardy and long-lived if given supplemental water in areas low in precipitation. Germination takes 2 - 6 wks. at either 40 or 70° F. It is susceptible to leaf spot in some situations.

Anthers: divaricate and explanate, dark; staminode lightly bearded at tip with pale hair, barely exserted

Names: honors Father Bernardo Cobo, a Spanish missionary and naturalist (1572 – 1659); Foxglove Penstemon; Wild White Snapdragon

Subgenus Penstemon, section Cristati

*P. comarrhenus* may be from 18″ - 2 ½′ tall with few stems and slender gray-green leaves. The flowers are broadly ampliate, a lovely, pale milky pink, lavender, blue or almost white and sometimes appear to spiral around the stem in an open thyrse. Stems grow erect but easily break or bend from the base if not grown with excellent drainage and full sun. Planting 2 – 3 seedlings together and supplying inconspicuous supports may prevent breakage where the sun is not as strong as in its native habitat. It is found blooming in late May through August in the dry Four Corners Region between 3,300 and 9,840′ in sandy soils and is easily cultivated, germinating after about 2 months chilling.

Anthers: widely divaricate with long, dense white hair; staminode bare or slightly hairy at tip, both included

Name: coma = tuft of hairs, referring to anther covering; Dusty Penstemon

Subgenus Habroanthus, section Glabri

***P. compactus*** is a short form of *P. cyananthus*, sometimes listed as a variety of it. It is usually about 6″ tall with small to medium-sized bright blue flowers, and is found in bloom in nc. UT and se. ID at 7900 - 9900′ between June and August. It is rare and seldom reported in cultivation but has been very popular in Scotland.

Anthers: dark, somewhat divaricate with a narrow opening and toothed sutures; slightly hairy; staminode bare or slightly bearded at apex, included

Names: Bear River Penstemon, Compact Penstemon

Subgenus Habroanthus, section Glabri

***P. concinnus*** has tiny light blue-violet flowers with purple guidelines and a prominently white-bearded throat. Two to four closely spaced clusters circle the stems that are usually less than 7″ tall in late May and June. Leaves are narrowly linear, rarely finely toothed, mostly basal. It is found in w. UT and adjacent NV at elevations betweeen 6300 and 7700′ in gravelly, alluvial soils and not reported in cultivation.

Anthers: explanate, blue, glabrous, exserted; staminode recurved with white or pale hairs, exserted

Name: Elegant Penstemon

Subgenus Penstemon, section Cristati

***P. confertus*** comes from the forests and woodland openings of s. Alberta and British Columbia, Canada and WA, OR, ID and MT from 4000 – 10,000′ and is variable in size of flowers and leaves. Several dense whorls of pale cream-colored or yellow flowers ring stems that rise from 8 - 20″ above a mat of bright green, smooth, finely toothed to entire leaves. It is easy in moist climates and spreads well in ordinary soil or sand beds in most of the northern US, Great Britain and Europe. Cold, moist conditions are needed for 8 weeks to germinate seed.

Cultivar:

'Kittitas' a dwarf form with deep yellow flowers

Anthers: widely divaricate, smooth, explanate; staminode bearded with brown hairs, included

Name: confertus = compressed; Yellow Procerus

Subgenus Penstemon, section Penstemon, subsection Proceri

***P. confusus*** is similar to *P. utahensis,* but shorter and flowers are smaller, red-violet or rose-lavender, with guidelines, and arranged in few-flowered whorls. Leaves are gray-green, entire and glaucous. It occurs in sandy, gravelly and clay soils with sparse vegetation from April until June in w. UT, NV, and e. CA between 3300 and 7300′. Seed germinates after 16 wks. of cold, moist stratification.

Anthers: divaricate, wide open, smooth; staminode may be smooth to densely hairy, both included

Name: confusus = puzzling

Subgenus Penstemon, section Peltanthera, subsection Centranthifolii

*P. coriaceus,* formerly known as *P. schaffneri,* is a branched sub-shrub that can reach 3′ and is native to San Luis Potosi, Aguascalientes, Zacatecas and Jalisco, Mexico with broad, slightly serrate, short, spatulate thick, leathery leaves, congested at the axils, and 1 ¼″ deep red-purple tubular flowers, with prominently exserted anthers, at the apices of the stems. It is similar and related to *P. kunthii* and *P. campanulatus.* It grows in rock crevices between 4900 and 8200′ and has not been reported in cultivation in the US.

Anthers: open wide, opposite exserted; staminode sparingly yellow-bearded

Name: coriaceous = with a rough, leathery texture

Subgenus Penstemon, Section Fasciculus, Subsection Campanulati

*P. crandallii* is a low, evergreen sub-shrub, 2 - 6″ tall and spreading to 1 foot or more, with flowering stems arising from an intricately branched, woody base. It is found in CO and UT between 6000 and 8850′, usually in pinyon/juniper woodlands, and is easy to grow in dry sandy and gravelly soils. Leaves are narrowly linear to spatulate, green or gray-green, closely spaced and up to 1 1/3″ long. From May to August, small flowers, lavender to bright blue, with open throats and a prominent orange staminode brighten the mats of foliage. The variety *atratus* has broader, obovate or spatulate leaves on stems that are more prostrate than the type, and has more presence in the garden. *Penstemon crandallii* has been successfully grown from WA to the east coast and in Great Britain. It is long-lived and can be multiplied by cuttings and division. Self-sowing is common in the southern Rockies. It germinates at 40°F. with 12 weeks cold, moist stratification.

Anthers: divaricate, opening widely with toothed sutures; staminode densely yellow-orange bearded, both more or less included.

Name: Crandall's Penstemon, honoring Charles Spencer Crandall (1852 – 1929), a Colorado botany professor, who collected it in 1897

Subgenus Penstemon, section Ericopsis, subsection Caespitosi

*P. cusickii* occurs in sw. ID and adjacent e. OR in dry sagebrush country at about 3600′. It usually is about 1′ tall with an open, few-flowered inflorescence of small, sapphire blue to lavender flowers above 1 - 3″ almost grass-like foliage that is softly hairy in May and June. It has been reported easy and long-lived in ID, but is little known elsewhere.

Anthers: sac-like, blue-black, narrowly open across the top; staminode white and glabrous, barely exserted

Name: Cusick's penstemon for William Cusick (1842 – 1922), plant collector and distributor of Great Basin Plants

Subgenus Saccanthera, section Saccanthera, subsection Heterophylli

*P. cyananthus* can be up to 3′ tall and is a beautiful, showy plant with many erect stems and smooth green leaves that form a basal rosette. Each stem bears a dense subsecund thyrse of 1″ bright blue, moderately ventricose-ampliate flowers from late May into August in its natural habitat. It is seen in n. UT, e. ID, and WY from 4900 – 10,500′ among aspens and on grassy slopes and road cuts where it receives frequent showers in the summer. Variety *subglaber* has narrower leaves. It has been widely praised by gardeners and germinates at cool temperatures after stratification for 16 wks.

Anthers: diverging, short-haired, opening from the outer ends only, included; staminode pale to dark orange-bearded, included

Name: cyan = blue; Wasatch Penstemon

Subgenus Habroanthus, section Glabri


*P. cyaneus* appears on dry, gravelly slopes and plains from c. ID to sw. MT and nw. WY at elevations of 4900 to 7900′, blooming from late May to early August. Inch-long, blue to purple secund flowers with a pale lower throat are closely spaced in a few-flowered thyrse on 1 - 2′ ascending stems above smooth, entire green leaves. It has been reported easy to grow from northern CA through the northern Rockies and in Scotland, even where temperatures fall well below 0°F. Foliage is attractive to rabbits and deer. Long-lived in most situations, it may rebloom if cut back after first bloom. Allow 8 wks. of cold, moist stratification for germination. It may bloom the first year if started early.

Anthers: opening only from the distal end and twisted, sutures finely toothed and finely hairy; staminode with short, pale bearding, both included

Name: Dark Blue penstemon

Subgenus Habroanthus, section Glabri


*P. cyanocaulis* is another blue-flowered penstemon from ec. UT and w. CO. It grows 1 - 2′ tall in dry pinyon/juniper country from about 4200 - 7900′. Flowers are small, of a beautiful, out-standing lavender-blue color and slightly ventricose in an open, whorled arrangement that can be found in May and June. Leaves are crisped, smooth, entire, somewhat glaucous, varying from glossy to dull. It has not been widely cultivated, but reported easy and beautiful. Seed germinates after 12 wks. of cold, moist stratification.

Anthers: widely divergent, somewhat twisted, having short sparse hairs, opening from distal end; staminode golden-yellow bearded and notched, just reaching the opening

Name: Bluestem Penstemon

Subgenus Habroanthus, section Glabri


*P. cyathophorus* has fleshy blue-gray leaves and bracts that surround the stout stem and cup the many closely spaced cylindric rings of small, funnel-form sky-blue to pink or lavender flowers. It is an early and profuse bloomer found in nc. CO and adjacent WY in dry, rocky sagebrush country between 7000 and 8500′ on clay loam soils. It has been successfully grown in CO. Stems are erect and up to 2′ tall. Allow 12 wks. cold, moist stratification to germinate.

Anthers: very obviously exserted, parallel sacs opening throughout; staminode densely bearded, extending upward and slightly exserted

Name: cyathophorus = cup-bearing

Subgenus Penstemon, section Coerulei

***P. dasyphyllus*** occurs in grasslands with gravelly soils between 4000 and 5500′ in sw. TX, s. NM, c. and e. AZ and Coahuila, Chihuahua and Sonora, Mexico. Several wiry 16 - 18″ stems are sparsely flowered with medium-sized, glandular, finely hairy blue-purple flowers, usually only one to a node, and all facing one direction. They can be found from April through October, depending on rainfall. Leaves are gray-green, covered with ashy down, narrow, folded and upward pointing. The plant is very difficult to find when not in flower. It germinates with 8 weeks cold, moist stratification.

Anthers: opening all the way across the longer side, toothed; staminode bare, included

Name: dasy = hairy and phyllus = leaved; Gila Penstemon

Subgenus Penstemon, subsection Chamaeleon


***P. davidsonii*** forms a dense, creeping woody mat with small, oval, evergreen, usually toothed leaves, with clusters of secund stems with large, keeled rose or lavender flowers rising one to several inches above the mat in the summer. This is a popular, easy and widely grown species for rock gardens in the northern states of the US, southern Canada, Denmark, Norway, Great Britain and Europe. A sunny situation and porous, gravelly soil with shielding from early morning sun is recommended. Germinates quickly at 70°F. without cold, moist stratification. It is found from 5600 to 12,000′ in n. CA, OR and WA and n. NV to British Columbia. Variety *menziesii* has smaller and more rounded leaves; variety *praeteritus* has longer flowers and more upright stems and var. *davidsonii* from the Cascade Mts. has entire leaves.


Cultivars:

'Albus' compact form of var. *menziesii* with white flowers

'Broken Top' 4″ x 18″, spreading, layering, with deep purple flowers

'Microphyllus' a form of var. *menziesii* with tiny, round leaves, violet-blue flowers

'Minnie' very floriferous form of var. *menziesii* with blue flowers

'Parma' form of var. *menziesii* with trailing habit, glaucous, toothed leaves, dk. violet flrs.

'Serpyllifolius' prostrate form of var. *menziesii* with very tiny toothed leaves, lilac flowers

'Mt. Adams Dwarf' smaller form of type variety


Anthers widely divaricate and explanate, covered with dense white woolly hair; staminode pale yellow-bearded, both included

Name: Davidson's Penstemon for George Davidson (1825 – 1911), astronomer and plant collector

Subgenus Dasanthera


***P. deamii*** is found in s. IL and IN in May and is quite similar to *P. digitalis*. The flowers are white (tinged purple sometimes), a little smaller, with very short sepals and are arranged in narrow panicles atop 3 - 4′ stems.

Anthers: divaricate, grey, opening throughout, sometimes with hair; staminode lightly bearded, just reaching opening

Name: Deam's Penstemon, honoring discoverer Charles Clemon Deam (1865-1953), author of an Indiana Flora

Subgenus Penstemon, section Penstemon, subsection Penstemon


**P. deaveri** is found in the White Mts. of AZ and NM around the Mogollon Rim from 7500 – 11,280'. Flowers are blue-lavender and secund on several erect stems to 24", appearing in May and June. It is very similar to *P. virgatus.* It is in cultivation in NM, well-liked but not long-lived.

Anthers: completely dehiscent, not explanate; staminode bearded with short golden hairs, slightly dilated

Name: Deaver's Penstemon, honoring Chester Deaver, authority on the flora of n. AZ

Subgenus Habroanthus, section Glabri


**P. debilis** is a charming, low, mound-forming species with small, glabrous and glaucous gray elliptic to oblanceolate stem leaves and no basal leaves. The small pale, pinkish-lavender, funnel-form, almost regular flowers face upward from a compact thyrse within the leaves. This species is found only in oil shale talus slopes at about 8200' in CO and may be listed as an endangered species. It was described in 1987. A few growers in Colorado are having success with it and describe it as a great plant that blooms profusely, dies to the ground in fall but comes back in the spring.

Anthers: bright magenta, divaricate, opening from distal end, surface slightly hairy; staminode slightly bearded, scarcely exserted

Name: debilis = weak stemmed; Parachute Penstemon for nearby town

Subgenus Habroanthus, section Glabri


**P. degeneri** has widely spaced clusters with a few small deep blue flowers in each, on several stems to 16" in June. It occurs in open juniper woodlands south of the Royal Gorge in CO and has not been reported in cultivation. It is a rare plant and may be endangered.

Anthers: widely divaricate, opening narrowly; staminode orange bearded, included

Name: honors Otto Degener (1899 – 1950), Colorado naturalist

Subgenus Penstemon, section Penstemon, subsection Humiles


**P. deustus** is a variable species, commonly found in arid, rocky locations from e. CA and OR to c. WA and east to NV, UT, WY, and MT between 2600 and 9,000'. It is a multi-stemmed plant, 4 - 16" tall, with variably toothed leaves that are smooth to sometimes hairy. The flowers are small, ivory or cream to yellow, sometimes with reddish guidelines in late spring and early summer. Many gardeners across the country have had success with it in poor gravelly soils. Allow 8 wks. for cold moist stratification. Variety *deustus* usually has a glabrous staminode, sometimes a maroon blotch in the throat; variety *pedicillatus* has small gray green sharply toothed leaves and forms a neat small clump. The flowers have a reduced, sometimes brownish upper lip. Variety *suffrutescens* is also short with oblanceolate leaves and variety *variabilis* is tall with narrow stem leaves and a bearded staminode.

Anthers: opposite and explanate, slightly exserted; staminode, bare or bearded, included

Names: deustus = scorched; Hot Rock Penstemon; Scabland Penstemon

Subgenus Penstemon, section Penstemon, subsection Deusti


***P. digitalis*** is a very popular tall species with broad panicles of medium to large white or pale lavender glandular, open bell-like flowers that may be found from May through August. It is native to the northern Mississippi River basin and has naturalized into the northeastern United States, Ontario and Quebec, growing in open woodlands, meadows and fields. It is easy to grow, long blooming, stiffly upright and long-lived almost everywhere, generally producing many seedlings. It is most effective planted in clumps. Fresh or stored seeds germinate readily at 70° with bright light. Height may be up to 5', but is usually between 3 and 4'. Foliage is thin, slightly toothed, dark green, maroon in winter. It will do well in arid locations with extra water.


Cultivars:

'Husker Red' a form with deep maroon foliage, flowers white (pale pink flowers have appeared on seed-propagated progeny)

'White Queen' has pure white flowers with no guidelines

'Lavender Queen' has large lavender flowers

'Pink Dawn' a pink-flowered form, 18" tall


Anthers: widely divergent and somewhat hairy; staminode, pale yellow-bearded, included

Name: for similarity to genus Digitalis; Foxglove Penstemon

Subgenus Penstemon, section Penstemon, subsection Penstemon


***P. diphyllus*** forms a rounded clump, 1 – 2 ½' tall with many slender stems of small light blue to lavender flowers in an open inflorescence that blooms over a long period. The narrow leaves are toothed to deeply cleft and dull green. It is found on rocky banks of the mountains of e. WA, ID OR and w. MT . It is a good garden filler and blooms long and late in the year. It is related to *P. triphyllus* and *P. richardsonii*. Allow 12 wks. for cold, moist stratification of seeds for germination.

Anthers: saccate with toothed sutures across top; staminode lightly bearded, just reaching the opening

Name: diphyllus = two-leaved

Subgenus Saccanthera, section Saccanthera, subsection Serrulati


***P. discolor*** is closely related and similar to *P. linarioides* but has racemes of tiny, pale pink to almost white flowers and silvery leaves. It is quite rare, found only on a mountain near Tucson in s. AZ between 6000 and 7500' from June to August. It shows well against dark rocks and has been cultivated in several areas. It lived 5 years in NE. Allow 12 weeks of cold, moist stratification to germinate seeds.

Anthers: widely divaricate; staminode golden orange-bearded, just reaching opening or somewhat exserted

Name: discolor = variegated, referring to upper surfaces of leaves gray, under side green

Subgenus Penstemon, section Ericopsis, subsection Linarioides


*P. dissectus* is native to Georgia pine barrens but has been grown all along the east coast of the US in poor, sandy, acid soils. It grows to 24″ and has few to several inch-long, pale rose-lavender to bright purple flowers with white markings on the lobes and maroon guidelines in the throat. It has been called the most attractive of the eastern penstemons. Stem leaves are deeply cut and almost fern-like, while basal leaves are broader and occasionally notched. It grows most gracefully in high shade, but is more compact and sturdy in sunny locations. The size of the clump increases yearly by stolons. It has been successfully grown near Puget Sound as well as on the east coast.

Anthers: divaricate with toothed openings, maroon; staminode lightly yellow-bearded, exserted

Name: dissectus = deeply cut

Subgenus Dissecti (the only species in the subgenus)


*P. distans* is an undistinguished species with small blue flowers on 1 - 2′ stems, only 1 or 2 at each of the 6 – 10 nodes in the inflorescence. It is found in nw. AZ at about 5000′ and has not been reported in cultivation.

Anthers: not diverging, barely opening; staminode densely bearded with orange-yellow hair

Name: distans = widely spaced, referring to nodes

Subgenus Penstemon, section Cristati


*P. dolius* is a very desirable plant for a rock garden or trough. Clusters of small, broad, pale blue flowers with white throats cover the slender gray-green, hairy oval leaves on mounded plants less than 8″ tall in May and June. It grows in dry, gravelly clay soil in UT and NV between 5000 and 7300′. Seeds germinate at 40°F after 6 – 12 wks. cold, moist stratification.

Anthers: widely diverging, narrow at the connective with toothed sutures; staminode has a dense tuft of pale yellow hair at the apex and sparse hair below, included

Name: dolius = barrel-shaped

Subgenus Penstemon, section Cristati


*P. duchesnensis* is similar to *P. dolius* and sometimes listed as a variety of it. It is shorter and more compact with shorter leaves and more erect stems and is found in eastern Utah only in the vicinity of Duchesne, where it blooms mid-June. It has upward-facing, red-violet flowers with blue lobes. Germination and growing conditions are the same.

Anthers: spreading but not explanate, opening narrowly; staminode densely bearded most of length, included

Name: of the vicinity of Duchesne, UT
Subgenus Penstemon, section Cristati


***P. eatonii*** has numerous pendant, slender scarlet tubes on many stout stems in May and June, ascending from a mass of deep green foliage. It normally grows to 2'. Although it is an arid land species from between 2750 and 6000' in AZ, UT and the Mojave Desert, it has performed well and been long-lived in the NW, the Rocky Mt. region and MI and east coast gardens as far north as MA. It has been used in highway plantings in ID and NM. Subspecies *undosus* has finely hairy rather than glossy leaves; subspecies *exsertus* has extended yellow anthers and may not be as hardy as the type. This is the earliest red penstemon to bloom in northern gardens. Stored seed germinates readily at 40°F. within 2 – 8 weeks.


Cultivar:
'Ritchfield Selection' multi-stemmed, erect form


Anthers: slightly divergent, opening from the distal end, S-twisted, included except in ssp. *exsertus*; staminode white, usually bare or with few hairs, included
Name: honors Daniel Cody Eaton, botanist at Yale Univ. (1834 – 1895), discoverer of the species
Subgenus Habroanthus, section Elmigera


***P. elegantulus*** is less than 1' tall and has several slender stems of small, deep blue flowers that have sparse white hairs on the lower throat, and appear in May and June above a compact crown of slightly serrate leaves. The species occurs in ID and e. OR along Hell's Canyon at about 5400', and has been reported to do well in the Puget Sound area. It is closely related to *P. albertinus*. It has germinated with 8 weeks cold, moist stratification.
Anthers: widely divaricate and opening widely; staminode orange-bearded, prominently exserted
Name: elegantulus = elegant
Subgenus Penstemon, section Penstemon, subsection Humiles


***P. ellipticus*** has large keeled orchid (sometimes white) secund flowers with a projecting white-bearded lower lip in the summer atop stems with smooth, firm, slightly toothed, elliptic green leaves. The flowers are similar to *P. fruticosus*. The stems rise to 8" above mats of woody stems that are usually buried in rock slides and crevices of the northern Rocky Mountains and the Canadian Rockies between 3000 and 9000'. It is said to grow well with a limestone substrate in cool regions along the Canadian border to Newfoundland. Allow 8 weeks for cold, moist stratification.
Anthers: covered with dense white wool; staminode bearded with long yellow hair, included
Names: Rockvine Penstemon, Alpine Beardtongue, Rocky Ledge Penstemon
Subgenus Dasanthera

*P. eriantherus* is usually 6 - 14″ tall or less with medium to large very inflated lavender, pink or orchid flowers with vertical lobes, prominent hairs at the throat and a very noticeable staminode. The entire plant has glandular hair, causing it to glisten in the sun and attract many insects. It is quite variable in flower size and color, leaf shape and size and amount of hairiness. The type has prominent guidelines also. It can be found blooming in May and June in arid areas from e. WA to ND, SD, ne. CO and also north into British Columbia and Alberta. Variety *cleburnei* is the smallest variety with prominent guidelines and few flowers that are constricted at the opening and do not occur in distinct rings. Variety *redactus* is also smaller, about 8″ tall, has pale lavender flowers and is found in MT, ID and OR. Variety *argillosus* has downy and sharply toothed leaves, deep purple-blue to red-violet flowers with an almost bare throat and included staminode and comes from e. OR. Variety *whitedii* has violet-purple flowers that are almost regular. Some consider them easy in the dry rock garden and others have found them difficult. Germination is best at 70°F after cold, moist stratification for 8 weeks. Deep sand or sand and gravel soils provide the best conditions for them.

Anthers: tan, open widely; staminode densely golden to orange bearded, exserted or at the opening

Names: eri = woolly; Crested Penstemon; Fuzzy Tongue Penstemon

Subgenus Penstemon, section Cristati


*P. euglaucus* has ½″ blue-violet, pale-throated flowers clustered in few-flowered to densely-flowered rings that are widely separated on slender stems that may reach 2′ above a dense mat of glaucous, glabrous, entire leaves. It grows on volcanic ash at about 4600′ in forest openings where it receives part shade, and blooms in July and August. It is native to the Cascades in OR and WA and has been in cultivation in England, Denver Botanical Garden and the Midwest in moderately rich soil as well as on the West Coast. It is larger than most of the Proceri and has been especially enjoyed when planted in large groups.

Anthers: widely divaricate, not explanate; staminode lightly pale-bearded, just reaching the opening

Name: euglaucus = completely glaucous; Glaucous Penstemon

Subgenus Penstemon, section Penstemon, subsection Proceri


*P. eximeus* is found in Baja CA near the Gulf of California and can be 7 - 8′ tall. The flowers, much like *P. palmeri,* are abruptly expanded, secund, pale pink to cream with red-violet guidelines. Most of the leaves are close to the base, sharply toothed and glaucous. Blooming occurs in May and June if there has been spring moisture. It has not been reported in cultivation.

Anthers: open wide, explanate; staminode short, bearded, not exserted

Name: eximeus = exemplary or exceptional

Subgenus Penstemon, section Peltanthera, subsection Peltanthera


*P. fasciculatus* is a species from sw. Chihuahua, Mexico with medium to large bright crimson flowers on many leafy stems rising to 20″ from woody rootstocks in August. The flowers usually have a white throat. Leaves may be either smooth and green or slightly gray with a minutely hairy surface. Small leaves cluster in the axils of the primary leaves. Foliage appears similar to *P. pinifolius*. It has been cultivated in CA and AZ where it is reported to be vigorous and attractive, but is not widely available.

Anthers: open wide, white and explanate; staminode bare

Name: fascicled = with clusters or bundles of leaves in axils that may become branches

Subgenus Penstemon, section Fasciculus, subsection Fasciculi


*P. fendleri* is an early bloomer with blue-violet flowers having slender, slightly curved tubes, rounded, flaring lower lobes and red-violet guidelines in 4 - 10 few-flowered, widely spaced whorls on one to a few erect stems reaching 20″. Leaves are lance-shaped, gray-green, glaucous and glabrous and clasp the stem. It grows well in sandy soils in TX, NM, OK, and KS and has been cultivated from CA to the Midwest. Cold moist stratification is required for about two months to germinate seeds. Several plants should be placed together for effective display.

Anthers: widely divergent, opening narrowly; staminode yellow-bearded, included

Name: Fendler's Penstemon, honoring August Fendler (1813 – 1883), noted botanical collector

Subgenus Penstemon, section Coerulei


*P. filiformis* is a rare, open subshrub to 20″ with small, bright blue flowers and almost thread-like leaves. It is found in a very limited area of n. CA at about 1500′. It has been successfully cultivated and reported on favorably in a few areas but seed is seldom available.

Anthers: sac-like, open halfway; staminode bare

Name: filiformis = threadlike

Subgenus Saccanthera, section Saccanthera, subsection Heterophylli


*P. filisepalis* has inch-long scarlet to deep red slender flowers with a few white hairs in the throat on 24″ stems. Leaves are slender with very small fascicles in the axils. It is from Chihuahua, Mexico and is quite rare. Seeds are seldom available.

Name: filisepalis = with thread-like sepals

Anthers: open flat, opposite; staminode has a dense, short yellow beard

Subgenus Penstemon, section Fasciculus, subsection Fasciculi


*P. flavescens* varies from 6 - 16″ in height and has small pale to bright yellow flowers in one to four verticillasters on stout stems above thick leaves which form a dense and sizable basal mat. The plant has good form, but is not showy. It often has only a single congested whorl of flowers at the top. Its native habitat is high in the Bitterroot Mts. of MT and ID, where it blooms in the summer. It may prefer acid soil. It is reported to be easily grown in Canada and Great Britain and northern states of the US and has good foliage and growth habit. Give cold, moist stratification for 12 weeks to germinate seed.

Anthers: red, moderately open, opposite; staminode yellow bearded at tip, included

Name: flavescent = yellowish

Subgenus Penstemon, section Penstemon, subsection Proceri

***P. floribundus*** is a rare plant from the Black Rock Desert of nw. NV. It is less than 1′ tall, and compact with narrow, medium to large flowers, pinched at the throat, dark blue on the face with a pale blue tube in a relatively long inflorescence for the size of the plant. Stem leaves have a prominent white mid-vein. There is no basal mat. It has not been reported in cultivation.

Anthers: barely exserted, horseshoe shaped, suture toothed, slightly twisted, dark in color; staminode white, smooth, included

Name: floribundus = with abundant flowers

Subgenus Saccanthera, section Saccanthera, subsection Heterophylli

***P. floridus*** is a robust and beautiful species from the desert foothills between 6000 and 8000′, north of Death Valley in CA and NV. Lanceolate leaves are blue-green with toothed edges on the lower ones. It has medium-sized, deep pink to rose-colored ventricose flowers, only 1 – 5 at each verticillaster in June and early July. Stems may be to 3′ tall. Variety *austinii* has slightly smaller and less inflated flowers that are more constricted at the throat with smaller lobes. Germinates after about 3 months of cold, moist stratification.

Anthers: opposite, explanate; staminode bare, both included

Names: Panamint Penstemon, Inyo Beardtongue

Subgenus Penstemon, section Peltanthera, subsection Peltanthera

***P. flowersii*** is a rare and threatened species, 3 - 10″ tall, found only in the clay badlands of ne. UT from 5000 - 5400′. Leaves are smooth, thick and blue-green, stems erect and flowers small, rose-pink in color.

Anthers: opposite, opening moderately; staminode has very short yellow-gold hairs at its recurved tip, included

Name: Flower's Penstemon for Seville Flowers (1900 – 1968), Brigham Young Univ. Botanist, who studied mosses extensively

Subgenus Penstemon, section Coerulei

***P. franklinii*** is a recently described species from Iron County, UT at 5500 to 6000′ with several stems less than 1′ tall, slender, finely hairy and narrowly attenuate-lanceolate leaves, glandular on the upper surface and occasionally toothed, and small to medium-sized blue to blue-lavender glandular-hairy flowers with purple guidelines and yellow bearding on the throat. It is closely related to *P. pinorum*.

Anthers: smooth, parallel, dehiscing end to end and across the connective, but not explanate; staminode bearded with flattened, golden hairs, included to slightly exserted

Name: honoring M. A. Franklin, Utah field botanist

Subgenus Penstemon, section Cristati

***P. fremontii*** grows on dry hillsides in the Uintah Basin of Utah, nw. CO and sw. WY between 4600 - 8000′ in May and June. It is common in pinyon/juniper habitat. Flowers are deep purple-blue, about 1″ long, almost regular, and large in proportion to the size of the plant, which may be 8 - 12″. Foliage is prominent and finely glandular-hairy. Allow 16 wks. for germination to occur.

Anthers: white, hairy, somewhat divaricate, opening from distal ends; staminode yellow or orange-bearded at apex, both included

Name: honors John C. Fremont (1813 – 1900), western explorer, "the Pathfinder"

Subgenus Habroanthus, Section Glabri

**P. frutescens** is now classified as **Pennellianthus frutescens**

***P. fruticiformis*** is a stiff, 1- 1 ½′ bushy, multi-branched wide plant with very narrow blue-green leaves and ventricose pale pink flowers with red-violet guidelines and exserted staminode in a loose, short inflorescence. It is found in desert washes between 4000 and 6000′ near Death Valley. It is reported easy to raise from seed, floriferous and neat by Rancho Santa Ana Botanic garden. Variety *amargosae* has smaller flowers and is found in NV. Cold stratification is not needed; it germinates readily.

Anthers: open almost flat; staminode densely bearded, exserted

Name: frutescent = somewhat shrub-like; Death Valley Penstemon

Subgenus Penstemon, section Peltanthera, subsection Peltanthera

***P. fruticosus*** is one of the most attractive penstemon species for large rock gardens. It is a shrubby plant, to 16″ tall when in flower and often broader than tall. It has keeled lavender to purple flowers, to 2″ in length that form secund clusters on the erect stems. Foliage is elliptical, usually toothed, dark green. It is common on rocky cliffs between 6500 and 8000′ east of the Cascade Range in OR, and in WA, MT, WY and British Columbia, where it may be seen in bloom anytime between May and August. It has been successfully cultivated from southern Canada and northern states to PA and New England and in Great Britain and Europe. It needs cold winter conditions with plenty of spring moisture. Will tolerate drier summer conditions. Protection from late winter sun is essential. It germinates at 70°F in 4 – 5 weeks. Variety *fruticosus* has slightly toothed leaves; variety *serratus* has a more mat-like habit, holly-like leaves and more compact form. Variety *scouleri* has larger flowers and narrower leaves.

Cultivars:

'Albus' is a dwarf form of variety *scouleri* with creamy-white flowers.

'Agog' has lavender flowers with an open throat, 6 - 8″ tall, and is a selection of var. *scouleri*.

'Amethyst' is a deep violet-flowered form of var. *scouleri*.

'Azureus' is a larger form of var. *scouleri,* to 12″ tall with lilac blue flowers, gray-green leaves.

'Charming' is a large form of pale pink-flowered var. *scouleri*

'Purple Haze' is a very floriferous form of var. *serratus* from the Univ. of British Columbia

'Holly' a delightful form of var. *serratus* with serrate and crisped, distinctive foliage; but not floriferous

'Jean' a form of var. *scouleri* with orchid flowers; 6 – 8″ tall

'Miss Spokane' is a lilac-blue-flowered form of the type species; 12 - 15″ tall.

'Shelly' is a pink-flowered form.

'Wallowa' is a compact form of var. *scouleri* with short, almost entire leaves, and normal flowers.


Name: fruticose = having characteristics of a true shrub

Anthers: covered with woolly hair, included; staminode lightly golden-bearded, included

Subgenus Dasanthera


**P. gairdneri** is a choice rock garden and trough plant that comes from ec. WA, OR and ID in June and July between 3250 and 5800′, blooming from late May into July. Slender, upward pointing ashy gray-green, mostly alternate leaves clothe many stems arising from a woody base. Flowers are medium-sized, usually secund, with wide-spreading lips in colors from white to pink or orchid, lavender and blue, often with a pale throat, in a narrow thyrse. The type species and subspecies *hians* are about 6″ tall. Subspecies *oreganus* is taller and more robust with larger flowers that are a soft blue with a cream-colored throat and leaves that are usually opposite. All are quite floriferous and have many sterile shoots that give a full base in the garden. May be deciduous in the mountains and semi-evergreen in cultivation in some locations. A warm spot in poor sandy soil is recommended. Germination takes about two to three months at 40°F.

Name: honoring Dr. Meredith Gairdner (1809 – 1835) amateur botanist, plant collector, physician

Anthers: widely divergent, not explanate; staminode yellow-bearded, barely exserted

Subgenus Penstemon, section Penstemon, subsection Gairdneriani


**P. gentianoides** is a Mexican species from the mountains sw. of Mexico City around 11,000′ south into Guatemala, generally in volcanic soil. Stems are usually 20 - 30″, but may be up to 6′ and are quite leafy with smaller leaves in the axils. The many medium to large flowers are purple or pink. The tube is campanulate. This plant is hardy in mild climate regions, probably not below USDA zone 7, rapid-growing and blooms abundantly.

Anthers: smooth, purple-black, not quite explanate; staminode slightly dilated with few short hairs, not exserted

Name: gentianoides = resembling a Gentian in shape; Gentian Penstemon

Section Penstemon, section Fasciculus, subsection Fasciculi


**P. gentryi** is another Mexican species from Chihuahua and nearby Sonora, closely related and similar to *P. campanulatus,* which is better known. It is distinguished by very narrow leaves. The flower color is pale lavender with a white throat and the stems are about 2′ tall.

Anthers: smooth and divaricate; staminode bare to minutely yellow-bearded

Name: Gentry's Penstemon for Howard S. Gentry (1903 - ), AZ botanist who specialized in Agaves

Subgenus Penstemon, section Fasciculus, subsection Campanulati


***P. gibbensii,*** from sc. WY, is a close relative of *P. cyananthus, P. saxosorum* and *P. fremontii.* It has several stems, 4 – 8″ tall with small to medium-sized clear blue flowers that are glandular and secund in a long raceme in June. Leaves are almost linear. It is found in barren sandy clay on slopes at about 6400′ and may be a threatened species. It has not been reported in cultivation.

Anthers: finely hairy, slightly divaricate, open only to the connective with toothed sutures; staminode sparsely yellow-bearded at apex, included

Name: Gibben's Penstemon, honoring its collector, Robert Gibbens, a Range Management student

Subgenus Habroanthus, section Glabri


***P. glaber*** has medium to large rich blue flowers with white throats and red-violet guidelines in 8 – 12 congested, secund verticils on stems that are usually 16 – 24" tall above a dense, glossy mat of basal foliage. The calyx is unusually short. Sometimes the stems are erect and sometimes spreading. Leaves are lanceolate, entire and bright green. The species is found in the wild between 6000 and 10,000′ from sw. ND, nc. SD and nw. WY to se. WY, nc. CO and w. NE., where it might be found blooming from late May into August. It is a popular species favorably reported from NH, VA, MI, SD, NE, and CA as well as the Rocky Mt. region. Paler color and sprawling are a problem in areas of high rainfall. Its native habitat is sandy to gravelly soils. Seed germinates at 40 or 70°F after being stored dry. *P. alpinus* and *P. brandegeei* are listed by some authorities as varieties of *P. glaber.* See descriptions under those names.

Anthers: with few short hairs, divergent; staminode bare or sparingly bearded with a rounded tip, included to slightly exserted

Name: glaber = glabrous, smooth; Smooth Penstemon

Subgenus Habroanthus, section Glabri


***P. glabrescens,*** found in n. NM and s. CO, is a mounding sub-shrub to 6″ with narrow linear leaves and small blue to lavender flowers with a showy staminode in late May and June. It is easy, long-lived and very pleasing for the rock garden. Germination takes about 12 weeks with cold, moist stratification at 40°F. Cuttings and divisions root easily. Some authorities list it as a subspecies of *P. crandallii.*

Anthers: divaricate and opening widely; staminode densely orange-bearded

Name: glabrous = smooth

Subgenus Penstemon, section Ericopsis, section Caespitosi


***P. glandulosus*** is a tall, outstandingly beautiful species, blooming from May to July, sometimes reaching 3 ½′. Unusually large, pale lavender flowers surround the stems in 3 to 6 dense clusters. The entire plant is covered with glandular hairs so that it is sticky and glistens in the light. The typical species has toothed leaves, but variety *chelanensis,* occurring in c. WA is shorter and has entire leaves. The original species is found in richer soil in WA, OR and ID up to 4600'. It is not difficult to grow and has been praised from ID to NM. Seed germinates at 40° in about 8 wks.

Anthers: white, hairy, sac-like with toothed sutures; staminode bare, dilated, exserted

Name: glandulosus = with gland-tipped hairs

Subgenus Saccanthera, section Saccanthera, subsection Serrulati


***P. glaucinus*** occurs only high in the mountains in sc. OR and was once considered an endangered species, but is no longer. It has not been reported in cultivation. It is 1' tall with small blue flowers in a few widely spaced rings, with only the top one or two rings densely flowered. It blooms in June and July. Leaves are thick, glaucous and usually bluish-green in color.

Anthers: open narrowly across the connective; staminode may be bearded or not, included

Name: Glaucous-leaved Penstemon

Subgenus Penstemon, section Penstemon, subsection Proceri


***P. globosus*** is an attractive member of the *Proceri* group that is fairly common in its native habitat of mountain meadows in ne. OR, ID and w. MT. It carries the largest flowers of the group, to ¾" long, usually in a single cluster, but may have up to four clusters of bright blue flowers on stems up to 24" from June to August. It is praised as a garden subject on the coasts and in Europe and Canada. Germinates in 12 wks. after cold, moist stratification

Anthers: divaricate, pouch-like, not open across the connective; staminode densely golden bearded, included

Name: Globe Penstemon

Subgenus Penstemon, section Penstemon, subsection Proceri


***P. goodrichii*** has small blue-lavender flowers with five equal, almost regular lobes flaring gradually from the tube. The flowers are downy and sticky in 3 – 6 few-flowered whorls on several 10 - 16" smooth stems in June. Leaves are almost linear and gray. It is found only in clay Badlands in ne. Utah between 5600 and 6200' and is possibly an endangered species. It has not been reported in cultivation.

Anthers: explanate; staminode densely golden-bearded, very short and included

Name: honoring Sharel Goodrich (1943 -  ) co-author of Flora of Utah and botanist with U. S. Forest Service

Subgenus Penstemon, section Cristati


***P. gormanii*** grows in northern British Columbia, the Yukon and Alaska from 3300 to 9800' and is similar to *P. eriantherus*. It grows up to 12" tall, is usually nearer 6". Flowers appear in June and are downy, small to medium in size and white to orchid-pink or blue-purple, almost campanulate, with guidelines and protruding staminode. Leaves are narrow and there are usually several stems arising from the crown. It germinates at 40° alternated with 70°F in 8 – 10 wks. and has been favorably reported on in MI and Europe.

Anthers: smooth, open wide, included; staminode yellow-bearded, exserted

Name: honoring Martin Gorman (1853 – 1926) who collected in the Northwest with T. J. Howell, author of the first Flora of Northwestern America, and also in Alaska

Subgenus Penstemon, section Cristati


*P. gracilentus* is a little known, late-blooming species from sc. OR to Lake Tahoe and adjacent NV. It has slender stems and small glandular-hairy blue to purple flowers that are arranged in sparse, widely-spaced clusters. Height is usually about 16″. It is found in open conifer woodlands around 6700′ in loose, stony soil rich in leafmold. A San Francisco grower reports it a delightful, long-lived plant.

Anthers: purple-black, sac-like; staminode moderately yellow-bearded, included

Name: Very Slender Penstemon

Subgenus Saccanthera, Section Saccanthera, Subsection Heterophylli


*P. gracilis* has small to medium-sized narrow, sticky-hairy lavender flowers, with an extended white-bearded palate, in a narrow thyrse in June. Each plant has a few stems to 18″ and lanceolate leaves that are slightly toothed. It is found on sandy and gravelly soils from British Columbia to Ontario and south to nw. IA and n. NM at about 6,000′. Although not showy, it is easy in cultivation, germinating in early spring. It is appropriately used in wild grass meadows because it competes well with sod-forming grasses and stands out among them.

Anthers: widely divergent with toothed edges on sutures; staminode densely golden-bearded, just reaching the opening

Name: Slender Penstemon

Subgenus Penstemon, Section Penstemon, Subsection Penstemon


*P. grahamii* is a charmer, ideally suited to troughs or a small, close-up rock garden. It has a cushion-like alpine appearance with dark green, elliptic leaves in a compact 4 - 8″ clump and upward-facing, ventricose-ampliate lavender flowers with a gaping mouth that are large in proportion to the plant. It occurs in a very limited dry area of broken shale soil in ne. UT and adjacent CO between 4600 and 6900′, blooming in late May and early June, and is considered threatened. It has been successfully grown in troughs in CO and is greatly admired.

Name: Graham's Penstemon, honoring Edward H. Graham (1902 – 1966) a botanist specializing in the Uintah Basin flora

Anthers: open fully, explanate; staminode exserted and densely golden-bearded

Subgenus Penstemon, section Cristati


*P. grandiflorus* is well-named, being one of the more spectacular species of penstemon. It may be found blooming in the Great Plains from e. MT, WY, and MN south to c. TX. Erect, stout stems are 2 - 4′ tall. Leaves are large, almost heart-shaped, gray-green, glabrous and glaucous. The flowers, sometimes almost 2″ long, of beautiful texture can be white, pink, lavender or blue and are distinctive in that the upper side of the flower is abruptly expanded but the lower side is flat. They are cupped by the leaves and bracts in many few-flowered whorls up the stem. This species is easy to germinate in about 8 wks. at cool temperatures and easy to handle as a seedling.  Plant in full sun in gravelly soil.  It is susceptible to leaf spot disease in wet climates and when over watered.  Gardeners from PA to NV have found it spectacular and very successful although it seldom lives more than 4 or 5 years.

Cultivars:

'Prairie Snow' a pure white form

'Prairie Palette' a seed strain that produces many colors from white, pink and red to dark purple. It also has a moderate degree of resistance to leaf spot.

Anthers: pale green, widely divergent but not explanate; staminode abruptly recurved at apex with minute orange hairs only at tip, dilated, just reaching the opening

Name: Shell-leaved Penstemon

Subgenus Penstemon, section Coerulei

*P. griffinii*  is a little-known, blue-flowered species, sometimes with a closed throat, from c. CO and n. NM, usually above 6000' in June and July.  It is related to *P. oliganthus*.  Several stems are 6 - 15″ tall with a loose thyrse of small to medium, slender blue flowers with a noticeable white palate and orange-bearded staminode.  It may be found in open fields or thin pinyon/juniper woodlands, and is just beginning to be cultivated.  It is easy to germinate.

Anthers: dark purple, widely divaricate, narrowly opened; staminode orange-bearded, barely exserted

Name: Griffin's Penstemon, honoring Alfred A. Griffin, a Colorado botanist and plant collector

Subgenus Penstemon, section Penstemon, subsection Humiles

*P. grinnellii* has medium to large ventricose-ampliate flowers similar to *P. palmeri* and is bee-pollinated, but differs in other respects.  It is bushy, 1 - 3' tall and can form a clump to 3' wide. Leaves are toothed and green, not connate, sometimes reported to have a whitish bloom.  The inflorescence is not as strict and flowers are more lavender than pink with distinct guidelines. They have no fragrance.  This species is found on dry rocky slopes in s. CA between 1640 and 9500' from April to August.  A subspecies, *scrophularioides,* comes from further north and grows taller.  This species has been grown in WA, NV and VA, and is highly recommended.

Anthers: widely divergent, opening full length; staminode densely yellow-orange bearded, exserted

Name:  for Fordyce Grinnell (1882 – 1943) entomologist

Subgenus Penstemon, section Peltanthera, subsection Peltanthera

*P. guadalupensis*  is found in c. TX on dry, gravelly soils and has small to medium white flowers with flared lobes  on 8 - 15″ stems in few-flowered verticillasters forming an open inflorescence from March to May.  Plants spread by underground roots.  Subspecies *ernestii* has somewhat broader leaves.  It is not known to be in cultivation.

Anthers, brown or black, smooth, explanate; staminode barely exserted, lightly yellow-bearded

Name: from Guadalupe River, TX
Subgenus Penstemon, section Cristati

*P. hallii* is an alpine species from above tree line of the Rocky Mts. in Colorado between 10,000 and 12,300', where it blooms in late June. It adapts well to garden conditions at lower altitudes and blooms earlier. The slender dark green leaves form clumps about 3" tall and short stems up to 8" bear clusters of over-sized, abruptly expanded violet to purple blooms. Surprisingly, it germinates readily at 70° without cold moist stratification. It is an early bloomer and does well in a gravel, sand and peat mix or gravel over sandy loam soil. It has been successfully grown from e. WA, NV, CO, NM, IA, and MI to PA and VA. In Scotland it is long-lived and long-blooming.

Anthers: smooth, dark purple, widely divergent; staminode orange-bearded, exserted

Name: honors Elihu Hall (1822 – 1882), Illinois botanist who collected plants from OR to TX

Subgenus Habroanthus, section Glabri

*P. harbouri* is another alpine, best in small rock gardens and troughs. It is a creeping plant, not over 6" tall, with small blue flowers, somewhat crowded and secund, just above the oval gray-green to green leaves. It is found from 10,000 – 13,500' in the high mountains of CO on scree slopes in July. It is reported to do well in OR and CO in sand, soil and granite grit mix. It is easily propagated from cuttings of the underground stems. May be deciduous in some areas. Germinates readily at 70°F.

Anthers: smooth, explanate; staminode broadened, densely orange-yellow bearded, just reaching the opening

Name: honors J. P. Harbour who participated in an expedition exploring Colorado in 1862

Subgenus Penstemon, section Penstemon, subsection Harbouriani

*P. harringtonii* is a 12 - 28" tall species with pink-lavender to bright blue flowers found in CO from Vail north between 7200 and 8000'. The flowers are small to medium in size and surround the stem in 5 – 10 verticillasters that are not congested. Foliage is glaucous. It is abundant in the small area where found. It is similar to *P. osterhoutii* and also has some characteristics of *P. cyathophorus*.

Anthers: sac-like, opening narrowly on side suture, one pair noticeably exserted; staminode broadened at tip, densely golden-bearded and barely exserted

Name: honors Dr. Harold Harrington (1903 – 1976) who published the first Colorado Flora in 1954

Subgenus Penstemon, section Coerulei

*P. hartwegii* is one of the largest flowered of the genus with intensely red-purple 2" narrowly expanded flowers having white throats and guidelines, on 5' erect, sometimes branching, stems. Leaves are slender and narrowly lanceolate, entire and bright green. This species is found in wooded highlands north of Mexico City between 6900 - 9200' near Hidalgo. Unfortunately, it has not proven hardy in the United States except in mild coastal climates. It can be greenhouse grown.

Cultivar:
'Albus', a fine plant with creamy buds that comes true from seed

Anthers: smooth, rounded, explanate; staminode smooth to moderately bearded
Name: honors Carl Theodor Hartweg (1812 – 1871), German-born botanist and plant collector
Subgenus Penstemon, section Fasciculus, subsection Fasciculi

*P. havardii* is a most attractive scarlet-flowered species from the Trans-Pecos region of w. TX, where it blooms in April and May and later if rain comes in the summer. The large, gray-green glabrous and glaucous entire leaves make a beautiful foil for many stems that may reach 5'. The flowers are glandular and more than an inch long, slightly constricted before flaring into almost regular lobes. They are often irregularly spaced in an open thyrse that continues to open new flowers over a long period. It has been successfully grown from Riverside, CA to Reno, NV and Falls Church VA. Late fall planting for some cold moist stratification outside or 8 weeks refrigeration are suggested. It has survived winters to 10°F., but not in USDA Zone 5.

Anthers: pale, explanate and exserted; staminode, bare, included
Name: honors Valery Havard (1846 – 1927) a French-born surgeon who served in the US Army and was an avid plant explorer and collector.
Subgenus Penstemon, section Peltanthera, subsection Havardiani

*P. haydenii* is now a rare and endangered federally listed plant but may one day be off the list, thanks to restoration efforts. It grows in the Sand Hills of NE and has been recently found in WY also. It is a sprawling to upright plant with long, tapering glabrous and glaucous gray-green leaves and fragrant milky-lavender inch-long flowers. The plant may be up to 20" tall and the inflorescence is compact with usually 6 – 10 closely spaced verticillasters of flowers circling the stem, but interrupted by tapering bracts extending well beyond the flowers. It is very hardy and had been quite widely grown before federal listing. Bloom is from mid-May to late June.

Anthers: divergent, opening all across; staminode densely golden bearded, included
Names: honors Ferdinand Vandeveer Hayden (1829 – 1887), geologist, plant collector and leader of the Rocky Mountain Survey; Blowout Penstemon
Subgenus Penstemon, section Coerulei

*P. henricksonii* has purple-red flowers similar to those of *P. barbatus,* but has broad leaves on stems up to 28". It is found in shaded oak/pine/fir forests between 6900 and 9000' in Coahuila, Mexico, but has not been reported in cultivation.

Anthers: open broadly from distal end with toothed sutures, exserted; staminode glabrous, dilated at apex, barely exserted
Name: honors James Henrickson (1928 – 1979), California botany professor and student of Chihuahuan Desert Flora

Subgenus Habroanthus, section Elmigera

**P. heterodoxus** comes from damp, high-mountain meadows of the Sierra Nevada in California and adjacent Nevada between 6500 and 12,800'. Very small, narrow, purple-blue flowers are arranged in 2 – 4 dense verticillasters on stems that may be from 3 - 8" tall in June and July. Variety *cephalophorus* can be 15" tall and have up to 6 or 7 clusters. It is found between 6800 and 10,800' at the southern end of the range. Variety *shastensis* is found at the northern end of the range between 6000 and 7900' and may be 2' tall and have more clusters. All have neat mats of entire, glabrous green foliage. They are desirable plants where moisture is adequate. Germination is good at 70°F.

Anthers: dehisce full length, glabrous, toothed along suture, just reaching opening; staminode yellow bearded, included

Name: heterodox = different from what is usually accepted; Sierran Penstemon

Subgenus Penstemon, section Penstemon, subsection Proceri

**P. heterophyllus** has been widely cultivated in this country and in Great Britain and Europe. It is a semi-shrub, 1 - 2' tall that blooms for a long period with many stems of medium-sized flowers that are a brilliant blue on the lobes fading into orchid pink tubes above narrow green leaves with fascicles. The flowers are arranged in open subsecund racemes. The type species has yellow buds but the yellow disappears from fully open flowers. This species is found from 160' to 5250' in CA on the coastal foothills from Humboldt Co. to San Diego and may be found in bloom from late May to August. Subspecies *purdyi*, found in the northern part of the range, does not have the yellow buds and has branches but rarely has fascicles. Subspecies *australis* has fascicles of fine leaves in the axils, is finely downy and is found in the southern part of the range. Germination takes 6 weeks at cool temperatures. It has been reported to survive -15°F and live many years with somewhat organic soil enriched with superphosphate and supplementary water in dry areas. It is easy from heel cuttings and is treated as an annual in many areas with wet summers where it blooms prolifically all summer and then dies out.

Cultivars:
'Blue Bedder' or 'California Blue Bedder', a form of var. *purdyi*
'Blue of Zurich' or 'Zuriblau', a "gentian blue" form

Anthers: sac-like, curved forward with teeth along the suture; staminode glabrous, included

Name: heterophyllus = varied leaf; Foothills penstemon; Ssp. *purdyi* is named for a longtime California plantsman, Carlton Purdy (1861 – 1945)

Subgenus Saccanthera, section Saccanthera, subsection Heterophylli

**P. hidalgensis** is from the mountains around Mexico City between 5900 and 7300'. Large red-purple to purple flowers with wide white throats in a leafy inflorescence top stems that may reach 6' or more. The plant is glandular hairy with irregularly toothed, heart-shaped leaves. It is in cultivation in Guatemala.

Anthers: divaricate, not explanate; staminode dilated and heavily bearded

Name: from the state of Hidalgo

Subgenus Penstemon, section Fasciculus, subsection Perfoliati


***P. hintonii*** is a rare species from the state of Guerrero, Mexico and somewhat similar to *P. campanulatus.* Leaves are strongly toothed, narrow to elliptic and widely spaced. Flowers are medium to large, purple, and campanulate, with a heavily bearded throat. Cultivation has not been reported in the United States.

Anthers: widely divergent, open narrowly; staminode dilated, bare, exserted

Name: honors George B. Hinton ( - 1943), plant collector

Subgenus Penstemon, section Fasciculus, Subsection Campanulati


***P. hirsutus*** has long been a popular garden species. Its natural habitat is from Quebec, Canada and MI south to VA and KY. It is easy to grow almost anywhere in the US, Great Britain and Europe. Many wiry, erect stems to 24″ carry open panicles of slender lavender to violet or pink inch-long flowers with an uplifted palate and closed white lips in May and June. The plants are glandular hairy and glisten in sunlight. Leaves are mostly basal, slender to moderately broad in the basal mat, green (turning maroon in winter), often finely toothed. A single plant a few years old can form a good clump but several planted together make a good display sooner. It is long-lived, self-sowing and reliable. Formerly, *pygmaeus* and *minimus* were listed as dwarf subspecies but are now considered just different forms. Almost any well-drained soil in sun or part shade with moderate watering in dry weather will suit this species. Seed should be stored at least 6 months and then given 3 months cold moist storage at 40°F before being sown in light at warm temperatures. Most plants seeded in January bloom the first year. Division of clumps is easy.


Cultivars:

'Albus', a white-flowered dwarf form like 'Pygmaeus'

'Dainty Violet', a strain of purple-flowered selections

'Gladwyne Strain', deeper colored varieties

'Minimus', a  dwarf form with erect stems, lavender flowers

'Pygmaeus', a dwarf form with short stems broadly angled, purple flowers; 4" tall

'Roseus', a pink-flowered form

'Tiny Tim', a 2″ tall form of 'Pygmaeus'


Anthers blue-black, smooth, opening across the connective; staminode golden bearded, slightly exserted

Name: hirsutus = covered with short stiff hairs

Subgenus Penstemon, section Penstemon, subsection Penstemon


***P. humilis*** is a variable small blue-flowered species, 8 – 20″ tall with leaves that vary from entire and smooth to slightly toothed and hairy, dark green or gray-green, usually with a basal mat. It is widely distributed from CA, NV, OR and WA to UT, WY and CO from 4950 to 11,000'. It is a good rock garden or low border plant in slightly enriched soil. Flowers are blue to deep blue-purple, moderately funnel-form, surrounding the short stems in separated clusters, and foliage is quite prominent. It may be found in bloom from May to July. Variety *obtusifolius* has slightly larger leaves that may be toothed; variety *brevifolius* is generally smaller with glabrous leaves. Germination takes place after 8 weeks of cold, moist stratification, but sometimes seeds need to be held over for a second year before germination occurs. Once started, the plants are very hardy, long-lived and easily divided.

Anthers: blue-black, smooth, opening full length; staminode orange-yellow bearded, included

Name: humilis = low-growing

Subgenus Penstemon, section Penstemon, subsection Humiles

*P. idahoensis* is a rather rare species from sc. ID and nw. UT. It has slender, erect, dark green, glandular strap-like leaves forming a clump from which several stems to 8″ tall of medium-sized deep blue flowers arise in June. The flowers are upward facing, secund, somewhat ventricose and glabrous. Germination is after 7 – 8 weeks of cold, moist stratification. Although it is found in tufa-like soil between 5350 and 5700', it has grown well and lived several years in sandy loam garden soil low in organic matter.

Anthers: moderately divergent, opening from the distal ends, not across the connective, covered with fine white hair; staminode smooth, included, bluish

Name: idahoensis = from Idaho

Subgenus Habroanthus, section Glabri

*P. imberbis* comes from a large area of c. Mexico: Guanajuato, Jalisco, San Luis Potosi and Zacatecas. It has sparse, narrow 1″ coral-red flowers with prominent pale anthers on stems two or more feet tall. Plant form is similar to *P. barbatus.* It is not known to have been cultivated in the United States.

Anthers, slightly divergent, opening from distal end, not across the connective; staminode bare, included

Name: imberbis = beardless

Subgenus Habroanthus, section Elmigera

*P. immanifestus* is a robust, stocky plant with smooth, entire gray-green leaves, erect stems to 2 ½', each bearing 4 – 11 somewhat congested verticils of small lavender to pink flowers in late May and June. It is found in the Great Basin Desert between 4900 and 6500' in w. Utah and e. NV. Germination requires cold, moist stratification, and sometimes does not take place until the second year.

It has not been widely cultivated but has been successful in NV, WA, MI and NM.

Anthers: divergent, opening full-length with finely-toothed sutures; staminode bearded with very short yellow hairs, just reaching the opening

Name: immanifest = unrevealed

Subgenus Penstemon, section Coerulei

*P. incertus* grows as a rounded shrub, 2 ½' tall and as broad, in the sandy washes and foothills into pinyon/juniper habitat in a large area on the western side of the Mojave Desert in CA between 3300 and 5600'. It is similar to *P. fruticiformis*. It has an open thyrse with narrow, finely toothed leaves and inch-long red-violet flowers with blue lobes. It was reported easily germinated in the Los Angeles area, floriferous and long blooming in rocky loam and full sun without additional irrigation. It has done well in se. WA but may not be hardy where temperatures fall below 15°F.

Anthers: divaricate, open full length but not explanate, finely toothed at suture; staminode densely bearded, included

Name: incertus = uncertain, doubtful

Subgenus Penstemon, section Peltanthera, subsection Peltanthera

*P. inflatus* is closely related and similar to *P. oliganthus*. It has small to medium-sized blue flowers with pale throats in up to seven widely spaced verticillasters on erect slender stems to 2', with glabrous green leaves and does not have a persistent basal mat. It is found in nc. NM in wooded areas between 7500 and 11,000', blooming in July. This species is not widely cultivated but easy and makes a good display with several plants together in partial shade in dry areas and sun in wetter climates. It is drought tolerant, hardy and long-lived.

Anthers: widely divergent, open across but not explanate; staminode orange-yellow bearded, included

Name: inflatus = enlarged, distended

Subgenus Penstemon, section Penstemon, subsection Humiles

*P. isophyllus*, from Puebla and Oaxaca, south and east of Mexico City, is a charming species with narrow-tubed 1 3/8" flowers. The numerous flowers are red to deep rosy-red or purplish-red with a white to pale cream throat, and have flared lobes and strongly marked guidelines. There is also a white form. Herbaceous stems may be decumbent or arching to 40" with narrowly elliptic to lanceolate, fascicled leaves. It is successfully grown in CA and other mild Mediterranean climate areas and in the Southeast where its foliage has remained green through the winter. It is widely used in hybridizing. Usually blooms in first year and may be used as an annual if started early in a greenhouse. May not be hardy below USDA zone 7.

Anthers: smooth and explanate; staminode bare to occasionally slightly bearded

Name; isophyllus = bearing only one type of leaf

Subgenus Penstemon, section Fasciculus, subsection Fasciculi

*P. jamesii* has medium to large broad, ventricose-ampliate lavender flowers with vertical lobes and a white line outlining the lip at the lower side of the throat. The lower lip is usually prominently bearded with pale golden hairs and the flower has red-violet guidelines. It may be up to 20" tall with several erect stems and 4 – 12 secund verticillasters and has narrow, gray-green barely toothed leaves and bracts. An attractive and drought tolerant plant, it does well in grasslands and dry rock gardens. It can be found in sandy and sandy-loam soils between 4500 and 7000′ in TX, CO, KS and NM, blooming in late May and June. Germination takes place after 12 weeks of cold moist stratifying or sowing outside in the fall in the Great Plains. A grower in southern France reports success with it as well.

Anthers: white, opening opposite and explanate; staminode bearded with long golden-yellow hairs, exserted

Name: honors Edwin James (1797 – 1861), a surgeon and naturalist with Long's Expedition to the Rocky Mts.

Subgenus Penstemon, section Cristati


*P. janishiae* is a short species that would fit well in a dry rock garden or trough. The small to medium-sized flowers vary from pink to red-violet and dull purple, are upward facing and ventricose ampliate, also distinctly bilabiate, with a large mouth and bearded lower lip. Few flowers are closely clustered in 2 – 5 verticillasters on several stems to 8″ tall. Leaves may be toothed toward the apex, gray-green and downy, small in proportion to the inflorescence. It is slow to germinate, requiring 8 – 12 weeks cold moist stratification, and not easy to maintain, but well worth the effort. It is found in clay soils in sagebrush and pinyon/juniper communities between 4200 and 7400′ in ne. CA, se. OR, n. and c. NV and sw. ID and grown in the Rocky Mt. States, blooming in late May and June.

Anthers: pale, widely divergent, explanate; staminode golden-bearded, recurved, and prominently exserted

Name: honors Jeanne R. Janish, botanical illustrator

Subgenus Penstemon, section Cristati


*P. kingii* is a rare small species with dark purple-blue to red-violet small to medium-sized glandular ventricose flowers and narrow hoary leaves. It is difficult to find in the dry sagebrush valleys and pinyon/juniper communities from 4950 - 9800′ in nc. and e. NV and se. OR from late May to July. It is usually less than 1′ tall with secund flowers. It has not been reported in cultivation.

Anthers: saccate, glabrous with toothed edges on the suture across the top; staminode smooth, exserted

Name: honors Clarence King (1842 – 1901), western explorer

Subgenus Saccanthera, section Saccanthera, subsection Heterophylli


*P. kunthii* is a late and long blooming species native to many areas of w. and c. Mexico to Oaxaca that has proven hardy over much of the United States and is popular for its attractiveness to hummingbirds. It forms an open, leafy fountain of branched stems 12 - 36″ tall with panicles of narrow, only moderately ampliate, dark red flowers, often with paler throats and interior guidelines. The leaves are variably serrate and have fascicles. It does well in sandy loam soils; does not need preconditioning to germinate. Bloom is from mid-summer to frost.

Anthers: explanate, glabrous; staminode somewhat dilated, slightly bearded, barely exserted

Name: honors Carl S. Kunth (1788 – 1850), botanist

Subgenus Penstemon, section Fasciculus, subsection Campanulati

***P. labrosus*** has scarlet flowers 1 ½″ long, narrowly tubular with lower lobes spreading downward and upper lobes forming a short hood in July. The leaves are mostly basal and upright. It is 12 - 24″ tall and forms a clump from creeping rootstocks after several years. Several plants together make a good display. It is found from s. CA into Baja CA in open pinyon/juniper and mixed conifer forest between 5000 and 10,000′. It germinates easily without treatment and lives 5 – 10 years in gravelly soil with some humus and occasional irrigation in light shade. It has been reported successful in southern CA and in England.

Anthers: opposite, opening narrowly from the distal end with minutely toothed edges, exserted; staminode glabrous, exserted

Name: labrosus refers to the prominent lips

Subgenus Habroanthus, section Elmigera


***P. laetus*** is a somewhat woody sub-shrub with narrow, gray-green leaves and an open inflorescence of 1 ¼″ exteriorly glandular purple-blue flowers in June and July. It may reach 2 ½′ but is usually shorter and sometimes sprawling rather than erect. It comes from dry open woods in the Sierras at elevations from 1300 to 8000′ in n. CA, OR and NV. Variety *sagittatus* has a slightly narrowed throat and longer, arrow-shaped anthers. Variety *leptosepalus* has longer sepals and is found at the northern end of the range. This species has been cultivated successfully in many areas.

Anthers: sac-like, with toothed opening across top, with a few long hairs on inner sides; staminode glabrous, not exserted

Names: laetus = cheerful, bright;  Sierran Penstemon, Gay Penstemon

Subgenus Saccanthera, section Saccanthera, subsection Heterophylli


***P. laevigatus*** is a tall, stiff species with an open thyrse of pale lavender or white inch-long flowers on stems to 28″. It is similar to *P. digitalis,* but not as large; is found in the wild from s. PA and NJ to FL and MS. Gardeners report it easy and good in sandy loam soil in woodland wild gardens from MI, IA and s. MO to PA. It is also reportedly quite drought tolerant.

Anthers: widely divaricate, smooth; staminode bearded, exserted

Name: from laevis = smooth, not hairy

Subgenus Penstemon, section Penstemon, subsection Penstemon


***P. laevis*** grows 1 - 3′ tall and has medium-sized rich blue to purple flowers in a narrow thyrse of 6 – 15 verticillasters that is sometimes somewhat secund. The flowers are glabrous, ventricose-ampliate and have distinct red-violet guidelines in the throat. Leaves are prominent, glabrous, and entire, bright green. It is found in UT in the vicinity of Zion National Park and may also be in adjacent AZ on the Kaibab Plateau at elevations between 5000 and 7100′, blooming in May and June. It is a dryland species.

Anthers: divergent, opening from the distal end, not across the connective, twisted, one pair just exserted; staminode golden-yellow-bearded, just reaching the orifice

Name: laevis = smooth; Smooth Penstemon

Subgenus Habroanthus, section Glabri

**P. lanceolatus**   is a scarlet-flowered species found in Mexico in the states of Aguascalientes, Nuevo Leon, Coahuila, Durango and Chihuahua; and in the US in s. TX, in or near Big Bend, and possibly in s. NM.  It has several stems to 20″, long narrow leaves with finely downy surfaces, an inflorescence with few flowers in a secund raceme, and blooms from July to October, after summer rains.  Flowers are about an inch long, glandular and tubular with small lobes.  It has not been reported in cultivation in the US.

Anthers: sac-shaped, dehiscent across top with fine teeth; staminode bare, not dilated, included

Name : from lance-shaped leaves

Subgenus Penstemon, section Chamaeleon

**P. laricifolius**   is a tiny plant from the dry plains of n. CO, MT and WY between 6000 and 9000′, blooming in late June and July, suitable for  rock gardens and troughs.  It is not showy, but totally charming with tiny tufts of grass-like foliage and many stems of full-faced, delicate cream, pink, orchid or lavender flowers and deeper colored buds rising to 12″ or less.  Lower stems extend outward in the garden so the tiny mound appears covered with flowers right to the ground.  Subspecies *exifolius* has clear white flowers and is usually less than 7″.  It is a dry land plant but needs spring moisture to bloom.  Germinates after 8 - 12 weeks of cold moist stratification.  It has grown well from NM and CO to MI, NY and Ontario; it has been long-lived in the west.

Anthers dark, opposite, opening narrowly; staminode with yellow bearding, slightly exserted

Name:  laricifolius = with larch-like leaves

Subgenus Penstemon, section Ericopsis, subsection Ericopsis

**P. laxiflorus**   occurs  from GA and FL west to TX in sandy, acid soils on woodland verges in April and is similar to *P. arkansanus*.  It has clusters of medium-sized, narrow, moderately ampliate, white to light pink flowers offset from the main stem on short branches forming open panicles.   The several stems are 12 - 28″ tall with lanceolate, finely toothed leaves and inflorescences 4 – 10 inches long.  The flowers have an extended lower lip, sometimes almost closing the mouth, lightly hairy with red-violet guidelines.  It has been cultivated in the south east but not reported elsewhere.

Anthers: dark, divergent, open all across with minute teeth along suture; staminode densely bearded with yellow hairs, exserted

Name: laxiflorus  = with loose or open flowers

Subgenus Penstemon, section Penstemon, subsection Penstemon

**P. laxus**   comes from the dry meadows of sw. ID at about 5800′.  Few-flowered, congested clusters of medium to dark, upward-facing small blue flowers with pale hairy throats top slender 1 - 2′ stems above mats of slightly gray-green leaves in late May.  From a distance it is said to look like an allium. It is reported to be easy to grow.

Anthers: explanate; staminode just reaching the orifice, smooth to lightly bearded

Name: lax = loose

Subgenus Penstemon, section Penstemon, subsection Proceri


***P. leiophyllus*** has 1″ glandular blue to purple flowers in a secund inflorescence of 2 – 17 verticillasters on one to several erect stems 8 to 28″ tall above narrow, glabrous green leaves. The flowers have white spots and red-violet guidelines in the throat. This species is found in sw.UT between 6000 and 11,900′ and blooms mid-to-late July and August. Two varieties are found in NV. Variety *francisci-pennellii* has larger flowers on stems less than 1′ and anthers that open from the distal end but not across the connective. Variety *keckii,* also less than 1′, has a shorter flower and is only found in the Charleston Mts. of NV. All three varieties have distinct white patches of gland tipped hairs on the inside edge of the lower lip and distinct red-violet guidelines. This is a dry upland species requiring 16 weeks of cold, moist stratification to germinate.

Anthers: white to blue, smooth, not open across the connective, with toothed sutures and just reaching the opening; staminode with a few short hairs, included

Name: leiophyllus = smooth leaved

Subgenus Habroanthus, section Glabri


***P. lemhiensis*** is a threatened species, found in ID and MT on rocky banks and wooded slopes or among sagebrush at around 7500′, with dark blue medium-sized flowers on stout stems 12 - 28″ tall. The inflorescence is often short, with flowers very close to the stem and appears in June and July. It has persistent thick basal leaves that may be smooth or covered with fine surface hair, and is long-lived in northern gardens when grown in rich soil. It is similar to *P. cyaneus,* but with narrower leaves. Seed germination takes place after 8 weeks of cold, moist stratification.

Anthers: narrowly open partway from the distal end, twisted, with few hairs and a finely toothed suture; staminode smooth, included

Name: lemhiensis =  from Lemhi County, ID

Subgenus Habroanthus, section Glabri


***P. lentus*** is somewhat similar to *P. angustifolius,* but the flowers are on short pedicels. It is 8 - 16″ tall with glaucous and glabrous, fleshy leaves and deep rose to red-violet, rather small flowers in 4 – 8 few-flowered verticillasters that are more or less secund and may or may not have hairs on the lower throat. Variety *albiflorus* (white-flowered) is found in the Abajo Mts. in se. UT only; the type species is found across the Four Corners region between 4900 and 8500′ in sandy or gravelly soil and blooms in May and June. It germinates after 12 weeks of cold, moist stratification and has been long-lived and very pleasing in dry gardens in the southwest.

Anthers:  widely divergent, opening narrowly; staminode somewhat recurved and dilated with yellow hairs at apex, just reaching the opening

Name: lentus = pliant, flexible

Subgenus Penstemon, Section Coerulei

**P. leonardii** is an especially fine low, compact plant to 1' with many small to medium-sized violet to blue flowers in 3 – 10 close verticillasters on many stems. It is found from se. ID to s. Utah in rock crevices and gravelly slopes between 6000 and 10,000', blooming in June and July. Variety *higginsii* has lavender flowers and occurs in sw. UT. This species is a dry land sub-shrub that has been reported successfully grown in several areas. It germinates after 8 weeks of cold, moist stratification.

Anthers: sac-like, open across the top with minute teeth and hairs; staminode slightly dilated, glabrous, white to blue, just reaching the orifice to slightly exserted

Name: honors Fred E. Leonard (1866 – 1922) plant collector and physician

Subgenus Saccanthera, section Saccanthera, subsection Heterophylli

**P. leonensis** is found in Nuevo Leon, Mexico in the Sierra Madre Oriental between 9800 and 11,000' in open pine forests. It has broad, inch-long bell-shaped glandular-hairy flowers that are red-violet on the upper surface and white on the lower throat and lips with deep red-purple guidelines. The 20" stems are many and leafy. The inflorescence is long, more or less secund, with one or two flowers open at each node at a time. It forms a very good-looking clump, has only been reported grown in England and se. WA, USDA Zone 6, where it performed well and is much enjoyed.

Anthers: opposite, explanate, glabrous; staminode dilated, bearded with long yellow hairs at apex

Name: from Nuevo Leon, Mexico

Subgenus Penstemon, section Fasciculus, subsection Fasciculi

**P. linarioides** is a popular species with rock garden enthusiasts because it is a neat and handsome plant all year. It has linear gray-blue-green leaves and small, upward and outward facing blue or lavender flowers, with a white throat and guidelines, (also sometimes with palate hairs) from May to August. The many stems may be upright to 1' or decumbent, becoming woody and matted after the first year. It is a hardy and long-lived species from the Four Corners region south to s. NM and s. AZ, found growing among sagebrush and in pinyon/juniper to ponderosa forest areas between 4500 and 10,000'. It is a dryland species that will do well in full sun or part-shade. It has been grown successfully from w. WA to MT, NE, MN, CT and NY to VA. Germination will take about 16 weeks of cold, moist stratification. Cuttings and divisions are easy. Variety *compactifolius* from near Flagstaff, AZ is more compact and often has deeper colored flowers. Subspecies *coloradoensis* and variety *sileri* are distinguished by microscopic features and locations where found. Subspecies *maguirei,* from the Gila Valley in s. NM and AZ, is distinguished by oblanceolate leaves.

Anthers: black, widely divergent opening moderately with toothed sutures; staminode golden-bearded and prominent with bright orange-gold hairs forming a tuft at the apex, barely exserted

Name: linarioides = resembling Linaria; Toadflax Penstemon

Subgenus Penstemon, section Ericopsis, subsection Linarioides

**P. longiflorus** is locally abundant on mountainsides near Beaver City, UT in June and July. One to several stems to 2' have medium-sized, light blue, white-throated flowers in a sparse, secund inflorescence of 3 – 6 verticillasters from June into July. It has not been reported in cultivation.

Anthers: open from the distal end, finely hairy; staminode white with a dense golden beard at apex, included

Name: longiflorus = long flowered

Subgenus Habroanthus, Section Glabri


*P. lyallii* forms large clumps, 18 - 32″ tall with many stems bearing large white to lavender flowers in a short secund inflorescence at the end of each stem. It blooms from early July through August on gravelly roadsides and steep rocky banks from 2100 to 8000′ in n. ID, nw. MT, sw. Alberta and se. British Columbia. The upper stems are herbaceous, not becoming woody, and the leaves are slender, lanceolate and finely toothed. It is reported one of the easiest to germinate and grow in appropriate climates. Growers in MT, WA, NY and eastern Canada praise it. It blooms earlier in lower elevations and bloom lasts several weeks in a rich silty loam soil with adequate moisture.

Anthers: explanate, covered with dense hairs; staminode slightly dilated, bare, included

Name: honors David Lyall (1817 – 1895), botanist on the Oregon Boundary Commission and in the Arctic

Subgenus Dasanthera


*P. marcusii* is found in a desert-like area in alkaline clay and gravel soils in c. Utah between 5200 and 6500′, blooming in May and June. It has several stems to 8″ with tiny funnel-form violet to blue or very pale flowers in 4 – 6 verticillasters arising from a basal rosette of usually smooth, narrow leaves. The flower lobes are almost regular and have guidelines inside the narrow tube, sparse bearding on the lower throat. This species has not been reported in cultivation.

Anthers: very short, glabrous, explanate; staminode very short, lightly yellow-bearded, included

Name: Jones' Penstemon, honoring Marcus E. Jones ( 1852 – 1934)

Subgenus Penstemon, section Cristati


*P. mensarum* is an early blooming dark, almost iridescent, purple-blue-flowered species from w. CO between 7000 and 9500′ that is winning new admirers every year. The flowers are small, somewhat ventricose, narrowed at the opening, and form a long, interrupted inflorescence on several stems to 3′ tall with narrowly elliptic smooth green leaves. It has been reported long blooming, the color not affected by cloudy, damp weather, adaptable to a wide variety of soils and long-lived from NM to MO, MI and VA. It germinates after 8 weeks' chilling and is not difficult to transition to the garden.

Anthers: sparse short hairs, open narrowly, not across the connective; staminode has long golden hairs, included to just reaching the opening

Name: mensarum = from tablelands

Subgenus Habroanthus, section Glabri


*P. metcalfei* is a leafy woodland species similar to *P. whippleanus,* but found only between 7500 and 9000′ in the Black Range in sw. NM. The 1″ flowers are pale blue-lavender with an extended, broad, hairy lower lip. The inflorescence is short and few-flowered above large, entire, ovate stem leaves. It has not been reported in cultivation.

Anthers: not explanate; staminode orange-bearded, included or barely exserted

Name: for collector O. B. Metcalfe (1879 – 1936) who published a Flora of the Mesilla Valley, NM

Subgenus Penstemon, section Penstemon, subsection Humiles


***P. miniatus,*** formerly ***P. apateticus,*** is a red-flowered, white throated species from Mexico that is found from Chihuahua to Oaxaca in open pine woodlands around 7800′. It forms a multi-stemmed clump with stems from 2 - 4′ tall, clothed with slender to broad, entire green leaves and topped with a long inflorescence of 1 to 1 ¼″ flowers which are seen in August and September after summer rains. It has not been reported in cultivation in the US.

Anthers: light colored, entire, glabrous; staminode glabrous, slender

Name: miniatus = red

Subgenus Penstemon, section Fasciculus, subsection Fasciculi


***P. miser*** is a small species found in sw. ID, NV, OR and n. CA in sagebrush deserts between 2460 and 4250′. It is less than 10″ tall with several stems arising from a basal clump of gray-green cinereous leaves to bloom in late May and early June. The flowers are small, abruptly ampliate, violet to pale or deep blue or purple, glandular, with a white-bearded lower lip in 3 - 6 congested, few-flowered verticils. It has not been reported in cultivation.

Anthers: variable in color, explanate, glabrous; staminode exserted, recurved, yellow-orange-bearded

Name: miser = wretched; Malheur Penstemon from type location, Malheur, OR

Subgenus Penstemon, section Cristati


***P. moffatii*** has small funnel-form blue to blue-purple glandular flowers, congested on stems usually less than 12" tall, held above sizeable tufts of oval, gray-green basal leaves. Although small plants, they are quite striking when blooming in May through early June against the dull clay, sand and gravel soils of c. UT and w. CO at elevations between 4200 and 5900′. Seed germinates after 12 weeks cold, moist stratification. This species is very good for a dry rock garden.

Anthers: open all across with toothed sutures, but not explanate; staminode moderately golden-bearded, just reaching the opening

Name: honors David Moffat, president of the Denver and Rio Grande RR

Subgenus Penstemon, section Cristati


***P. mohinoranus*** is a rare species from Chihuahua, Mexico and is similar to *P. barbatus*. It has slender scarlet tubular flowers that are lighter within and have guidelines and sparse white bearding on the somewhat reflexed lower lobes. They are held away from the main stem, usually one or two blooming at each node. Stems are about 3' tall with narrow leaves and are found toward the southern end of Chihuahua in open pine woodlands at 7000′. It has not been reported in cultivation in the US.

Anthers: glabrous, explanate; staminode bare, somewhat dilated

Name: from type locality, Cerro Mohinora, Chihuahua, Mexico

Subgenus Penstemon, section Fasiculus, subsection Fasciculi


***P. monoensis*** has small rose-purple to wine-red glandular flowers in a congested inflorescence of 4 – 8 verticillasters above short stems and narrow, elliptic leaves covered with downy, glandular hairs, giving them a very gray appearance. It is found only on the dry, rocky hills and sandy washes surrounding Owens Valley, between 3800 and 6000′ in CA. It is similar to *P. calcareus;* neither has been reported in cultivation.

Anthers: smooth except for toothed sutures, opening distally; staminode yellow-bearded, barely exserted

Name: monoensis = from Mono County; Mono Beardtongue

Subgenus Penstemon, section Cristati


***P. montanus*** commonly forms leafy clumps in rock scree at elevations from 5000 to 10,500′ in n. UT, c. and e. ID, w. MT and w. WY. It has glandular, gray-green, ovate, usually toothed leaves on stems 2 – 8″ with flowers usually paired near the apex of stems, and no basal clump. Flowers are medium to large, strongly ridged, with upper lobes projecting and the lower ones white-bearded, and may be pink, blue or lavender. Subspecies *idahoensis* has narrower, gray to almost white leaves that are covered with dense hairs and either less toothed or entire, but it is variable in flower and leaf. It blooms in habitat in July and August. Cultivation is not easy but rewarding for rock gardeners. Stored seed germinates at 70°F and has been grown successfully in WA, OR, ID, CO and Scotland. A mix of turkey grit and peat in a crevice garden with afternoon shade or deep gravel on a north-facing slope is recommended.

Anthers: densely white-woolly, explanate; staminode smooth to sparsely white-bearded, included

Name: montanus = of the mountains

Subgenus Dasanthera


***P. moriahensis*** is a little-known species from e. NV between 8200 and 9200′. It is found in dry sagebrush and mountain mahogany to pinyon/juniper and ponderosa pine communities. The plant has several stems to 20″ with few basal leaves and 1″ blue flowers in a few secund verticillasters in June and July. The flowers are somewhat ventricose and glandular. The leaves are entire and narrowly oblanceolate. It has not been reported in cultivation.

Anthers: somewhat divaricate, opening from the distal end, with finely-toothed sutures and long tangled white hairs on the sides; staminode bearded with a few white hairs, included

Name: moriahensis = from Mt. Moriah, the type location

Subgenus Habroanthus, section Glabri

*P. moronensis* is found in Zacatecas, Mexico and grows in volcanic soils at about 7500′. It has broad, toothed, finely hairy leaves with small leaves in the axils, and 1″ purple flowers that are quite abruptly inflated on several stems to 20″. It has not been reported in cultivation in the US.

Anthers: divaricate, opening moderately but not explanate; staminode bearded at apex, included

Name: for location where found, Sierra Morones

Subgenus Penstemon, section Fasciculus, subsection Perfoliati


*P. mucronatus:* see *P. pachyphyllus*


*P. multiflorus* is found in scrub oak and pine woodlands in FL and GA, but has proven hardy in MI, VA and OR. Several stems to 2 ½′ bear many medium-sized, abruptly ampliate white flowers (occasionally pale lavender) in open panicles above leaves that are reduced in size up the stem. It is an excellent plant for perennial borders; germinates easily after 8 weeks cold, moist stratification. Loose soil with organic matter and additional water are recommended in dry climates.

Name: multiflorus = with many flowers

Anthers: black, opening narrowly near the connective; staminode has pale hairs at the apex, included

Subgenus Penstemon, section Penstemon, subsection Multiflori


*P. murrayanus* can be found in sandy soil in pine woods and open prairies of the Ozarks, e. TX, LA, OK and AR. in mid-to-late summer. It can be up to 6′ tall, but is usually less when several stems develop. It is a striking plant with many rounded glabrous and glaucous broad stem leaves that become connate-perfoliate near and within the inflorescence. The tubular, gradually ampliate flowers are medium to large and bright coral red with exserted green anthers. The stems are often red-purple and usually upright, bearing a few flowers on pedicels above the encircling leaves in each verticillaster. The inflorescence is very long, opening new flowers as it elongates, so that it is in bloom for a long period. This is an easy plant, moderately long-lived, germinating best with at least 5 weeks of cold moist stratification. It should be given loose soil and supplementary water in dry areas. Occasionally pale pink sports appear. This species has been grown from NM and AZ to the Midwest, MN, MI, VA and Long Island and praised everywhere.

Anthers: well-exserted, moderately divergent, opening wide; staminode bare, included

Name: honors Johann Andreas Murray (1740 – 1797), student of Linnaeus and later professor of botany and medicine

Subgenus Penstemon, section Peltanthera, subsection Havardiani


*P. nanus* forms tufts of narrowly ovate, gray-green, entire to finely-toothed leaves with a few flowering stems to 4″, each with a tight cluster of quite small, upward-facing glandular, red-violet to blue-violet flowers with a prominent staminode. This is a rare desert species from western Utah found in gravelly limestone alluvial soils in sparsely vegetated shadscale to pinyon/juniper communities between 5200 and 7020′, blooming in May and June. It has been brought into cultivation by specialists and is best in a dry trough. Germination takes place after 12 weeks of cold moist conditions. Light is necessary.

Anthers: remaining horseshoe-shaped, opening narrowly from end to end; staminode just reaching the opening, densely bearded with short orange-gold hairs

Name: nanus = dwarf

Subgenus Penstemon, section Cristati


*P. navajoa* occurs in ponderosa woodlands from 8,200 – 10,350′ on Navajo Mountain in s. Utah. It is 12 to 16″ tall with pale blue, somewhat ventricose-ampliate flowers, less than 1″ long, blooming in July and August. The secund inflorescence is raceme-like, with one or two upward-facing flowers at up to 7 nodes. Leaves are slender, glabrous. It is rather rare and has not been in cultivation.

Anthers: opening narrowly, not across the connective, glabrous or with long hairs, exserted; staminode glabrous, slightly dilated, not exserted

Name: from type location, Navajo Mountain

Subgenus Habroanthus, section Glabri


*P. neomexicanus* is somewhat like *P. virgatus* in that it has a long secund inflorescence, no basal mat and a flower with red-violet guidelines that is rounded on both upper and lower sides. The few stems are up to 28″ tall and the flowers, lavender-blue to medium blue, with a white line at the lower edge of the throat, sometimes bearded, are about 1 ¼″ long. Leaves are linear to narrowly lanceolate. This species is widely cultivated. It is from the southeast mountains of NM between 6000 and 9000′ elevation, where it blooms in July and August. It germinates after 8 weeks of cold, moist stratification. Several plants should be placed together for a good effect and additional water applied in dry periods.

Anthers: open wide but not explanate, exserted; staminode smooth, dilated and notched, exserted

Name: neomexicanus = New Mexico Penstemon

Subgenus Habroanthus, section Glabri


*P. neotericus* comes from dry, open pine woods in n. CA, where it grows on volcanic soils or red clay between 3300 and 7300′ elevation, but it is rather uncommon. It is similar to *P. laetus* and *P. azureus.* All have buds that are brown or purple with yellow at the tip. *Penstemon neotericus* forms a woody-based sub-shrub to 2′ tall with numerous erect and wiry stems and narrow bluish-green stem leaves. The glandular flowers are medium to large with a red-violet tube and blue face. White lines mark the lower lip. It blooms in July and August. Seed germination takes 12 weeks of cold, moist conditions. It has been grown in CA, OR and se. WA and is liked by gardeners there.

Anthers: sac-like with toothed opening across top, barely exserted; staminode glabrous, included

Name: neotericus = recent in origin; Plumas County Penstemon

Subgenus Saccanthera, section Saccanthera, subsection Heterophylli

***P. newberryi*** is a favorite of rock gardeners, and of all California flower lovers, where its bright flowers appear in July and August in the mountains from 4000 to 10,000′. Short, one-sided clusters of brilliant rosy-red flowers stand above a foliage mat of leathery, finely toothed leaves. The plant in bloom can be 12 to 18″ tall. The medium-to-large flowers are keeled dorsally with a gradually expanded tube and forward projecting upper lip; color may vary from rosy to crimson. Subspecies *berryi* is found in OR and has larger purple flowers with included stamens; subspecies *sonomensis* has darker-colored flowers and is found at high elevations in Sonoma County, CA. The type species is also found in NV. This species germinates easily after 8 weeks of cold moist stratification but is not easy to keep in hot climates. In cooler areas it thrives in coarse sand and full sun in cool dry locations and should be protected from winter sun. Ground fir and cedar bark or pine needle mulch are also good in dry areas where they do not hold moisture for long periods. Plants have lived 20 years in Scotland.

Anthers: yellow to white-wooly, exserted; staminode yellow-bearded, included

Name: honors Dr. John. S. Newberry (1822 – 1892) participant in an early California survey; Mountain Pride

Subgenus Dasanthera

***P. nitidus*** is an early-blooming light to medium blue-flowered dryland species that should be more widely known. Usually 6 – 12″ tall, several stems have beautiful, glaucous blue-green leaves and 4 – 10 congested verticillasters of small funnel-form flowers, sometimes with pink tubes. It is found from se. British Columbia, s. Alberta, w. Manitoba and MT, ND, SD and n. WY in clay and gravelly soils in the plains and prairies at 3500′ in the northern Rocky Mts. from April through May. It germinates after 8 weeks cold, moist stratification and performs well where it gets plenty of moisture until after bloom ends and new growth is well along. It may then be kept dry through the summer. It is not a long-lived plant but off-shoots can be taken after the second year to perpetuate it. Space plants 6 inches apart for a good display. It has been grown from e. WA and n. NM to MT, NE, MN, MI and MA. Variety *polyphyllus* has more erect and less compact flower clusters and may reach 2′.

Anthers: dark, widely divergent, opening widely; staminode, dilated, recurved with golden hairs at apex, included to barely exserted

Name: nitidus = shining or handsome

Subgenus Penstemon, section Coerulei

***P. nudiflorus*** is found only in nc. AZ in pine woods between 4500 and 7000′. It has 1″ pale orchid to lavender flowers with hairs at the lower throat; flowers are on long pedicels in a short inflorescence above rather bare stems with glabrous and glaucous, entire lanceolate leaves forming a small clump at the base. If several plants are closely spaced, a good-looking clump results. This species does well in se. WA, has bloomed for 4 years and self-sows. Give 12 weeks cold, moist stratification. This is a dry-land species but needs winter moisture.

Anthers: widely divergent, opening moderately but not explanate; staminode lightly bearded, somewhat exserted

Name: nudiflorus = with naked flowers

Subgenus Habroanthus, section Glabri

*P. occiduus*   is a rare Mexican species from sw. Chihuahua and Durango.  It is similar to *P. gentianoides* with campanulate lavender flowers, slightly longer than 1″, in a loose inflorescence. Several stems may reach 24″.  It has not been reported in cultivation in the US.

Anthers: widely divaricate, moderately open; staminode lightly bearded

Name: occiduus refers to its location in the Sierra Madre Occidental

Subgenus Penstemon, section Fasciculus, subsection Fasciculi


*P. oklahomensis*   has slender white flowers, about 1″ long, with a closed mouth and yellow-bearded lower lip.  Flower buds are pale yellow.  Stems are 16 to 22″ tall with the flowers held in an open inflorescence of only 3 – 6 verticillasters. Leaves are lanceolate, the lower ones toothed. It is found in the Osage Plains of central OK from north to south, in red clay and sandy loam soils.  It is an easy plant to grow, usually blooming in its first year.

Anthers: widely divaricate and open; staminode densely bearded with orange-gold hairs, barely exserted

Name: oklahomensis = from Oklahoma

Subgenus Penstemon, section Penstemon, subsection Penstemon


*P. oliganthus*   has slender glandular blue or blue-purple flowers with a white throat and guidelines, lower lobes flared forward and longer than upper. The flowers are ¾″ long, few and widely spaced on several stems to 2′.  Stem leaves are narrowly lanceolate and basal leaves are persistent.  Several plants together in part shade make a nice display.  It is found in n. AZ, n. NM west of the Rio Grande and up to c. CO in mountain meadows between 6000 and 8000′ from late May to August. Germination occurs after 8 weeks of cold, moist stratification.

Anthers: black, widely divaricate, opening moderately; staminode short, densely orange bearded, included

Name:  oligo = few-flowered

Subgenus Penstemon, section Penstemon, subsection Humiles


*P. ophianthus*   has flowers similar to those of  *P. jamesii,* but smaller, in late May and June. They are ¾″ long, much inflated, pale to medium lavender or blue-lavender with vertical lobes and guidelines.  Plants are usually less than 1′ tall with narrow gray-green leaves, with 4 - 7 more or less secund verticillasters, sometimes quite congested.  They are found between 4900 and 7900′ in sandy, gravelly or clay soils in the Four Corners region to c. UT, among sagebrush, pinyon/juniper, and ponderosa pines.  Germination takes 6 – 8 weeks at 70°F.

Anthers: glabrous, explanate; staminode densely bearded, thrust well forward

Name:  ophi = snake-like

Subgenus Penstemon, section Cristati


*P. osterhoutii*  and *P. pachyphyllus*  are very similar with glabrous and glaucous fleshy broad leaves and small to medium-sized, gradually flared blue to lavender flowers in well-separated verticillasters on stems to 28″.  *P. osterhoutii* is found on sagebrush slopes in nw. CO and adjacent UT between 5500 and 7200′ in June.  Old seed germinated quickly at 70°F.

Anthers: widely divergent and open full length; staminode much broadened and recurved, barely exserted

Name: honors George Everitt Osterhout (1858 – 1937) Colorado lumberman and amateur botanist

Subgenus Penstemon, section Coerulei


*P. ovatus*  has performed well in gardens all across the northern part of the US and adjacent provinces of Canada, down to MO, PA and VA, and in higher elevations in the southern Rocky Mts.  It grows  west of the Cascade Mountains in OR, WA and British Columbia in damp, rocky openings of the woods between 3000 and 6000′, where it blooms in May and June.  Several leafy stems to 3 ½′ bear many ¾″ bright blue flowers in clusters on wide spreading cymes.  The leaves are bright green and toothed, oval to lanceolate.  Soil with organic matter and regular but not continuous watering and occasional division will keep it going for many years, even in dry climates. Old seeds germinate readily at 70°F under light.

Anthers: almost explanate; staminode yellow-bearded, slightly exserted to just reaching opening

Name:  Ovate or Broadleafed Penstemon

Subgenus Penstemon, section Penstemon, subsection Humiles


*P. pachyphyllus*  is common and showy around the Grand Canyon in AZ, north into UT, CO, NV and WY.  It is usually about 1 - 2′ tall with 5 – 10 close to widely spaced cylindrical verticils of small lavender, blue or purple flowers in May and June.  Leaves are thick, moderately broad and often mucronate, glabrous, entire and glaucous gray-green.  It is a dryland species found between 4500 and 10,500′ in gravelly or sandy soil, with a prominent basal mat.  The type variety's staminode is quite broad with dense hairs.  Variety *mucronatus* is less than 1′ tall, has a sparsely bearded staminode, blue flowers with prominent guidelines and nearly round leaves with a small, pointed tip.  Some authorities consider this a separate species.  Variety *congestus* has a narrow, densely hairy staminode, darker blue to purple flowers and narrower, lanceolate leaves.  Seed germinates at 40 or 70°F in 2 – 3 months.  Has been in cultivation and reported generally to live 3 – 4 years.

Anthers: opposite, not explanate; staminode broad, recurved and  bearded, just reaching opening

Name: Thickleaf Penstemon

Subgenus Penstemon, section Coerulei


*P. pahutensis,* is found only in the Grapevine Mts. of NV between 6250 and 7550′ in pinyon/juniper woodlands.  It has several 7 - 10″ stems with a secund inflorescence of up to 13 sparsely flowered verticillasters of small to medium-sized blue flowers in June and early July above narrowly elliptic or lanceolate glabrous and entire leaves.  This species has not been reported in cultivation.

Anthers: diverging but not opposite, opening from the distal end with toothed sutures; staminode densely golden-bearded, just reaching the opening

Name: for type locality, Pahute Mesa in Nye County, NV; Pahute Penstemon
Subgenus Habroanthus, section Glabri


*P. pallidus* is an eastern species, entirely glandular, with small, pale lavender to white flowers with guidelines in a short, open, triangular panicle on stems to 22″ tall with toothed, lanceolate leaves in a basal mat and up the stem. Its native range in the MS and OH River valleys has been extended up into New England. It has grown well in OR for five years.

Anthers: divergent, open across the connective but not explanate; staminode yellow bearded, slightly recurved, exserted

Name: pallidus = pale

Subgenus Penstemon, section Penstemon, subsection Penstemon


*P. palmeri* is a spectacular plant for dry country gardens, widely grown throughout the mountains and deserts of the west. It has been used for roadside planting in several states. Several to many stems that can be 2 – 5′ tall bear long secund inflorescences of pale to deep pink, medium to large-sized ventricose ampliate flowers above an often bushel-basket-sized clump of glaucous, toothed foliage. The flowers have red-violet guidelines from the lower lip into the thoat and an intense clover-like scent that makes them extremely attractive to bumble-bees. The upper leaves of the stem are connate-perfoliate. Variety *eglandulosus* has glabrous stems and pedicels where the type has glandular-pubescent stems. The species is native only in the CÁ, UT, NV and AZ deserts between 2600 and 8950′, where it can be in bloom from May to August, but has been widely cultivated in NM, CO, ID and e. WA and has been successfully grown in NE and Manitoba. It will withstand temperatures near 0°F. It is not long-lived but will usually bloom well for two years and produces copious amounts of seed that can be germinated without refrigeration.

Anthers: widely divaricate, open all across, white, smooth; staminode moderately dilated and yellow-bearded, recurved, well-exserted

Name: Palmer's Penstemon for Dr. Edward Palmer (1831 – 1911), botanical explorer and ethnobotanist

Subgenus Penstemon, section Peltanthera, subsection Peltanthera


*P. papillatus* is a little known species found only in Inyo and Mono Counties of CA between 6550 and 8900′ in dry, pinyon/juniper and lodgepole pine woodlands. The glandular blue-violet flowers are 1 ¼″ long, somewhat ventricose, bare on the palate, upward-facing, in 3 – 6 few-flowered, wide clusters on stems to 16″ with gray, almost cinereous leaves, the lower ones with winged petioles. It has not been reported in cultivation.

Anthers: horseshoe-shaped, opening across the top with toothed sutures; staminode lightly yellow-bearded at apex, included

Name: papillate = bearing microscopic bumps; Inyo Beardtongue

Subgenus Saccanthera, section Saccanthera, subsection Heterophylli

***P. parryi*** can be up to 4′ tall and blooms in March and April in its home in s. AZ and n. Sonora, Mexico between 1500 and 5000′. Many stems bear ¾″ funnel-shaped, almost regular flowers in bright shades of rose, pink or magenta above slender, pale, glabrous and glaucous gray-green leaves. It is widely planted in AZ and has been successful in the Willamette Valley of OR and in VA where the temperature does not usually get near 0°F. Seeds do not need chilling and germinate well in a few days at 70°F.

Anthers: pale and widely divergent, explanate; staminode yellow-bearded, included

Name: honors Charles C. Parry (1823 – 1890) amateur botanist and physician

Subgenus Penstemon, section Peltanthera, subsection Centranthifolii

***P. parvulus,*** formerly a subspecies of *P. azureus*, is found blooming from c. CA to sw. OR on mountain slopes between 1640 and 7200′ from late June to August. This low, sprawling plant has mats of glabrous, ovate to spatulate blue-green leaves from which rise erect stems from 8 - 14″, bearing ¾ to 1″ deep blue flowers and maroon to yellow buds in a loose, subsecund inflorescence. Germination requires 12 weeks of chilling. The plant has been praised in CA, OR and se. WA, but not reported on outside that area. It is long-lived, spreading by rooting branches. If cut back it will rebloom. It is reported to take temperatures to 15°F for short periods, and does not like muggy weather.

Anthers: sac-like, open across top and most of sides, inner margins hairy; staminode glabrous, included.

Name: parvulus = very small

Subgenus Saccanthera, section Saccanthera, subsection Heterophylli

***P. parvus*** inhabits dry sagebrush-grassland communities in s. UT between 7200 and 11,500′, where it blooms from late June through July, and has not been reported in cultivation. It is considered a threatened species. Stems 8 – 10 ″ tall arise from basal rosettes of slender leaves. The small flowers are glandular, blue to dark blue, in 3 – 8 subsecund verticillasters.

Anthers: open narrowly, smooth, one pair exserted; staminode white, glabrous slightly dilated, just reaching the opening

Name: parvus = small; Aquarius Plateau Penstemon

Subgenus Habroanthus, section Glabri

***P. patens*** is a beautiful small-flowered dryland species, similar to *P. utahensis,* that is found in Mono and Inyo Counties of CA and adjacent Clark County in Nevada between 6250 and 9900′ among sagebrush, pinyon/juniper and ponderosa pine communities. Leaves are thick and fleshy, glabrous, glaucous and entire with a few stems bearing lavender or pink to magenta upward-facing flowers in a broad, loose thyrse of 5 or more secund verticillasters rising to 16″ in May and June. It requires scarification and 8 weeks of cold, moist stratification to germinate. Gerdeners in CA have success with it but it has not been reported in other areas.

Anthers: divaricate and fully open with toothed sutures but not explanate; staminode, lightly bearded with yellow-orange hairs, dilated and recurved, included

Name: patens = open, spreading

Subgenus Penstemon, section Peltanthera, subsection Centranthifolii

*P. patricus* has several ascending stems up to 10″ tall with a few upward-facing small to medium violet flowers in 3 – 6 verticillasters on each stem in July. Leaves are small and narrowly elliptic, with no basal rosette at bloom time. It is found in wc. UT and adjacent NV. It was at one time a subspecies of *P. leonardii* and is similar. There are no reports of it in cultivation.

Anthers: horseshoe-shaped, opening across the top with toothed sutures, just reaching the opening to exserted; staminode white, glabrous, included

Name: Dad's Penstemon, named by Dr. Noel Holmgren to honor his father, Dr. Arthur Holmgren

Subgenus Saccanthera, section Saccanthera, subsection Heterophylli

*P. payettensis* has erect, wand-like stems to 28″ with a congested inflorescence of small to medium-sized, deep blue flowers in 4 – 10 or more wide close clusters. It is much like *P. pennellianus,* but has broader leaves that are glabrous, entire and somewhat thickened. It is found in ne. OR and c. Idaho between 5900 and 8200′ on dry, gravelly slopes up to open woodlands, in bloom between late May and August. Germination requires light and 12 weeks cold moist stratification. It is a beautiful garden plant, but not always long-lived.

Anthers: open from distal end, not across connective, with minute teeth, just reaching the orifice; staminode smooth or sparsely yellow-bearded, included

Name: Payette Penstemon from type location, Payette National Forest in Idaho

Subgenus Habroanthus, section Glabri

*P. paysoniorum* grows from a woody base, with several decumbent or ascending stems rising to 6 or 8″ with a short secund inflorescence of 2 – 6 verticillasters of small lavender blue flowers. Leaves are glabrous and entire, narrowly lanceolate to almost linear, often folded and crisped. It is found on dry sagebrush covered hills, in sandy creek bottoms and on chalk bluffs between 6400 and 7500′ in sw. WY. It germinates in 12 weeks with light, responds well to very sandy soil and is very floriferous, the color sometimes changing to pink or lavender in cultivation. It is an excellent plant for the dry rock garden.

Anthers: blue-black with short sparse pale hairs, opening from the distal end, not across the connective, with toothed sutures; staminode pale yellow bearded, included

Name: Paysons' Penstemon, honoring Dr. Edward B. Payson (1863 - 1927), botanist at the University of Wyoming, and Mrs. Payson.

Subgenus Habroanthus, section Glabri

*P. peckii* is one of the easiest penstemons to grow, although it is quite rare in its native habitat of dry, open pine woods on sandy soil on the eastern slopes of the Cascade Mts. in OR. Flowers are tiny, glandular, slender and may be white, pink, blue or lavender. The erect stems to 2′ hold 3 – 10 verticils open in July. Foliage is slender and deep green and may form a large basal clump over several years. It germinates with 6 weeks of cold moist stratification and usually blooms the first year from seed.  It is hardy and long-lived, often reblooming if cut back, and self-sows readily.

Anthers: glabrous and explanate; staminode yellow-bearded at apex, included

Name: Peck's Penstemon, honoring Morton Peck (1871 – 1958), botanist and author of an Oregon Flora

Subgenus Penstemon, section Penstemon, subsection Proceri


*P. penlandii*  is considered an endangered species, limited to one location in CO on selenium-rich soil. It is similar to *P. paysoniorum*.  The stems are about 10″ tall, the inflorescence secund and sparsely flowered with small blue flowers.

Anthers: explanate, sutures toothed, not open across the connective, moderately hairy; staminode included, sparsely bearded with pale orange hairs

Name: Penland's Penstemon in honor of C.W. T. Penland (1899 - 1982), Colorado botanist

Subgenus Habroanthus, section Glabri


*P. pennellianus*  grows in the Blue and Wallowa Mts. of se. WA and ne. OR.  Large, conspicuous clumps of vivid blue to purple 1 ¼″ long flowers in June and July atop stout stems to 20″ with large, glossy green leaves.  In its native habitat of rocky slopes between 4000 and 5400′, it frequently appears as a single stem, but in cultivation many ascending stems make a spectacular show with 3 – 10 many-flowered clusters in a continuous cylinder. Close in appearance are *P. glaber* and *P. payettensis.*  A basal mat is maintained throughout the year. Germination is slow, sometimes not until a second spring.  Plants are not long-lived, but well worth renewing every few years.

Anthers: open from distal end with toothed sutures, s-twisted, sparsely hairy; staminode bearded apically with short hairs, included

Name: Pennell's Penstemon honors Frances Whittier Pennell  (1886 – 1952) curator of Botany at the Academy of Natural Sciences in Philadelphia and leading taxonomist of Scrophulariaceae

Subgenus Habroanthus, section Glabri


*P. perfoliatus*  is a rare Mexican species from the southern state of Oaxaca at elevations around 10,000′.  Plants have broad, serrate leaves that are connate-perfoliate on the upper stem, which is about 40″ tall.  The entire plant is glandular-hairy, except for the flowers that are less glandular but have villous hairs in the throat.  The violet to lavender flowers form rings with broad bracts cupping them in an interrupted inflorescence.  Cultivation in the US has not been reported.

Anthers:  divaricate, open all across, not explanate; staminode dilated, slightly bearded

Name: perfoliate = leaf pairs are joined at the base so stem passes through them

Subgenus Penstemon, section Fasciculus, subsection Perfoliati


*P. perpulcher*  has small to medium bright blue flowers, usually in a long inflorescence on several stiff, erect stems to 2′ in late May and June. The flowers are closely spaced and somewhat secund in up to 14 verticillasters.  Narrowly lanceolate leaves are entire, bright green and usually glabrous. It is found in the plains and foothills along the Snake River in ID between 2100 and 6560′. It has not been reported in cultivation.

Anthers: divaricate, opening from distal end with toothed sutures, sometimes with hairs; staminode yellow-bearded, included

Name: perpulcher = very beautiful

Subgenus Habroanthus, section Glabri


*P. personatus* is a rare and threatened species from the dry hillsides west of the Sierra Nevada Range in California near Chico between 4900 and 5900′. The plant is about 2′ tall with an open panicle of a few upward-facing slender 1″ red-violet to lavender and white flowers with small, closed white lips. The leaves are broad, ovate, some finely toothed, and well below the inflorescence. It has not been reported in cultivation.

Anthers: opening all the way across; staminode densely yellow-bearded at apex, included

Name: personate = closed

Subgenus Cryptostemon ( the only species in the subgenus)


*P. petiolatus* is a floriferous and charming low, shrubby penstemon from limestone cliffs between 3300 and 5600′ in sw. UT and adjacent NV. It may reach 8″ and spread into a broad clump with small, pale gray-green glabrous and glaucous toothed leaves smothered by magenta pink flowers in May, June and July. The foliage is attractive all year. The many stems each have a short inflorescence of 2 – 4 secund verticillasters of small, glandular flowers with prominent pale yellow staminodes. This plant has been grown in the Denver, CO area and n. NM and has survived below zero F temperatures for several years. It requires light to germinate at 70°F.

Anthers: glabrous, explanate; staminode widely dilated, with sparse yellow hairs, barely exserted

Name: referring to leaves with stems or petioles; Crevice Penstemon

Subgenus Penstemon, section Peltanthera, subsection Petiolati


*P. pinifolius* is a small shrubby evergreen that is well-known and widely grown. It comes from sc. NM, se. AZ and adjacent Mexico and is found in gravelly and sandy soils on rocky slopes between 6000 and 8500′ The short, needle-like evergreen foliage is dense and forms a clump variable in height to 1′ and almost twice as broad. Many stems with few leaves may rise to 16″ on older plants and bear a narrow secund raceme of hummingbird-attracting scarlet tubular flowers with forward-extending upper lobes and lower lobes that spread downward and outward. The throat has conspicuous yellow hairs. Yellow and orange sports are sometimes found. It blooms in habitat from May to August. Seeds germinate readily with 8 weeks cold, moist stratification preceding warmer temperatures. New plants can also be grown from cuttings and division. It is long-lived, long blooming and hardy from the west coast to New England and in Great Britain, Scandinavia and Europe. It is suggested that a south facing exposure among rocks that collect heat be used in northern climates.

Cultivars:

'Compactus' a short dense form with red flowers

'Magdalena Sunshine' yellow-flowered sport with bright green foliage found near Magdalena, NM

'Mersea Yellow' very similar plant from sport in a garden in England

'Shades of Mango' sport with flowers varying yellow to orange to red as they age

Anthers: widely divergent and explanate, concealed under upper lobes; staminode yellow bearded, included

Names: Pineleaf Penstemon; Needleleaf Penstemon

Subgenus Penstemon, section Fasciculus, subsection Fasciculi

**P. pinorum** is a little-known species from Utah, not reported in cultivation. It is locally abundant under pinyon and juniper trees between 5600 and 5800' in the Pine Valley Mts. of sw. UT, but because of limited range is considered a threatened species. It ranges from 3 - 8" tall and has small glandular blue-violet flowers with a bearded throat in 5 – 7 interrupted verticillasters and narrow, sharply toothed leaves.

Anthers: dehiscing full length and across connective, remaining parallel; staminode densely bearded with pale orange hairs; well exserted

Name: pinorum for Pine Valley, UT

Subgenus Penstemon, section Cristati

**P. plagapineus** comes from 8550 to 9500' on the western slope of the Sierra Madre Occidental in Durango, Mexico. It is a multi-stemmed branching plant with large narrowly oval entire leaves and large brilliant red flowers but is not known to be in cultivation in the United States.

Anthers: smooth and explanate; staminode slender and smooth, included

Name: plagapineus = place of pines

Subgenus Penstemon, section Fasciculus, subsection Fasciculi

**P. platyphyllus** forms large clumps to 24" with many erect stems bearing upward-facing small to medium-sized lavender, violet or purple flowers in a wide, subsecund thyrse of 4 – 8 few-flowered verticillasters from June to August. It is reported to be slightly fragrant. Leaves are firm, green, elliptic, deciduous and prominent in the clump. There are no basal leaves. It is found between 4300 and 7900' elevation on dry, rocky slopes in nc. UT in Wasatch and Duchesne Counties. It is a splendid dry garden plant, but it tends to be floppy in typical garden conditions. Germination takes place after 12 weeks in cold, moist stratification. It has recently been seen in nurseries in UT.

Anthers: sac-like, open across the top with toothed margins; staminode white or blue-tipped, smooth and exserted

Name: platyphyllus = broad-leaved

Subgenus Saccanthera, section Saccanthera, subsection Heterophylli

***P. potosinus*** has large, broad, glandular red-violet flowers with a pale throat, no guidelines, and bearding on the palate. Stems are hairy, to 40″, leaves broadly spatulate, short, sometimes with toothed margins, sometime with fascicles. It is found in the mountains around Guanajuato and San Luis Potosi, Mexico, where it blooms in July and not known to be in cultivation in the United States.

Anthers: widely divaricate, open full length; staminode is broadened distally, sparingly yellow-bearded, included

Name: from type location, San Luis Potosi

Subgenus Penstemon, section Fasciculus, subsection Campanulati


***P. pratensis*** has small pale blue to white flowers in 2 - 5 interrupted verticils on several stems to 20″ in June and July. It is similar to *P. rydbergii* except for color. It forms basal mats of glabrous, lanceolate leaves in its natural habitat in moist meadows between 4900 and 9000′ in sw ID, se. OR and adjacent NV. It appears to hybridize with *P. watsonii* and *P. humilis,* but no reports of cultivation have been found.

Anthers: widely divergent and open; staminode densely golden-bearded, just reaching orifice

Name: pratensis = growing in meadows.

Subgenus Penstemon, section Penstemon, subsection Proceri


***P. procerus*** has six named varieties from 2 – 16″ tall. Tiny or small flowers cluster in one to several rings about the ascending to erect stems and have been reported as fragrant. The usual color is blue, but violet, purple, white, cream, and pink can also be seen in the wild. The throat is white within, often white rimmed on the lower lobes and white or yellow-bearded. They may be in bloom from May to August, depending on elevation. *Penstemon procerus* variety *procerus* can be found from s. Alaska and Yukon to Saskatchewan, the Northwest and south to c. CO between 6450 and 11,800′. It is the tallest variety and has a mat-like base usually with many sterile shoots as well as flowering stems. Variety *tolmei* is found in the Olympic and Cascade Mts. of WA and British Columbia from 5000 to 7000′. It has a loose mat with leafy stems only 2 - 6″ tall, and one or two clusters of flowers. This is an especially popular rock garden plant. Variety *formosus* is also between 2 and 6″ tall, another rock garden favorite, with usually only a single cluster of flowers and a leafy mat with 1″ leaves. It is found from the Wallowa Mts. in OR to NV and Yosemite in CA between 8200 and 11,800′. Variety *brachyanthus* can be from 4 - 16″ tall and is found between 4560 and 7870′ from n. CA into WA. Variety *aberrans* is found only in sc. UT and can be from 4 - 14″ tall with oblanceolate stem leaves. It and variety *modestus,* from Elko County, NV, that is about the same height are probably the most tolerant of dry conditions. All varieties germinate easily with 8 weeks cold, moist stratification. Some may germinate at 70°F. They are long-lived and spread slowly to make handsome clumps. They are tolerant of most soils and generally prefer regular watering. They have been widely praised from southern Canada and the west coast through the midwest to New England and as far south as NC; also in Great Britain and Europe. Good drainage and a half-day of sun in damp climates to part shade in sunny areas are recommended.

Cultivars:

'Roy Davidson' a pink form of var. *tolmei*

'Nisqually Cream' a creamy white form

Anthers: widely divergent and open; staminode densely golden-bearded, just reaching the orifice

Name: Littleflower Penstemon

Subgenus Penstemon, section Penstemon, subsection Proceri


*P. procumbens* was for years listed as a variety of *P. crandallii,* and also as a form of *P. caespitosus,* but is now recognized by many as a species. It is found at about 9800' in wc. CO and has been a popular addition to rock gardens for years. It forms trailing mats, 1 - 2" high with procumbent stems that spread over and around rocks and root as they go. The ovate leaves are 3/16" wide at most and ¾" long, including the ¼" petiole. The small upward-facing violet to blue flowers with pale throats lie on the mat and appear in the garden in May and continue into June. This species survives in dry conditions but is most attractive and floriferous with supplemental water. Germination takes about 12 weeks of cold, moist stratification. Cuttings and layering work very well. It is adaptable to most climates with some shade in dry areas. It is often called 'Claude Barr', after a well-known early plantsman of the Great Plains

Anthers, black, opening narrowly; staminode orange bearded, included

Name: procumbens = prostrate

Subgenus Penstemon, section Ericopsis, subsection Caespitosi


*P. pruinosus* is a clump forming plant 4 - 16" tall with gray-green, glandular-hairy, toothed ovate to lanceolate leaves and small deep blue-purple flowers in 3 – 7 loose, many-flowered clusters in May and June. It is found in dry areas of British Columbia and c. WA east of the Cascade Mts. at about 2100'. It is easily germinated at cool temperatures in 6 – 8 weeks and is long-lived, very attractive and desirable in dry gardens. It has not been reported in the east or Europe.

Anthers: divergent and opening widely but not explanate; staminode yellow-bearded, just reaching the opening

Name: pruinose = frosted, with a whitish bloom on surfaces; Chelan Penstemon

Subgenus Penstemon, section Penstemon, subsection Humiles


*P. pseudoparvus* is a charming short relative of *P. oliganthus,* with a few stems 4 to 12" tall bearing a few small, upward-facing, glandular blue to purple flowers with a large lower lip and pale throat. Several plants together make a pleasing display. Dark green, broadly elliptic leaves with a distinct midrib form a basal mat and stem leaves are almost linear. It is found at about 9500' in the mountains of sc. NM, but is not common and is rarely available.

Anthers: opposite and open across but not explanate; staminode orange bearded, included

Name: pseudoparvus = like *P. parvus* or false *P. parvus*

Subgenus Penstemon, section Penstemon, subsection Humiles

***P. pseudoputus*** is similar to *P. virgatus,* except that it is shorter and has no palate hairs. It is found between 7900 and 8900′ in the open meadows and aspen-spruce forests of n. AZ and s. UT on sandy loam in the summer. It is between 6 and 16″ tall with small, glabrous, white-throated blue to purple flowers in a secund raceme and narrow, usually rolled, leaves. Seeds are available but it has not been reported in cultivation.

Anthers: opposite, opening narrowly with toothed sutures, exserted; staminode white, smooth, dilated, exserted

Name: pseudoputus = like *P. putus;* Kaibab Penstemon

Subgenus Habroanthus, section Glabri

***P. pseudospectabilis*** is a gorgeous specimen plant in the southwest and can be grown over a wide area. It is a desert/mountain species but will survive temperatures below 0°F. It is found in CA, NV, AZ and NM between 2000 and 7000′, where it may be in bloom from April through June, and has been cultivated in VA, CO, e. WA and e. OR as well as in the area where it is found. In cultivation it can reach 4′ with many stems and large, broad gray-blue, glabrous and glaucous toothed leaves which become connate on the upper portion of the stem. The medium to large glandular flowers are pendant and usually deep pink to brilliant magenta in a long, open thyrse. The flowers are somewhat ventricose to funnelform, with lips abruptly flaring at right angles to the tube, and may or may not have guidelines in the throat. This species blooms over a long period and often reblooms after heavy summer rains or with a short period of irrigation. In VA it did well for many years in a mound of equal parts of sand, compost and pea-gravel. It is quite long-lived and the evergreen foliage remains attractive in the winter. Ssp. *connatifolius* is found in the eastern part of the range, has greener leaves and does not have glands on the calyx and pedicels. This species is closely related to *P. floridus.*

Anthers: explanate; staminode usually glabrous but sometimes with a few hairs, included

Name: pseudospectabilis = resembling *P. spectabilis*; Nevada Penstemon; Desert Beardtongue; Mojave Beardtongue

Subgenus Penstemon, section Peltanthera, subsection Peltanthera

***P. pudicus*** has medium to large, glandular, upward-facing blue to blue-violet flowers with a pale tube in 3 – 6 few-flowered verticillasters on erect or ascending stems from 8 to 20″ tall in late June and July. The basal leaves are oblanceolate to rounded, stem leaves narrowly elliptic to linear, glandular and entire. It is only found in s. NV on slopes in pinyon/juniper communities between 7600 and 9000′. It has not been reported in cultivation. It is related to *P. papillatus.*

Anthers: sac-shaped, opening across the top with toothed sutures; staminode densely golden-bearded at apex, included

Name: pudicus = modest

Subgenus Saccanthera, section Saccanthera, subsection Heterophylli

***P. pumilus*** has a neat gray-green basal clump of linear to spatulate, cinereously hairy leaves and small, glandular blue-purple flowers closely spaced on short stems from 2 - 5″ tall. It is an ideal plant for small dry rock gardens or troughs. It is found in sc. ID between 4600 and 6500′ on gravelly plains and flats, blooming late May into June. It is said to cover the ground in some locations within its range. It has been in cultivation but is not an easy species.

Anthers: widely divergent and wide open; staminode sparsely golden-bearded, included

Name: pumilus = dwarf; Dwarf Penstemon

Subgenus Penstemon, section Cristati

*P. purpusii* is a good crevice, trough and rock garden plant with densely hairy foliage on mostly decumbent or prostrate stems which may take root. Flowers are glandular, sharply keeled, red-violet to deep blue-purple with a violet tube and distinct white lines on the ridged throat, up to 1″ in length. Lower leaves are rounded and finely toothed; upper ones oval to lanceolate. It is found on n. CA peaks from 4900 to 7900′, blooming in late July and early August. It is reported to survive temperatures to 0°F with no winter snow cover in hot, dry exposures. Success in growing it has been reported in WA, OR, CO, NM, MA and Czechoslovakia and growers have praised its showy flowers and moderate persistence. In some areas it reseeds vigorously. It may require an acidic soil.

Anthers: sac-like, open most of their outer edge, with toothed sutures, hairs on inner side; staminode glabrous, included

Name: honors Carl A. Purpus (1851 – 1941) botanist and plant collector; Snow Mountain Penstemon

Subgenus Saccanthera, section Saccanthera, subsection Heterophylli

*P. putus* see *P. virgatus*

*P. radicosus* is a few-flowered species between 8 and 16″ tall that is found in Yellowstone National Park and surrounding states from CO, UT and NV to MT, ID and WY between 4600 and 8200′ from late May to July. It may be found in open woodlands or slopes with sagebrush or pinyon/juniper communities in dry areas. The plant has a woody caudex but herbaceous stems with slender leaves and no basal rosette. Flowers are small, glandular and blue-purple on the dorsal side but white ventrally with a projecting and larger lower lip that is sparsely bearded. This species has a long blooming period and dies back after bloom then sends out new growth in the fall. The flowers are glandular and the foliage covered with very fine down so that it appears gray-green. This plant has not been reported in cultivation.

Anthers: dehiscing full length with toothed sutures, not explanate; staminode dull gold, included

Name: radicosus = with many roots; Matroot penstemon

Subgenus Penstemon, section Penstemon, subsection Humiles

*P. ramaleyi* is found only in sc. CO and has similarities to *P. crandallii* and *P. glabrescens*.

Sometimes it is listed as a subspecies of *P. crandallii*. Stems are erect to 8″ with flat or involute very slender linear leaves that are more than 1″ long, and small blue flowers, usually from one side of each node. It is said to be deciduous and has no trailing stems but little is known about it as a garden subject.

Anthers: short, not explanate; staminode yellow-bearded, not exserted

Name: honors Dr. Francis Ramaley (1870 – 1962), Colorado botanist

Subgenus Penstemon, section Ericopsis, subsection Caespitosi

***P. ramosus*** is a rare scarlet-flowered species found in sw. NM and se. AZ that is closely related to a Mexican species, *P. lanceolatus*. It has branched stems to 20″ with few slender leaves and few 1½″ tubular orange-scarlet to deep red glandular flowers, often with the lower lobes folded to points. It blooms in June, dies back to the ground over winter and sends up new growth in the spring in se. WA.

Anthers: open almost throughout but not explanate, twisted; staminode included

Name: ramosus = branching

Subgenus Penstemon, section Chamaeleon

***P. rattanii*** is the largest flowered of subsection *Humiles*, and may reach 4′ in its native location in coastal ranges of n. CA and w. OR between 3000 and 4500′ in humus-rich soil. Stems have broad, toothed and glabrous clasping leaves. Basal mats can be 2 - 3′ wide. It blooms from May to August. The inflorescence is glandular, with spreading cymes bearing several rose-lavender 1″ flowers that are abruptly ampliate and have a white-bearded, long lower lip. Subspecies *kleei* is found in CA redwood forests that are drier. It is being grown in se. WA and is reported very nice in part-day shade with a mulch, producing great flowers. It germinates after 12 weeks cold, moist stratification.

Anthers: divaricate, opening narrowly; staminode with long pale hairs, well-exserted

Name: honors Volney Rattan (1840 – 1915) who published an early California Flora

Subgenus Penstemon, section Penstemon, subsection Humiles

***P. retrorsus*** is a small dryland species found only in w. CO at about 5700′. Many stems are 4 - 8″, ascending to erect, with narrow leaves that are about 1″ long and oblanceolate or narrowly elliptic. The leaves are covered with down (under a magnifying glass the hairs can be seen to be pointing backward instead of upward) that makes them appear quite gray. Small blue flowers are one or two per node on the upper third of the stems. Germination occurs after 12 weeks of cold, moist stratification. This is a difficult species but well-liked for dry rock gardens and long-lived, spreading to a foot or more.

Anthers: widely divergent, opening narrowly; staminode orange-yellow-bearded, included

Name: retrorsus = turned backwards

Subgenus Penstemon, section Ericopsis, subsection Caespitosi

***P. rhizomatosus*** is a small and rare species found only in White Pine County in NV on talus slopes between 9900 and 10,700′, where it blooms in July. It was first published in 1998. It is 3 - 8″ tall, with minutely hairy spatulate to oblanceolate leaves and small to medium-sized glandular-hairy violet to red-violet flowers with a protruding lower lip. It is related and similar to *P. kingii,* but will probably never be in cultivation.

Anthers: purple-black, sac-shaped; staminode slightly dilated, bare and barely exserted

Name:  for the woody rhizomes above the taproot from which stems arise
Subgenus Saccanthera, section Saccanthera, Subsection Heterophylli


**P. richardsonii**  is a late-flowering sub-shrub that may be erect to sprawling and has distinctly serrate to almost dissected leaves.  It is extremely variable in growth habit, size, leaf shape and suface, and flower color. Plants may flower from June to August or later. Variety *richardsonii* is found from the Columbia River Gorge in c. WA into British Columbia.  It has deeply cleft leaves and flowers more than 1″ long with a bearded staminode.  Variety *dentatus* has broader, somewhat glaucous leaves that are not deeply cut, also has flowers more than 1″ long with a bearded staminode and is only found in a small area of nc. OR.  Variety *curtiflorus* is found in a larger area of OR and has smaller flowers with a bare or almost bare staminode.  Some plants are too large for a rock garden but are very attractive in the border.  They are found at elevations from 4300 to 7300′, in rock slides, crevices in rock walls and in woodlands and have been cultivated successfully from the west coast to the east coast from ME to VA.  Flower color may be rose-pink to lavender, violet or blue, and white sports appear occasionally.  It may be in bloom from May to frost, depending on location.  It germinates readily with 6 weeks of cold moist stratification, can take cold and dry conditions in sun or part shade in the garden, is quite long-lived and self-sows readily.

Anthers: horseshoe or sac-shaped, opening across the top and partway down the sides with toothed sutures; staminode slightly exserted, bare to bearded depending on variety, slightly exserted

Name: honors Sir John Richardson of Scotland (1787 – 1865) naturalist, zoologist, polar explorer

Subgenus Saccanthera, Section Saccanthera, Subsection Serrulati


**P. roezlii**  resembles *P. laetus* but has smaller flowers from late May into July.  Stems may reach 20″ but are usually shorter with an open, few-flowered thyrse of 4 – 12 verticillasters, in an airy effect.  The flowers are small, glandular, blue to blue-violet.  Leaves are gray-green, slender, downy.  It is found between 2300 and 8200′ on gravelly slopes in c. and sw. OR, NV and n. CA. It has been popular in the west and in England and Germany.

Anthers: horseshoe-shaped, dehiscing across the top and upper part of the outer sides with hairs at inner sides; staminode broadened at apex, just reaching opening

Name: honors Benedict Roezl (1824 – 1885) plant collector

Subgenus Saccanthera, section Saccanthera, subsection Heterophylli


**P. rostriflorus,** long known as *P. bridgesii,* has been in cultivation for many years and bridges a gap between the low-growing scarlet-flowered *P. pinifolius* and tall scarlet-flowered *P. barbatus.* All grow in dry conditions and gravelly soil and will take cold temperatures.  All have produced yellow and orange color variations in the wild.  *P. rostriflorus* is usually about 16″ tall with a woody base and slender leaves.  Flowers are in an open thyrse and about 1″ long with forward thrusting upper lobes and narrow, downward flaring lower lobes, the outer two curling backward. It occurs in CA, Baja, NV, UT, CO, AZ and NM from 3300 to 10,950′.  It is long-lived and long-blooming, often June through August, and has been grown from OR and WA to CO, NM, NE, MA, VA and also in England. Seed germinates after 8 weeks of cold, moist stratification.

Anthers: sac or horseshoe-shaped, opening across the top 1/3 with toothed sutures, exserted; staminode glabrous, included

Name: rostral = beaked, Beaked Beardtongue

Subgenus Saccanthera, section Bridgesiani


***P. rotundifolius*** is a little-known Mexican species from the state of Chihuahua, usually found hanging from rock cliffs. Rounded or almost triangular, glabrous and glaucous blue-gray leaves, with long petioles on the lower ones, are distinctive, with prominent veining, similar to *P. alamosensis*. The flowers are scarlet and tubular with small lobes.

Name: Round-leaved Penstemon

Subgenus Penstemon, section Peltanthera, subsection Havardiani


***P. rubicundus*** has robust stems to 4', medium to large-sized glandular orchid, pink or rose-colored flowers with a bearded palate and toothed, fleshy, lanceolate gray-green leaves. The plant is similar to *P. palmeri* but the flowers are not ventricose and the inflorescence is a subsecund and open thyrse. It is found only in the mountains of w. NV in canyons between 4600 and 9350', blooming from June to August. It is considered more beautiful than *P. palmeri* by some gardeners, but does not have the fragrance. Allow 12 weeks cold, moist stratification for germination.

Anthers: opening narrowly; staminode exserted, somewhat recurved, golden bearded

Name: rubicund = rosy; Wassuk Penstemon

Subgenus Penstemon, section Peltanthera, subsection Peltanthera


***P. rupicola*** catches the eye from Mt. Ranier to OR and n. CA, where its masses of bright rosy flowers hang from crevices in dark rock cliffs from May through July. It may be found from 4000 to 7700'. The small leaves are leathery, ovate, finely toothed, evergreen and glaucous on low, woody, creeping stems. Slender, medium to large flowers rise above the foliage in a short secund thyrse to less than 6". Sports are sometimes red or white. This is a very popular plant in cold and moist climates where it is found in many rock gardens. It is said to do well in sun to part shade with acid soil that is coarsely gravelly with small amounts of leafmold and pine needle duff. It is reported to do well in s. Canada and most northern states and high altitude areas in the Rocky Mts., on the east coast and in Great Britain, Scandinavia and n. Europe. Stored seed germinates after 3 – 8 weeks at 70°F. It is easily propagated by cuttings and by layering.


Cultivars:

'Albus', a white form

'Diamond Lake', comes in a range of pinks; variable from seed

'Myrtle Hebert', a deep pink form with gray-green foliage, less prone to die-back

Anthers: exserted, explanate, covered with wooly hairs; staminode more or less bearded, included

Name: rupicola = rock-dweller, Cliff Penstemon

Subgenus Dasanthera


***P. rydbergii*** is a small-flowered species, similar to *P. procerus*, with slender stems to 28″ and a basal mat of thin, glabrous green leaves. It may be found from CA to east of the Cascade and Blue Mts. of OR and WA to MT, WY, CO and NM between 4600 and 11,450′. Most often it grows in mountain meadows and along streams and prefers a moist climate. Variety *rydbergii* is found throughout the range, variety *oreocharis* on the west side of the range and variety *aggregatus* through the center of the range. Differences are in anther cells, calyx, and amount of fine hairs. Flowers appear in high elevations in July and August and are quite small, blue to purple, with a densely bearded palate and are arranged in 1 - 6 congested but widely spaced verticils. Growers in moist climates find it long-lived and pleasing. Germination requires 12 weeks of cold, moist stratification.

Anthers: open across the connective, sometimes toothed, black; staminode golden-bearded, just reaching the opening

Name: honors Pehr Axel Rydberg (1860 - 1931), a botanist from Sweden who worked at the NY Botanical Garden for many years

Subgenus Penstemon, section Penstemon, subsection Proceri


***P. saltarius*** is a species found at about 8500′ in open woodlands in Durango, Mexico with short stems (to 15″) bearing a few medium to large, ventricose, glandular, violet to purple flowers after summer rains. Leaves are slender, glabrous; basal leaves few at bloom time. This species has not been reported in cultivation in the United States

Anthers: widely divaricate, not explanate; staminode smooth, included

Name: for type location, El Salto, also for collector Dr. U. T. Waterfall, (salto de agua, in Spanish)

Subgenus Penstemon, section Fasciculus, subsection Racemosi


***P. saxosorum*** is similar to *P. subglaber,* but with small flowers and shorter stems. Both have a narrow, crowded, secund inflorescence with flowers usually blue or blue-purple. *P. saxosorum* is found on dry, rocky slopes between 7500 and 8400′ in s. WY and nw. to c. CO, usually in a clump of stems to 24″ with a basal mat of glabrous green leaves. It has not been reported in cultivation.

Anthers: reaching the opening, somewhat hairy; staminode densely bearded with long yellow hairs, barely exserted

Name: saxosorum = of rocky places

Subgenus Habroanthus, section Glabri


***P. scapoides*** has medium sized slender, glandular lavender, purple or blue flowers in a few-flowered open thyrse on thin, almost leafless stems to 16″ above a basal mat of densely hairy, ovate gray-green leaves. It occurs between 6600 and 10,500' among sagebrush and pinyon-juniper east of Yosemite Park in CA and has not been reported in cultivation.

Anthers: horseshoe-shaped, open across top and part of sides with toothed sutures; staminode dilated and with pale yellow hairs, included

Names: scapoides, like a scape (with a naked stem); Inyo Penstemon

Subgenus Saccanthera, section Saccanthera, subsection Heterophylli


**P. scariosus** has a few ascending to erect stems 6 - 20" tall with small to medium-sized blue flowers arranged in a subsecund thyrse of 3 – 6 few-flowered vertcillasters above a basal mat, and stem leaves that are slender, glabrous, crisped and entire. These beautiful flowers are found between 4950 and 10,430' from late May to July. Variety *scariosus* is found in central Utah; variety *albifluvis* is found in ec. UT and has smaller pale blue to lavender flowers. Its basal leaves disappear at bloom time. This variety is considered a threatened species. Variety *garrettii* also has smaller blue flowers, and is found in sc. UT. Variety *cyanomontanus* has glandular blue purple flowers and is found along the CO border. This species may take 16 weeks of cold moist stratification to germinate, but is a good garden subject for most northern gardens.

Anthers: not widely divaricate, not open across the connective, with toothed sutures, sparsely white-haired, exserted; staminode with sparse yellow bearding, just reaches the opening

Names: scarious = of thin membranous texture (the sepals); Plateau Penstemon

Subgenus Habroanthus, section Glabri


**P. secundiflorus** has medium-sized pink to orchid or lavender flowers in a secund inflorescence on several erect stems to 20". Basal and stem leaves are entire, pointed, blue-green, glaucous and glabrous, and the inflorescence may have 3 – 10 closely spaced but not crowded verticillasters. Flowers are only slightly expanded until the equal, rounded lobes abruptly flare at right angles to the throat. Some plants have guidelines but not all. Some authorities consider a blue-flowered species found in the Arkansas River area of CO as a subspecies and others list it as a species, *P. versicolor. P. secundiflorus* is found from WY to NM in the eastern plains, foothills and lower elevations of the Rockies betweeen 5400 and 9000' in gravelly and sandy soils, blooming in May and June. It is of easy cultivation, germinating with 6 weeks cold, moist stratification and is long-lived, forming many-stemmed clumps. It has been widely grown throughout its native range and also with success from MN and MI to ME in sand beds.

Anthers: widely divaricate, opening narrowly; staminode dilated and deeply notched, recurved and densely bearded with golden-orange hairs, very prominent, just reaching the opening

Name: Sidebells Penstemon

Subgenus Penstemon, section Coerulei


**P. seorsus** is found in e. OR and adjacent ID between 4900 and 6600' on dry sagebrush flats and low hills. It has many stems less than 1' tall with very narrow, downy gray stem leaves that are barely noticeable and many non-flowering shoots, also with narrow leaves, at the base. The flowers are lavender to violet, glandular, upward-facing, small, narrowly tubular, with small lobes barely flaring, in a narrow thyrse with 1 or 2 flowers at each of 4 – 7 nodes in late May and

June. This would probably be a nice species for the dry rock garden, but has not been reported in cultivation.

Anthers: widely divergent, opening full-length; staminode exserted, densely bearded with short yellow hairs

Names: seorsus = separate (reference unclear); Short-lobed Penstemon

Subgenus Penstemon, section Penstemon, subsection Gairdneriani


*P. sepalulus* occurs in dry, rocky and gravelly soils from Zion National Park to Salt Lake City, Utah between 4900 and 7250'. In June and July it has 1″ lavender, moderately ventricose-ampliate upward-facing flowers on many erect, branching stems, almost forming a bush, to 30″ tall, with very narrow, rather glaucous, entire leaves. It has been grown from Oregon to NY and reported attractive and long blooming. It germinates after 12 weeks of cold, moist stratification and is also easy from cuttings.

Anthers: blue-black, sac-like, opening across the top with toothed sutures: staminode white, smooth, slightly dilated, just reaching the opening

Name: Littlecup Penstemon, referring to small sepals

Subgenus Saccanthera, section Saccanthera, subsection Heterophylli


*P. serrulatus* is an attractive, bushy plant from s. AK, British Columbia, WA and OR, where it grows on the wetter western side of the mountains from 300' to 3600' and is in bloom in early summer. It has large glossy serrate leaves on stems to 28″ each with a short, congested thyrse of many small to medium-sized blue to purple flowers at the apex, or sometimes with several clusters on cymes held close to the main stem. This is a vigorous, free-blooming and well-liked plant in moist climates where it blooms for a long time, reblooms after being cut back, and frequently self-sows. Often there are sports in white, pink and orchid. It likes acid to neutral, loamy, well-drained soil and part-day shade.

Cultivar:
'Albus', a white-flowered form

Anthers: horseshoe-shaped, opening across the top with toothed sutures; staminode dilated, lightly yellow-bearded, slightly exserted

Names: serrulatus = somewhat serrate leaves; Cascade Penstemon; Coast Penstemon

Subgenus Saccanthera, section Saccanthera, subsection Serrulati


*P. skutchii* has an open inflorescence and is a hummingbird pollinated species that has long, pendant, gradually inflated tubes with nearly regular, rounded lobes in a deep reddish maroon. The plant is usually 3' tall but may be up to 6' and has lanceolate, entire leaves. It is found only in a limited area of Guatemala at elevations around 11,000', where it blooms in August.

Anthers: divergent and explanate; staminode slightly dilated, almost glabrous

Name: honors Alexander F. Skutch, a botanist and ornithologist who specialized in plants and birds of Central America

Subgenus Penstemon, section Fasciculus, subsection Fasciculi

***P. smallii*** has long been a popular eastern species. It is grown all across the country from the west coast to Canada, and LA and MS, ME to SC and in England and Europe. It is one of the showiest of the eastern species with many orchid to red-violet flowers with an extended pale, bearded lower lip. The flowers are born in open panicles on bushy plants that can be up to 3′ high, but are usually about 2′ tall. They stand up well, have no pest or disease problems and are long blooming. They also self-sow prolifically, but are not difficult to remove where unwanted. Seeds germinate with light in about 2 weeks at 70° and generally the plants bloom the first year. They can be placed in full sun or part-day shade and mix well with lilies and daylilies. They are not long-lived but self-sow readily anywhere they have enough moisture. Older plants are less floriferous than young plants.

Anthers: widely divergent, opening moderately; staminode densely orange-bearded, just reaching the opening

Name: honors John K. Small (1869 – 1938), botanist, herbarium curator

Subgenus Penstemon, section Penstemon, subsection Penstemon


***P. spatulatus*** is a 10″ tall relative of *P. procerus* with ½″ glandular-hairy violet flowers in 1 – 4 dense interrupted clusters. The flowers may have a pale blue face and are somewhat pendant. Leaves are narrow, entire and glossy green on the stem, spatulate in the basal mat and can spread widely. This is a rare species from the Wallowa Mts. at about 9000′ in July and August. It has been reported well-liked in Scotland and England. Germinates in 8 weeks with cold, moist stratification.

Anthers: widely divergent, opening narrowly; staminode densely golden-bearded, just reaching the opening

Name: spatulate, referring to basal leaf shape

Subgenus Penstemon, section Penstemon, subsection Proceri


***P. speciosus*** is a beautiful western species found between 100′ and 10,500′ in CA, OR, WA, ID, NV and UT. It has medium to large broadly ampliate flowers that are violet on the tube and sky blue or deeper on the face, paler in the throat, distinctly bilabiate. Stems may be few to several, ascending 8″ to 2 ½′ with a long inflorescence of 4 – 12 close but not crowded subsecund verticillasters from May to July. Leaves are usually glabrous, narrowly lanceolate on the stem and broader and oblanceolate at the base. Seeds take 8 – 12 weeks cold, moist stratification to germinate; plants need a well drained dry location, but winter and spring moisture. Sand and gravel beds are recommended. A very desirable form of *Penstemon speciosus* was for a long time called subspecies *kennedyi*. The flowers were large but it was usually less than 8″ tall, often with the stem ascending rather than erect. It is no longer considered a subspecies because plants produced from its seed may be normal in height.


Cultivar: 'Kennedyi'

Anthers: dehiscing from the distal end, s-twisted, toothed sutures; staminode included, may be bare or bearded

Names: Beautiful Penstemon; Showy Penstemon, Royal Penstemon

Subgenus Habroanthus, section Glabri


***P. spectabilis*** is a spectacularly beautiful species from the deserts around Los Angeles, CA and into the Baja Peninsula. Many stems to 4' have blooming flowers for half their length. Flowers are 1 ¼" long, ventricose-ampliate, with red-violet tubes shading into blue lobes. Leaves are broadly lanceolate, sharply toothed, glabrous; upper stem leaves are connate-perfoliate. It may be found from 380' to 7900' in dry washes and on hillsides among chaparral from late April to July Subspecies *subinteger* from Baja has entire leaves. Variety *subviscosus* has a slightly glandular-pubescent inflorescence. The species germinates without chilling and is a popular garden feature where temperatures do not go below 10°F. It has been grown in s. CA, s. AZ and in Albuquerque, NM. It has also been successful in VA on a mound of equal parts compost, sand and pea gravel.

Anthers: pale, moderately divergent, opening narrowly with toothed sutures; staminode bare or with few hairs, included

Name: spectabilis = highly visible, notable

Subgenus Penstemon, section Peltanthera, subsection Peltanthera


***P. stenophyllus*** is found in AZ and Chihuahua, Sonora and Durango, Mexico between 4000 and 5500' in grasslands. Slender stems to 28" bear an open thyrse of blue-purple flowers that are a little longer than 1", almost campanulate, with guidelines in the throat and lobes flaring forward and somewhat ruffled. Leaves are widely spaced on the stems and very narrow. It is reported to bloom after summer rains.

Anthers: not widely divergent, opening at distal ends with toothed sutures; staminode dilated, bare, included,

Name: stenophyllus = narrow-leaved

Subgenus Penstemon, section Chamaeleon


***P. stephensii*** is found only in the eastern Mojave Desert of CA on slopes between 5600 and 9200' and is rare. It has stems to 5' with finely toothed glabrous green lanceolate leaves up the stem, the upper ones connate-perfoliate. Flowers are less than 1" long, narrowly tubular, flesh pink to rose, magenta or lavender. The inflorescence is subsecund and narrow. This species has not been reported in cultivation.

Anthers: glabrous and explanate; staminode glabrous, included

Name: honors Frank Stephens ( 1849 – 1937) CA mammologist and plant collector

Subgenus Penstemon, section Peltanthera, subsection Peltanthera


***P. strictiformis*** is found in the Four Corners region between 4900 and 6900', blooming in June and July. It is similar to *P. strictus* but generally a smaller more compact plant with smaller flowers and leaves. The flowers are about ¾" and often a lighter shade of purple or blue. The inflorescence and flowers are glabrous and subsecund to secund, with 5 – 9 verticillasters. Leaves are narrow, entire, green, not forming a spreading basal mat. This is a desireable garden plant, not as vigorous as *P. strictus*, more drought tolerant, but not as widely available.

Anthers: open from distal end, not across the connective, sparsely hairy; staminode bare to moderately yellow-bearded, included

Name: strictiformis = with a narrow form

Subgenus Habroanthus, section Glabri

*P. strictus* is found at higher elevations, between 6700 and 10,750′ and over a broader range, into northern WY and CO, east into the Rockies, and the Sangre de Cristo and Sandia Mts in NM. The flowers are over 1″ long, moderately ventricose-ampliate and usually deep purple-blue with upper lobes forming a porch over the throat. Stems are usually about 2′ tall. The inflorescence is long, narrow, secund, and the flowers closely spaced, appearing in June and irregularly thereafter. Leaves are dark green, entire, slender to spatulate, and form a basal mat that expands to one or two feet in a few years. It is long-lived and is easily divided to increase stock. Seeds germinate either at 40° or 70°F. It does well in full sun or part shade, but may become floppy and paler in shade in moist climates.

Cultivar:

'Bandera', a deep purple form

Anthers: widely divergent with long tangled hairs, opening narrowly from the distal end, not across the connective, with toothed sutures, one pair often exserted; staminode bare to moderately hairy, included

Name: strictus = narrow

Subgenus Habroanthus, section Glabri

*P. subglaber* has glandular, medium-to-deep blue flowers, about 1″ long, in an interrupted, subsecund inflorescence on stems from 10 to 30″ from June to early August. Leaves are smooth, green and entire. It may be found in moist or dry sites in UT, ID and WY between 6000 and 10,000′. It is reported good in gardens in e. WA, MT, MN, CO and NE, hardy and long-lived. Germination requires 8 weeks of cold, moist stratification.

Anthers: widely divergent, opening moderately with toothed sutures, not across the connective, with short white hairs on sides, more or less exserted; staminode yellow-bearded at apex, more or less exserted

Name: subglaber = almost smooth

Subgenus Habroanthus, section Glabri

*P. subserratus* is a beautiful blue-flowered species from the east side of the Cascade Mts. in WA and just into OR. Flowers are slender tubes with flaring lobes, less than ¾″ long, in 3 – 10 interrupted clusters on stems to 2 ½′ tall, appearing late May through July. Leaves are finely toothed, glossy green to finely downy. It is found in wooded areas in partial shade and has been successfully grown on the east coast as well as in its native habitat. Germination takes 8 weeks of cold, moist stratification.

Anthers: opening narrowly, not across the connective, with toothed sutures; staminode orange bearded, included

Name: subserratus = not quite serrate

Subgenus Penstemon, section Penstemon, subsection Humiles

*P. subulatus* has slender scarlet tubes with small flaring lobes that are held almost horizontally or slightly pendant on stems to 24″. It is found in southern AZ between 1500 and 4500′, blooming in April. Leaves are narrow, widely spaced and grey-green. In cultivation in s. AZ and s. NM, it has formed large, many-stemmed, showy clumps and bloomed over a long period. Seed germinates after 12 weeks of cold, moist stratification.

Anthers: pale, widely divergent opening throughout; staminode bare, included

Name: subulatus = awl-shaped

Subgenus Penstemon, section Peltanthera, subsection Centranthifolii

*P. sudans* is a close relative of *P. deustus* with tiny white to cream-colored flowers with dark guidelines in up to 18 distinctly separate verticillasters on several stout stems to 28″ in June and July. Leaves are ovate, toothed and strongly glandular so that they have a clammy feel. There are no basal leaves at bloom time. It is found between 3950 and 5600′ in open rocky places in Lassen County, CA and adjacent NV. It has not been reported in cultivation.

Anthers: white, glabrous, almost explanate; staminode white, glabrous, included

Name: sudans = sweating

Subgenus Penstemon, section Penstemon, subsection Deusti

*P. superbus* lives up to its name with coral to carmine flowers in many widely-spaced rings on upright stems that range from 2 - 4′. The glandular flowers are ¾″ long with an almost regular face and small opening. The inflorescence may have 15 or more interrupted whorls. Leaves are thick, ovate, glabrous and glaucous. The basal clump may be 12″ wide but usually is absent at bloom time. It is related and similar to *P. wrightii* and *P. parryi*, but larger in all parts. It is native to se. AZ, sw. NM and the states of Sonora and Chihuahua, Mexico between 3500 and 5000′, blooming in April. It has been cultivated in CA, OR, WA and VA as well as NM and AZ and while not long-lived, it is a treasure that should be tried by anyone from USDA zone 5 1/2 or higher in sandy soil with good drainage and full sun. Supplemental water is necessary in low deserts. It germinates without chilling.

Anthers: widely divergent, explanate; staminode pale, not dilated, with few short hairs, included

Name: superbus = superb or magnificent

Subgenus Penstemon, Section Peltanthera, Subsection Centranthifolii

*P. tenuiflorus* is very similar to *P. hirsutus* with wiry stems one to two feet tall and slender tubular flowers with a closed mouth. It can be all white or the tube tinged with pink or lavender.

The flowers form an open thyrse above finely toothed or entire thin dark green leaves. It is found in sandy soils in AL, MS, KY and TN. It has not been reported in cultivation.

Anthers: widely divaricate, opening widely, smooth; staminode yellow-bearded, exserted

Name: tenuiflorus = slender-flowered

Subgenus Penstemon, section Penstemon, subsection Penstemon


*P. tenuifolius* is a bushy subshrub to 18″ that has almost needle-like leaves and small to medium broadly ampliate strongly purple flowers with pale throats in a sparsely flowered open inflorescence on many branched stems. Leaves are narrow and in ssp. *minutifolius* very similar to *P. pinifolius.* It is found on the central plateau from Puebla to San Luis Potosi at about 7000′. It has not been reported in cultivation.

Anthers: Open full length; staminode with short hairs at the apex

Name: tenuifolius = thin-leaved

Subgenus Penstemon, section Fasciculus, subsection Racemosi


*P. tenuis* produces a delicate open panicle of many flowers on wiry stems 16 – 36″ tall. The flowers are ¾″ long, abruptly inflated, pink to orchid or red-purple above a large clump of thin, finely-toothed basal leaves. This species is found in wet woodland soils in AR, e. TX, LA and OK in May and has been praised by gardeners from c. TX to northern gardens and in England and Europe where moisture is plentiful. It germinates readily and blooms late in the same year. It has been raised as a greenhouse plant in some areas.


Cultivar:

'Betty's Choice', has lavender flowers and is a sturdy plant with many stems


Anthers: widely divaricate, opening wide, smooth; staminode lightly bearded, just reaching the opening

Names: Sharp-sepal Penstemon, Gulf Coast Penstemon

Subgenus Penstemon, section Penstemon, subsection Penstemon


*P. tepicensis* is a little-known species from a mountainous area of the west coast of Nayarit, Mexico. It has inch-long violet to purple bell-shaped flowers with hairs on the lower throat in an open, spreading thyrse on hairy stems with large, toothed leaves. It has not been reported in cultivation in the United States.

Anthers: open moderately across the connective, widely divaricate, glabrous; staminode dilated and bearded

Name: from type location, Tepic, Nayarit, Mexico

Subgenus Penstemon, section Fasciculus, subsection Campanulati


*P. teucrioides* has small blue flowers and linear leaves with short flowering stems rising from woody, decumbent stems bearing the flowers only 2 - 5″ above the ground. The crowded leaves are microscopically hairy, giving them a gray appearance. The flowers are narrowly tubular, nearly ¾" long with a white palate. This is the most floriferous of the section *Ericopsis* with flowers totally covering the mat at peak bloom in good garden conditions. It is found in c. and wc. CO between 7200 and 10,000', where it blooms in June and July, but has been widely cultivated from WA to NY and in Great Britain. It germinates in 8 weeks and is long-lived, spreading into mats 2' wide. Sand or scree beds in full sun are recommended and acidic, neutral and alkaline soils all seem satisfactory.

Anthers: glabrous, fully dehiscent, not explanate, staminode slender, bearded, included

Name teucrioides = resembling Teucrium; Creeping Penstemon

Subgenus Penstemon, section Ericopsis, subsection Caespitosi

**P. thompsoniae** is well suited to troughs because the plant is so small that it would be easily lost in a rock garden, and should be appreciated at close range. Leaves that are covered with fine appressed hairs on both surfaces and appear gray are often less than ½" long by ¼"wide, thick, almost succulent in appearance and erect on tufted stems to 4" or sprawling stems. The flowers are larger than the leaves, red- violet to blue violet, glandular, with a white rimmed throat and sparsely yellow-bearded lower lip. Plants are found in high deserts in CA, NV, UT and AZ. Flowers are borne within the tuft on variety *thompsoniae,* on elongated stems in variety *desperatus* and on erect, leafy stems with thyrse-like panicles in ssp. *jaegeri.* All are found between 4900 and 9800', blooming in May and June.

Germination requires 12 weeks of cold, moist stratification. This species loves hot, dry conditions and has been successfully grown from eastern WA to NY.

Anthers: black, glabrous with toothed sutures, open across but not explanate, more or less exserted; staminode orange bearded, more or less exserted

Name: honors Ellen Powell Thompson, sister of John Wesley Powell

Subgenus Penstemon, Section Ericopsis, Subsection Caespitosi

**P. thurberi** has branching stems with small, slender green leaves and many pink to rose or bluish-lavender tubular flowers in open racemes that make an excellent display from April through August with sufficient rain. The form of the plant is similar to that of *P. ambiguus,* but the salverform flowers have a more expanded and deeply colored throat and pale lobes that are not as regular. The plant may reach 30" tall and as wide. It is found from CA and Baja to NM in sandy soils around 4000'. It may not be hardy below 10°F but has been grown in moderate climates from CA to PA and VA and blooms over a long period. Fresh seed germinates without chilling in less than 2 weeks. The plants die back and can be cut to the woody base each year to make way for fresh growth in the spring.

Anthers: small, divaricate and explanate; staminode smooth

Name: honors George Thurber (1821 – 1890), botanist with the Mexican Boundary Survey

Subgenus Penstemon, section Ambigui

**P. tidestromii** is a rare and threatened species from central UT found between 5350 and 8200' in desert scrub and pinyon/juniper communities. It has several erect stems to 20" with 4 – 11

secund verticillasters having in each a few small, moderately ampliate flowers with violet to lavender throats and spreading blue lobes in June. Leaves are finely hairy and gray-green.

Anthers: black, not open across the connective, with toothed sutures; staminode yellow-bearded, included

Name: honors Ivar Tidestrom (1864 – 1956) botanist with USDA and Smithsonian, authored an early Flora of AZ and NM

Subgenus Habroanthus, section Glabri

*P. tiehmii* is found on a high elevation, steep talus slope only on Mt. Lewis in Lander County NV. It is a close relative of *P. kingii,* with small, glandular violet flowers on several stems that are only 4 - 8″ tall from mid-June to early August. It was described and published in 1998 and should not be collected because of its rarity.

Anthers: sac-shaped; staminode bare, exserted

Name honors Arnold Tiehm (1951 -  ) botanist and collector in the Great Basin for the NY Botanical Garden

Subgenus Saccanthera, section Saccanthera, subsection Heterophylli

*P. tracyi* is a rare and distinctive small plant with a flat basal rosette and stem leaves that are small, obovate, mainly entire and leathery. The small pink flowers with densely bearded throat are tightly clustered in a single or few whorls in July and August. This plant is found at about 7000′ in Trinity County, CA in rock crevices and has been reported successfully grown in CA, VA, Scotland and Gothenburg, Sweden.

Anthers: widely divaricate, explanate; staminode sparsely bearded at apex

Name: honors Joseph Prince Tracy (1875 – 1953) plant collector

Subgenus Penstemon, section Penstemon, subsection Deusti

*P. triflorus* has leafy stems to 2′ topped with glandular, medium to large white, pink or rosy-red flowers with striking guidelines in differing patterns. It is an extremely variable species that may have an open inflorescence or a narrow one, subsecund to encircling, and few to many flowers. Leaves are irregularly toothed to entire and form a large basal clump at bloom time. It is related to *P. cobaea*, but not as hardy or large-flowered. It is found in c. TX in dry limestone cliffs in April and May and widely grown from there to the CA coast. Subspecies *integrifolius* has lavender flowers, bearding on the staminode and entire leaves. This species is not hardy in USDA zone 5, but popular where it is not subject to wet winter and spring conditions. It has survived and flowered well for several years in VA.

Anthers: widely divergent, explanate; staminode bare to lightly bearded, included

Name: triflorus = three-flowered; Hill Country Penstemon

Subgenus Penstemon, section Cristati

*P. triphyllus* forms an open subshrub to 30″ and may spread as wide, blooming from May to July. Leaves are variably toothed and may be 1 – 4 (usually 3) at a node. Small flowers are lavender to blue-lavender, trumpet-shaped with guidelines and bearded throat in a very open thyrse on many stems. It blooms early to mid-summer for a long period and is long-lived. It is found around 1600' in basalt cliffs in the Snake River drainage from e. ID to WA and OR. Seed germinates after 12 weeks of cold, moist stratification. The plant becomes straggly late in the summer and may be sharply cut back. It makes a good filler in a border.

Anthers: sac-like, opening across the top with toothed sutures; staminode densely bearded, exserted

Name: triphyllus = three leaved

Subgenus Saccanthera, section Saccanthera, subsection Serrulati

*P. tubaeflorus* has 1" glistening, glandular white flowers in a long, narrow, encircling inflorescence that may be interrupted or not from May to July. The stems can be from 10 to 36" tall, usually one to a few. Leaves are entire, glabrous, broadly lanceolate. This species is very hardy and floriferous and is found in prairies and moist woodlands from WI, NE, KS, OK, TX and AR to LA and has naturalized into the east. The flowers are trumpet-shaped with almost regular faces and no guidelines. Several plants together are needed for a good display but they should not be crowded. Plants are easily divided. It germinates with 8 weeks cold, moist stratification.

Anthers: black, widely divergent, explanate; staminode sparsely yellow-bearded, included

Name: tubaeflorus = trumpet-flowered

Subgenus Penstemon, section Penstemon, subsection Tubaeflori

*P. tusharensis* is found only in c. UT between 7050 and 10,000' on subalpine slopes in sandy or gravelly soils. It is closely related to *P. caespitosus* and sometimes listed as *P. caespitosus* ssp. *tusharensis* or as a synonym of *P. caespitosus* var. *suffruticosus*. Flowering stems may be ascending to 5" from decumbent older woody stems. Tiny ½" leaves are oval and gray-green with fine, appressed, downy hairs on the upper surface. Flowers are blue to blue-violet, small and upward-facing from several nodes on each stem and may appear from June to August.

Anthers: almost explanate with toothed sutures; staminode golden bearded, included

Name: from the type location Tushar Plateau

Subgenus Penstemon, section Ericopsis, subsection Caespitosi

*P. uintahensis* is an alpine plant that grows between 9000 and 12,500' in the Uintah Mts. of UT. It is found in humus-rich, gravelly soil and has a short, subsecund inflorescence of small, medium blue-purple flowers with pale throats and fine guidelines on stems 2 - 8" tall above a mat of strap-like, entire, glabrous green leaves in July. Older plants bear many stems of flowers. It has been grown in troughs in Scotland, in e. WA, n. NM and in a mountain garden in AZ. Germinates after 4 weeks of cold, moist stratification.

Anthers: divaricate, opening narrowly, not across the connective, with finely-hairy sides and toothed sutures; staminode pale yellow, somewhat dilated, included

Name: Uintah Mountains Penstemon

Subgenus Habroanthus, section Glabri

*P. unilateralis*  see *P. virgatus* var. *asa grayi*


*P. utahensis,* a very showy and attractive plant, blooms from early April to June between 4000 and 7500′ in desert canyons and on mesas in pinyon/juniper country of CA, UT, NV and AZ.  It has glistening, glandular, small to medium-sized pink, rosy or carmine-red flowers on several stems to 20" tall in a long, subsecund inflorescence. The flowers are tubular-salverform with the face densely glandular at the throat.  Leaves are entire, sometimes crisped, gray-green and glaucous with a basal rosette at bloom time.  It is reportedly a temperamental species, but well worth having.  Seed germinates at cool temperatures after 8 weeks of cold, moist stratification.

Anthers:  pale, divaricate, explanate; staminode broadened at tip, usually beardless, included

Names:  Utah Firecracker; Utah Bugler; Utah Penstemon

Subgenus Penstemon, section Peltanthera, subsection Centranthifolii


*P. venustus*  is  a lovely clump-forming species from dry, rocky cliffs and roadside cuts between 3000 and 7250′ in e. OR, WA and w. ID that may be 12 - 32" tall. It usually has several to many upright stems with toothed, smooth, lanceolate leaves and no basal mat.  The medium-sized, broadly ampliate, glabrous flowers are lavender to violet in a long inflorescence of 4 – 10 subsecund verticillasters from May to August.  Seed germinates after 8 weeks of cold, moist stratification. This is an easy, long-lived and long-blooming species that has been praised in dry and moist climates from w. WA to OH and VA.  Part-day shade is recommended.  It dies to the ground over winter.

Anthers:  sac-like, opening across the sparsely toothed top, with hairs on inner sides and filament, exserted; staminode with few white hairs at apex, somewhat exserted

Name: venustus = beautiful

Subgenus Saccanthera, section Saccanthera, subsection Serrulati


*P. versicolor*  is related and similar to *P. secundiflorus* and considered a subspecies of it by some authorities.  It is found in the Arkansas River Valley of sc. CO from 5000 to 8000′ in May and June.  Leaves are entire, elliptic to ovate, glaucous and glabrous, and the flowers almost regular, sky-blue to blue-lavender on one to a few stems 10 - 14" tall with 4 – 8 subsecund, usually close but not crowded, verticillasters.  It is a beauty that is easy in dry gardens and long-lived.  It germinates after 6 – 8 weeks cold, moist stratification at cool temperatures.

Anthers: widely divaricate, opening narrowly, across the connective but not to the ends; staminode dilated, recurved, densely golden-bearded, just reaching the opening

Name: versicolor = showing a variety of colors

Subgenus Penstemon, section Coerulei


*P. virens*  makes rounded clumps that are almost covered in small blue flowers in the foothills of the eastern side of the Front Range in CO and WY from 5500 – 10,500′ in late May and to July at higher elevations.  It is often found in acid pine duff.  The funnel-form flowers are light to dark blue on many ascending to erect stems to 10″ tall (occasionally more) with 3 – 6 distinct or close verticillasters and a basal clump of bright green, almost entire leaves.  This is a gem for rock gardens, easy and long-lived in almost any soil and situation from WA and n. NM to SD, MI, OH, PA, and New England to VA, and in Great Britain. It may be grown in full sun in the east and midwest, but tolerates part shade in the west. In some areas the basal mat disappears over winter. Stored seed germinates after 6 weeks cold, moist stratification at 40°F.

Anthers: widely divaricate, opening nearly to but not across the connective; staminode densely bearded with stiff golden hairs, included

Name: virens = green; Blue-mist Penstemon

Subgenus Penstemon, section Penstemon, subsection Humiles

*P. virgatus* is an extremely variable species with a few erect stems to 32″ tall with slender strap-like leaves and no basal mat. The former *P. unilateralis* is now recognized as *P. virgatus* var. *asa-grayi*. The flowers may be small to medium in size and white, pink, blue or purple, broadly ampliate and with red-violet guidelines into the throat in a long, secund inflorescence in summer. It is found in NM and CO between 6500 and 8500′. Variety *asa-grayi* has larger flowers, usually purple, and broader leaves. Variety *putus* has narrow leaves, white or almost white flowers. This species germinates with or without stratification and is easy and well-liked from WA to VA.

Anthers: divaricate, dehiscing completely but not explanate; staminode sometimes dilated, smooth, just reaching the opening to exserted

Name: virgate= wand-like; Wandbloom Penstemon

Subgenus Habroanthus, section Glabri

*P. vizcainensis* has been found only on the southern tip of the Baja Peninsula, a very low rainfall area, in sandy arroyos at low elevations. It may be as much as 7 ½′ tall. Leaves are bright green, toothed, lanceolate. The flowers are less than an inch long, funnelform to ventricose, deep pink to rose-purple in a very long, narrow inflorescence. It has not been reported in cultivation.

Anthers: widely divergent, explanate; staminode smooth to sparsely bearded, dilated

Name: from type location, Vizcaino Peninsula, Baja California, Mexico

Subgenus Penstemon, section Peltanthera, subsection Peltanthera

*P. vulcanellus* is another Mexican species from the area of Durango, where it grows in rocky, volcanic soil and blooms in July. It has many stems about one foot tall with low branches to give it a bushy effect and small narrow, crisped leaves. The flowers are about 1″ long, lavender to purple, glandular, broadly ampliate with small lobes in a narrow raceme-like inflorescence. It has not been reported in cultivation.

Anthers: widely divergent, explanate; staminode smooth, slightly dilated

Name: vulcanellus = little Fire-god

Subgenus Penstemon, section Fasciculus, subsection Racemosi

*P. wardii* is a rare and threatened species that grows in clay and gypsum in the pinyon/juniper covered foothills of the Sevier Valley in c. Utah between 5495 and 6810′ and blooms in July. It may be up to 18″ tall and has entire, spatula-like leaves that are densely cinereous and 3 – 10 closely spaced verticillasters that are secund and few-flowered with inch-long ventricose, glandular, blue to lavender-blue flowers with pale throats. It has not been reported in cultivation.

Anthers: divergent, opening from the distal end, slightly toothed at sutures and slightly s-twisted; staminode smooth, somewhat enlarged at apex, included

Name: honors Leslie F. Ward (1841 – 1913)

Subgenus Habroanthus, section Glabri


*P. washingtonensis* grows in moist flats and wooded slopes in nc. WA between 6100 and 6800'. It has a well-developed basal mat of shiny green leaves and many stems 4 to 10″ tall bearing one to four dense clusters of tiny, deep blue-purple glandular flowers in July and August. Occasionally off-white forms are seen. It has been garden grown in northern climates and is well-liked for rock gardens but is on the state's threatened list.

Anthers: widely divergent, almost explanate; staminode bearded lightly to heavily, included

Name: from the state of Washington

Subgenus Penstemon, section Penstemon, subsection Proceri


*P. watsonii* has a short inflorescence of small violet to blue flowers on cymes and pedicels that are held close to the main stem to form 3 – 6 loose, interrupted verticillasters above a clump of narrowly lanceolate leaves from June to August. The several stems may be up to 24″ tall. This species is found in dry, rocky soils from nw. AZ, NV, UT and CO to ID and WY from 5400 to 10,430'. It has been reported easy to grow from WA to NE and more tolerant of drought than others in its subsection.

Anthers: widely divergent, not explanate, with toothed sutures; staminode densely yellow-bearded, just reaching the opening

Name: honors Sereno Watson (1826 – 1892), who participated in several western surveys and later worked under Asa Gray at Harvard University

Subgenus Penstemon, section Penstemon, subsection Proceri


*P. whippleanus* can be found from 5000 to 12,000' in aspen groves to alpine tundra of the Rocky Mountains in ID, MT and WY, NV, UT, CO, n. AZ and n. NM, blooming from late June to August. It ranges in height from 8″ to 2', rarely more, with erect, leafy stems from a basal mat of thin, finely-toothed ovate to lanceolate leaves. The stems bear one to several clusters of 1″, narrowly campanulate flowers with an elongated lower lip. Colors that are most unusual from cream to pale lavender, dark violet, wine red and grape-purple and glandular hairs that catch the light make them a photographer's delight. A careful selection of seed is necessary. Germination requires 3 months cold, moist stratification. This species does require moisture and has been grown successfully in CO, MT, MI, NE, Great Britain and Germany in neutral to acid soils. Some report it grows and spreads too fast! Division is easy. Although it is a late bloomer in the mountains, it can bloom as early as late April in low elevation gardens.

Anthers: widely divergent, explanate; staminode dilated, bare to yellow-bearded at apex, exserted to included.

Name: honors Amiel Whipple (1818 – 1863), engineer, botanist, boundary surveyor and Civil War general.

Subgenus Penstemon, section Penstemon, subsection Humiles

*P. wilcoxii* grows in open coniferous woods from e. OR and WA through ID into w. MT, blooming from May to July. It is similar to *P. ovatus* but grows east of the Cascade Mts. in drier environments. The small to medium-sized blue flowers with an extended and bearded lower lip are numerous, and form a loose, wide thyrse on leafy stems to 3'. Leaves are toothed to entire, variable in shape but generally lanceolate or ovate. Germination may require 12 weeks of cold, moist stratification. It is reported easy to grow in northern climates. Gardeners report that it looks best against a dark background because of the openness of the inflorescence. It seems to do well in any loose soil.

Anthers: widely divergent, not explanate; staminode strongly yellow-bearded, exserted

Name: honors Earley Vernon Wilcox (1869 – 1950) who collected the type plant at Kallispell, MT

Subgenus Penstemon, section Penstemon, subsection Humiles

*P. wislizenii* has 1 - 3' stems with a subracemose inflorescence of 1" scarlet tubular flowers with small lobes that flare only slightly. The flowers are slightly glandular and have no bearding in the throat, but do have guidelines. Leaves are narrowly spatulate and sparse, mostly basal. This species is found in nw. Mexico in the Sierra Madre Occidental region and south to Sinaloa.

Anthers: divaricate, opening from the distal end only, exserted; staminode abruptly dilated, exserted

Name: honors Frederick A. Wislizenius (1810 – 1889), botanist and physician

Subgenus Habroanthus, section Elmigera

*P. wrightii* grows 2 - 3' tall in the grasslands north of Big Bend National Park in TX. It has pink to carmine flowers in a long, narrow, interrupted inflorescence similar to *P. superbus,* but fewer flowered generally, blooming in April and May. The flowers are almost 1" long, regular, with rounded, overlapping lobes. Leaves are glaucous and glabrous, entire, ovate, sometimes mucronate, and clasping. This plant is not long-lived but if started early or in the fall in mild climates good bloom can be had the first year and it may survive winter temperatures to 10°F. Germination does not require chilling. It is cultivated in sw. TX, s. AZ, s. NM and s. CA and in VA.

Anthers: red to maroon, open wide but not explanate; staminode golden-bearded, included

Name: honors Charles Wright (1811 – 1885), who participated in the Mexican Boundary Survey and reported many new species

Subgenus Penstemon, section Peltanthera, subsection Centranthifolii

*P. yampaensis* is closely related to *P. acaulis* and sometimes listed as a subspecies of it, but appears more robust, with flowers slightly larger and more numerous appearing in June. They are reported to be lilac or blue-lavender rather than the clear blue of *P. acaulis* and barely extend above the foliage. Leaves are narrowly oblanceolate, cinereous, in dense clumps with no stem showing. This species is found in Moffat County, CO at 6200'. The plant is about 2″ in height and should be used in troughs or atop a wall so it can be appreciated in close-up. Germinates after 12 weeks cold, moist stratification

Anthers: divaricate, not explanate, toothed at sutures; staminode golden-bearded, exserted

Name:  from the vicinity of the Yampa River

Subgenus Penstemon, section Ericopsis, subsection Caespitosi

## Descriptions of the Larger Classification Divisions

To make use of the classification system, you need to learn what characteristics distinguish the different groups within each division and subdivision. It will then be easier to visualize them. The following are descriptions of the larger groups.

The subgenus **Dasanthera** is made up of long-lived low, shrubby species with good-sized flowers and anthers covered in dense, woolly hair. They have leathery evergreen leaves, with the exception of *Penstemon lyalli*, which has herbaceous, willow-like, finely toothed leaves and tends to be 20" or higher. They are found in the Pacific Northwest of the United States and southwestern Canada, with the exception of *P. newberryi*, which extends into California and Nevada. They are usually found in the mountains on and among rocks or talus and prefer a cool climate, neutral to acid soil, and good drainage with generous moisture and humidity. The flowers are numerous and showy and come in shades of bright pink and lavender to purple, with white sports appearing occasionally.

The subgenus **Saccanthera** are found in Utah, Nevada and California and are distinguished by the saccate or sac-like anthers which open across the top. The only red one is *Penstemon rostriflorus*, in its own section, Bridgesiani. The Serrulati have violet to lavender flowers and toothed foliage. The Heterophylli have entire foliage and flowers that often shade from a red-violet tube to blue lobes. Others have entirely blue flowers. All perform well with a modest amount of water, although *P. serrulatus* prefers moist soil.

The subgenus **Habroanthus** have anthers that diverge but do not become opposite and are usually smooth, but some have a few hairs, and they are divided into two sections. The Glabri are generally blue to purple, have fairly large flowers with wide throats and are some of the most beautiful blues and purples in the plant world. Many are upright spikes, frequently secund or subsecund. They come from the central and northern Rocky Mountain and Intermountain regions, prefer moderately alkaline soils and are drought tolerant. The Elmigera are red-flowered and their narrow tubes attract hummingbirds. They are from southwestern states and Mexico and are also drought tolerant.

The section **Coerulei** are noted for their bluish-glaucous foliage that is substantial and stout spikes of flowers that are in pastel colors, sometimes full cylinders and sometimes secund. They are very drought tolerant, occurring in alkaline soils that may be sand, gravel or clay, and are plants of the Great Plains, Great Basin and Rocky Mountains from Canada to New Mexico.

Section **Cristati** are generally small plants with moderately large flowers that are covered with glandular-hairs, giving a crystalline appearance, and often have prominent golden staminodes protruding from their throats. They are found from the eastern edge of the Great Plains into the arid Intermountain Region, like full sun and are very drought tolerant, except for *Penstemon triflorus* and *Penstemon cobaea* that are from the eastern side of the region and only moderately drought tolerant.

The section **Ericopsis** are small leaved, evergreen, very low, woody-based plants that are very drought tolerant, with few to many small, usually blue flowers, found west of the Front

Range of the Rocky Mountains in poor alkaline soils. They often grow under or protected by shrubs and evergreens.

The Section **Fasciculus** consists of species from Mexico with red or purple flowers that have generally not yet been widely brought into cultivation in the United States. The exception is *Penstemon pinifolius,* found also in New Mexico and Arizona, a low plant with very narrow scarlet flowers and needle-like foliage, that is widely grown across this country and in other countries.

Section **Peltanthera** are usually large, tall plants with many long spires of pale or bright pink to bright red flowers. Their foliage is usually glaucous, thick and leathery, sometimes with toothed edges. They are found from Mexico into the desert parts of the Intermountain Region as far east as Texas. Spectacular in appearance, very drought tolerant, needing bright sun, and easy in poor soils where it is dry most of the time, they are not long-lived but are must-have penstemons that tolerate quite cold temperatures.

Most of the subsection **Humiles** are small to moderate-sized plants, generally with slender blue flowers that have a long lower lip, in an open inflorescence and have many flower bearing stems. Leaves are toothed, sometimes barely so. Their anthers open opposite and across the connective. They are found from high elevations in the Rockies to lower elevations on the west coast. Some are more drought tolerant than others and most will do well with some shade in the southwest. They are very long-lived generally.

The subsection **Penstemon** species are found in the Mississippi River Basin and eastward and are mid-sized to tall plants that are easy to grow with adequate moisture in sun or shade all across the country. They have anthers without hairs that open from end to end. They are tolerant of most soils, surprisingly drought tolerant with part-day shade even in the high desert, and long-lived. Many northern species will take very cold temperatures if there is adequate moisture in the ground. Most have many stems with large open panicles of white to pink, rose or lavender, small to medium-sized flowers and are in bloom over a long period.

Subsection **Proceri** species are easy to distinguish from other penstemons because the flowers are small and clustered in whorls or false whorls, that are widely spaced on the stem. Their leaves are always entire. Most occur in moist regions or areas with heavy winter snow cover. They may be from a few inches to two feet tall and are found in the northwestern quadrant of the United States into Canada, from the Rockies westward.

See Appendix 5 for the species lists in each classification.

# Chapter 3

## Penstemon Hybrids

Hybrids may be classified as natural hybrids or hybrids that originate from controlled crosses. Natural hybrids occur in the wild, usually only where the ranges of different species overlap. These hybrids are often referred to as hybrid colonies or hybrid swarms. Sometimes it is difficult to distinguish between those that are sports or forms varying from the type and those that are true hybrids between species. Natural hybrids may also occur when different species are grown in close proximity, as in gardens, nurseries or field trials where cross-pollination is likely to take place, especially if there are some hybrids already in the vicinity.

Hybrids from controlled pollinations are made by plant breeders, both professional and amateur, and are popular and widely available. They may be bred for garden worthiness, hardiness, pest resistance, growth habit and aesthetic characteristics. Many hybrids are more vigorous than their parents. They also can be more adaptable to typical garden conditions. Those included here are by no means all that exist, but are ones that have been registered with the American Penstemon Society plus others that are currently available in nurseries. Everyone who names and releases a new hybrid or cultivar is strongly encouraged to register the name with the American Penstemon Society. (See the form in the appendix).

We are dividing hybrids into two main groups, **American** and **European** or large-flowered Penstemons, and a third mixed group, which we are calling **Bedding Penstemons**. The American hybrids have been developed in the United States and Canada and will be further divided according the Penstemon subgenera and sections to which they belong. European or large-flowered hybrids have been developed in Great Britain, continental Europe and recently by breeders in the milder climates of the west coast of America and New Zealand. They were created by crossing several Mexican and Guatemalan species and later *P. cobaea* was added to the germ plasm. They tend to be less hardy than the American hybrids. They have been available and very popular in mild climates where they can be successfully grown from USDA Zone 6 and above. Bedding Penstemons are half-hardy hybrids that are sold as seed strains in many catalogues and nurseries. They are usually treated as annuals, started in the fall in mild climates, and make a wonderful display in beds where they are massed, because they branch well and continue sending up new flower heads over a long period.

## American Hybrids

## Dasanthera Subgenus Hybrids

Subgenus Dasanthera contains the first species of penstemons to evolve.* They are found in the northwestern United States and Alberta and British Columbia in Canada. Most are low-growing shrubby plants and the hybrids are crosses between the species *P. cardwellii, P. fruticosus, P. davidsonii, P. barrettiae* and *P. rupicola.* As mentioned above, sometimes it is difficult to say whether some named varieties are just different forms or true hybrids.

*Dr. Andrea Wolfe of Ohio State University in a personal communication

Penstemon x 'Blue Mink' is a cross between *P. rupicola* and *P. fruticosus* with rosy-purple flowers and leaves that are gray in summer and edged with a fine red line.

Penstemon x 'Breitenbush Blue' is a vigorous but compact natural cross between *P. cardwellii* and *P. davidsonii* that grows to about 6" with flowers almost 1 ½" long.

Penstemon x 'Cardinal' is from *P. rupicola* and *P. cardwellii* with red flowers, 12" x 12".

Penstemon x 'Crystal', a cross between *P. barrettiae* and *P. cardwellii, is* a compact, hardy shrub with translucent white flowers and light green foliage.

Penstemon x 'Edithae', is a cross between *P. barrettiae* and *P. rupicola,* which has rose-red flowers and small leaves.

Penstemon x 'Grape Tart', a robust cross between *P. cardwellii* 'John Bacher' and *P. davidsonii* ssp. *menziesii*, has two-toned lavender flowers and shiny green foliage.

Penstemon x 'Pat' is a natural hybrid, suspected to be of *P. rupicola* and *P. fruticosus,* that grows to 10" and has rather glaucous leaves and bright pink flowers.

Penstemon x 'Pink Dust', a cross between *P. davidsonii, P. fruticosus* and *P. rupicola* has light pink flowers and rather silvery-gray leaves.

Penstemon x 'Pink Holly', a multiple cross between *P. fruticosus, P. davidsonii, P. rupicola* and *P. rupicola 'albus',* has bright pink flowers and toothed, bluish foliage.

Penstemon x 'Six Hills' is a hybrid of *P. rupicola* with an unknown partner, bearing bright pink flowers.

Penstemon x 'Snoqualamie Hybrid', a cross between *P. fruticosus* and *P. rupicola* with rose-lilac flowers, has an erect habit of growth and short green leaves; it is vigorous and easy to propagate.

Penstemon x 'Wax Works', a cross between *P. cardwellii* 'John Bacher' and *P. davidsonii* var. *menziesii* 'Albus', has thick, shiny, deep green leaves and masses of bright white flowers.

Penstemon x 'Winter Frost' has pale pink to lavender flowers and is a multiple cross of unknown Dasanthera species. It is a dwarf, gnarled shrublet with dense, glaucous, toothed foliage.

**Penstemon Section Hybrids**

Hybrids in this section are not common but bring some differences in height and color to a massed bed of penstemons.

Penstemon x 'Dusty', a cross between *P. confertus* 'Kittitas' and *P. peckii,* has bright yellow flowers.

Penstemon x 'Goldie', a cross between *P. confertus* and *P. euglaucus,* has bright yellow flowers.

Penstemon x 'Rose Queen', a cross of *P. calycosus* and *P. digitalis,* is tall and erect with deep pink flowers.

## Section Cristati Hybrids

Penstemon x 'Prairie Splendor' is a seed propagated line with large campanulate flowers that come in mixed pastel colors, from white to pink, rose and lavender. It is the result of crosses of *P. cobaea* and *P. triflorus.*

## Peltanthera Section Hybrids

These hybrids are found in the wild, but are not generally available as seed or in nurseries. In gardens where several of the Peltantheras are grown, hybrids are not uncommon.

Penstemon x *palmeri x spectabilis* occurred in an Albuquerque, NM garden.

## Habroanthus Section Hybrids

The two large sections of Habroanthus are Glabri and Elmigera. Glabri have blue and purple flowers (occasionally white or cream) and are usually secund; Elmigera have flowers in a variety of shades of red. Most of the hybridization that has been done in Canada and the United States has been between species in these two sections. The results are great hardiness and erect or vase-shaped plants with numerous stems and flowers.

Penstemon x 'Arroyo' is a cross between 'Prairie Fire' and *P. cardinalis* with red flowers and has a high degree of disease resistance.

Penstemon x 'Cambridge Mix' is a *P. barbatus* cross with pink and salmon colored shark's head shaped flowers.

Penstemon x 'Elfin Pink' is a *P. barbatus* hybrid with salmon-pink shark's-head shaped flowers, and grows 12 - 15" tall.

Penstemon x 'Flathead Lake' originated in the wild, parentage unknown, but is believed to be a cross of *P. barbatus* with *P. glaber, P. strictus* or another of the section Glabri. It has pink or red flowers with a shark's head shape and deep green lanceolate leaves. Many other hybrids have been produced using it as the receptor.

Penstemon x 'Indian Jewels' is a 'Flathead Lake' hybrid strain in many colors also sold as seed.

Penstemon 'Marshall Hybrids' were developed in Manitoba, Canada and are extremely hardy with a range of colors and sizes.

Penstemon x 'Mesa' is a cross of 'Flathead Lake' and a Habroanthus species producing red-purple flowers with deep purple guidelines that is very disease resistant.

Penstemon x 'Praecox Nana' is similar to 'Flathead Lake' but was developed in England.

Penstemon x 'Prairie Dawn' is a multi-species hybrid with non-secund flowers of pale, clear pink and grows to 28".

Penstemon x 'Prairie Dusk' is a cross of 'Flathead Lake' and *P. strictus* with deep purple flowers of shark's-head shape, two feet tall with a persistent mat of basal foliage and is disease resistant.

Penstemon x 'Prairie Fire' is a cross between 'Flathead Lake' and a *P. grandiflorus* hybrid with bright red flowers, strong stems and evergreen foliage.

Penstemon x 'Rondo' is a broad-leaved and many-colored mix of sturdy non-secund, erect flowers, 12 to 16" tall.

Penstemon x 'Rose Elf' is a deep pink, low-growing form of 'Flathead Lake' sold as a seed strain.

Penstemon 'Saskatoon Hybrids' is a Canadian strain available as plants or seeds in many colors.

Penstemon 'Scharf Hybrids' is a Canadian strain of 'Prairie Fire' crossed with *P. cardinalis* available as seeds or plants in many colors and of varying heights.

Penstemon x 'Utah State' is a vigorous grower with red-purple flowers developed at Utah State University; also known as the Pollard Hybrids .

## Section Coerulei Hybrids

There have been only a few hybrids among these species, usually involving *P. grandiflorus* and *P. murrayanus*. Many are no longer to be found.

Penstemon 'Fate Hybrids' have 2 - 3' stems and pale to medium colors in flowers with slender throats and with the *P. grandiflorus* form.

Penstemon x 'Prairie Jewel' has 2 - 3' erect stems with flowers in white, lavender, rose pink and deep purple-violet, and is a vigorous plant similar to *P. grandiflorus*. Available as a seed strain

Penstemon 'Seeba Hybrids' have 2 -3' erect stems with flowers in deep colors, similar to *P. grandiflorus* in form.

## Sections Peltanthera and Fasciculus

Penstemon x 'Mexicana' is a multi-cross strain developed by Bruce Meyer in Washington. It is a very hardy and disease resistant hybrid with dark green leaves bearing flowers in many colors from pink to purple with strongly marked throats.

Penstemon x 'Mexicali' is a cross of P. X 'Mexicana' with 'Sensation Hybrids', a half-hardy American hybrid in many colors, also created by Bruce Meyer, and has proven to be hardy to USDA Zone 4, producing bushy plants, bearing many campanulate flowers with wide-open white throats over a long period. 'Red Rocks' and 'Pikes Peak Purple' are trademarked named selections from within the 'Mexicali' hybrids. They have done well from Zone 4 - 8 in dry and humid climates.

**European or Large-flowered Hybrids**

The striking and gorgeous European hybrids were first produced from Mexican species *P. hartwegii* and *P. gentianoides. P. campanulatus, P. isophyllus, P. kunthii* and *P. cobaea* were incorporated into their parentage later. Most of these are not hardy species in USDA Zone 5 and the resulting hybrids are also less hardy, but some variation does exist in their hardiness. These hybrids are usually only planted in Zone 6 and above, and may or may not be long-lived. Most do their best in rich, loose soil that is moisture retentive, but still porous. They can become dessicated quite easily so are not successful in very dry climates. They are killed by abrupt drops in temperature and wet winters so it is always a good idea to have cuttings ready for replacement if you are in an area where the temperature is borderline for them. In appropriate climates they will bloom from June until November. Unfortunately, names are frequently not registered and there is disagreement about the names of many hybrids. You can purchase seed packets of large-flowered hybrids that will produce many similar to the named large-flowered hybrids and they are easy to grow in appropriate climates.

Penstemon x 'Alice Hindley' grows to a height of 3 - 4' and a width of 2' in rich garden soil and produces many large flowers with lavender tubes shading to blue-lavender lobes and a clear white throat. It has survived 15° F.

P. x 'Bev Jensen', sometimes listed as 'Ben Jensen', has broad red-violet flowers with a deep colored collar around the pale throat and striping within.

P. x 'Blackbird' is an outstanding dark, wine-red-flowered plant with long flowers loosely arranged on many willowy stems to 4' tall and 3' wide, with long, narrow, widely spaced leaves.

P. x 'Blue Midnight' ('Midnight') has deep blue-purple flowers and grows to 2 or 3'.

P. x 'Cerise Kissed' has vibrant red lips and a white throat on short compact plants 2' by 15". It blooms from summer until first frost.

P. x 'Cherry' has slender red tubular flowers gracefully arranged on 2 - 3' stems.

P. x 'Cherry Glow' has coral-red flowers in profusion on stems to 4' and blooms over a long period.

P. x 'Coral Kissed' is 2' tall by 2 ½ ' wide with large white flowers having coral-pink edges and buds.

P. x 'Elizabeth Cozzens' has orchid to lilac medium-sized flowers with red-violet striping in the throat. It is about 2 ½ by 2 1/2' at maturity.

P. x 'Evelyn' has slender pink flowers on fine-leaved bushy plants, 2 - 2 1/2' by 12 - 18".

P. x 'Firebird' or ('Schoenholzeri') or ('Ruby') has deep red flowers with a pale exserted staminode on a 3' bushy plant with burgundy stems.

P. x 'Garden Star' grows to 3' by 3' with 1" pale-throated pink flowers and bright green foliage.

P. x 'Garnet' or ('Andenken an Friedrich Hahn') is a very floriferous, 3' bushy plant with bright crimson flowers, marked with deeper stripes in the throat, and slender leaves.

P. x 'Ghent Purple' is only 15 - 18" tall with smaller flowers of plum purple with white throats striped in purple and serrate leaves.

P. x 'Hidcote Pink' is a free-flowering, robust plant to 3 1/4' by 3' with rose-pink flowers having white throats with numerous red markings.

P. x 'Hopley's Variegated' is a 2 ½ x 2 ½' plant with cream markings on the leaves and blue lavender flowers with white throats and purple markings.

P. x 'Joy' has salmon-colored flowers with white throats and broad foliage on plants 3' by 3'.

P. x 'King George V' has salmon-colored flowers with white throats streaked with red. It is an old hybrid from England that only grows to 20".

P. x 'Mother of Pearl' has pale lavender flowers with red striping in the throat and grows to 3'.

P. x 'Papal Purple' grows to 18" and has deep purple-red campanulate flowers in short panicles with good foliage that persists through the winter.

P. x 'Peace' grows to 2' and has pink buds that open to almost white flowers with pale pink lobes.

P. x 'Pennington Gem' has deep pink, gradually flaring flowers with white throats and forward extending lobes. It grows to better than 2' in favorable conditions.

P. x 'Purple Passion' has white-throated purple flowers on 3', stiffly upright stems in dense whorls. It was introduced from New Zealand.

P. x 'Raspberry Flair' is a 2' by 2' compact plant with densely-flowered stems of large lavender-purple flowers with red streaking in white throats.

P. x 'Rubicundus' has very large scarlet and white flowers up to 2 ¼" long on 2' stems. It is not like the species *P. rubicundus*

P. x 'Scarlet Queen' is a seed strain with large white-throated, scarlet flowers on 2 ¼' plants

P. x 'Snowstorm' ('White Bedder') has a bushy growth habit to 2 ¼' and almost pure white flowers. It is available as a seed strain.

P. x 'Sour Grapes' is a shorter plant, 2 - 3', having large flowers with blue-lavender tubes shading to pale red-violet lobes, a pale throat and guidelines within. There are several plants sometimes given this name. The original has not been identified so do not be disturbed if you acquire one with this name that is somewhat different.

P. x 'Stapleford Gem' is an erect plant to over 2' with numerous leafy stems and pale purple-blue campanulate flowers that shade to pink lobes and have a white throat with maroon markings.

P. x 'Thorn' has rather narrow leaves, grows to 2 ½' and has flowers with a cream-white tube and pink lobes.

P. x 'Wine Kissed' has large white-throated, deep red flowers on 2' stems forming broad clumps.

There are many other named hybrids in this group and nursery catalogs from the list in the appendix and other sources should be consulted for additions.

## Bedding Penstemons

These are half-hardy hybrids of various heights that are usually raised to be used as annuals. They have flowers all around the stem and come in a wide range of colors. Many are seed strains. They require good, rich, warm, well-drained soil and regular watering and will bloom continuously over a long season if dead-headed regularly. They may be purchased as ready-to-bloom plants in many nurseries. In mild climates they can be set out in the fall to begin blooming in April. In colder climates they can be started in the greenhouse in February, potted into 3" pots when they are about an inch tall, fertilized and grown on to be hardened off and set in the garden in late April or May. They have names such as 'Jingle Bells', 'Floradale Giants', 'Hyacinth-flowered', 'Petite Bouquet', 'Early Bird', 'Sensation' and 'Rainbow' mixes or seed strains.

**Chapter 4**

**Selecting, Growing and Caring for Penstemons**

What kinds of penstemons would you like to grow? Become familiar with the many types available. Plan where you want to use them. Consider what soil and sites you have and whether you will have to amend the soil or build up the area with better soil or sand and gravel to give penstemons the good aeration and drainage most require. Think about how much care you want to give them. One of the best things about penstemons is their low care requirement. Generally it is best to start with plants that are widely available in local nurseries. When you have had success with these you will want to go on to try many more and see just how many you can grow. You will become a 'penstemaniac'! **Don't be afraid to experiment, since penstemons are frequently more adaptable than would be expected based on native habitat!** The cultural limits of most species and varieties have <u>not</u> been determined and you may have micro-climates or soil conditions that will make it possible for you to grow many more than you would expect.

**For the Traditional Perennial Border** If you want to interplant with other garden classics and you live in an area that has a fairly mild climate, Zone 6 and above, you will probably want to select from the large-flowered European hybrids, west coast and eastern species and their cultivars. If you live in an area that has a more severe climate, Zone 5 and below, you will want Canadian and US hybrids, northern, mid-western and eastern species and their cultivars. The zone you are in does not tell you everything about what you will be able to grow, but it is a first indicator to assist beginners in selecting species. Generally it is best to start with plants that are widely available in local nurseries.

**For Pots and Containers** There are penstemons that will perform well in pots and bloom for a long time where the air is moderately humid. They may be discarded at the end of the outdoor season or severely cut back and brought into a cool storage area. The ones called Penstemon 'Gloxinoides' or European Hybrids and bedding types come in a riot of colors on the red side of the spectrum from deepest purple to the palest pink and white. Beautiful orchid and blue *Penstemon heterophyllus* and its named cultivars are also good choices for pot culture.

**As Annuals** Some penstemons can be used as annual bedding plants. They are half-hardy hybrid strains that come in many colors and heights. They bloom for a very long period and perform best in areas with a long, mild summer and fall. A few are hardier than others and may live and thrive for several years. Seeds need to be started in late fall and early winter in mild climates, or plants may be purchased and set out after the weather has settled. Look particularly for seed mixtures that have been bred for fully round, multi-stemmed plants. Those mentioned for use in pots are also useful as annuals.

**For Low Care** If you want plants that will require the least amount of soil preparation and watering, choose the wild species that grow in areas of similar conditions of soil, temperature and precipitation to yours from the lists in the appendix. Many can be reliable perennials for years. They can be planted with other local wildflowers from like locations in native grass fields and lawns, as colorful specimen plants or along walls and paths. Look for new garden styles that use penstemons in contemporary garden magazines and books. Penstemons' drought tolerance has made them an especially popular subject in recent years.

**For Rock Gardens, Slopes and Raised Beds** These sites provide ideal conditions for the greatest variety of species. You need to decide whether you will keep it fairly dry or water regularly. This will influence your selection of species to grow. Those from the northern states and alpine areas will perform better if watered regularly by normal precipitation or irrigation, especially in the spring. Those from normally arid regions can perform well if watered infrequently, perhaps not at all! This will depend on your soil and precipitation.

In general, the size of the rocks you have available and the size of the garden will determine which species will be best for you. With boulder-sized rocks, you can use penstemons that grow two to five feet tall! Large rocks can also be used to shelter smaller plants from full sun. Many penstemon species are particularly good in these situations because they have evergreen basal leaves that are attractive through the winter. They might turn a rich maroon or be covered with a downy surface that reflects light. There are also many with leaves in shades of gray, gray-blue and gray-green and almost white.

**Troughs** should be considered by those who are fond of miniature plants, don't have much room or cannot stoop to tend a garden. They are containers made of concrete, peat and perlite in any shape and 6 - 10 inches deep, that are usually raised off the ground so that tiny leaves and flowers can be appreciated without kneeling. The top of a stone retaining wall with crevices between stones offers a similar possibility. There are many charming small penstemon species that fit either type of location.

**To Attract Hummingbirds, Butterflies and Bees** The many southwestern species in all shades of red are well-known for their attractiveness to hummingbirds and should be planted near windows and outdoor sitting areas. **Please do not plant them if cats are around!** Butterflies are also attracted to many penstemons and bumblebees love the fat flowers of *P. palmeri,* which should be planted where its honey-like fragrance can be enjoyed. (Some people are highly allergic to bee stings and flowers that attract bees should not be planted where people will brush against them!)

**Soils**

Whatever style of garden and penstemons you select, you should have soil that is well aerated and drains quickly. This may mean digging deeply for a perennial bed or building a raised bed above the surroundings with a mix of coarse sand and fine gravel. It should be about 6" deep if you live in an area where precipitation is high or if your soil is an impervious clay. Many eastern and mid-western gardeners grow a great variety of penstemons, even species from arid sites, by building beds of sand and gravel above their normal soil or by creating slopes. Roots will travel down to anchor the plant in the soil, but the crown, the most vulnerable part of a plant, will be protected from standing water. Even in arid locations, the garden area selected should have good drainage, and often the plants will perform better and bloom longer if some humus and fine gravel and/or coarse sand are incorporated into the soil. Fine gravel will reduce capillary action in the soil and slow evaporation from the surface. Soil amendments such as peat moss and manure should be avoided, especially in dry climates. The best amendment is homemade compost (leaf mold and mushroom compost are also used) but it should be only a small percentage, except where you are growing hybrids. The American and Canadian hybrids do well in average to good soils but the large-flowered hybrids from milder climates require soil that is porous and holds enough moisture that plants never totally dry out. Most penstemons do not seem to be fussy about the soil pH, although slightly alkaline soils seems preferred by many species and hybrids. If your soil is quite acidic, it would be good to add some, pumice, ground oyster shell or something else that would bring it nearer to neutral.

## Exposure

The majority of penstemons thrive in full sun, but some prefer or tolerate sun for only part of the day or filtered sun. This has usually been mentioned in the descriptions. Where you live will have a great influence on how much light your penstemons receive.

In high precipitation areas and those with many cloudy days, the greatest amount of sun exposure possible will produce plants that grow erect and with the brightest, clearest colors from the hybrids, midwestern and western species. Eastern species that are paler in color will grow well and show to good advantage in areas of partial shade. Choosing an area with good drainage and where air moves freely about the plants will also be beneficial, and you will probably not be troubled with diseases. Most penstemons are well able to withstand wind and rain damage and will not need staking if they have all the light they need.

At high altitudes and in hot climates, many species that grow in full sun in their native locations often will bloom longer and fuller where they are shaded part of the day. There are a few tall-growing species such as *Penstemon comarrhenus* that do need full sun all day to develop strong stems that will not break off at the base when exposed to wind. Eastern species and hybrids will do well where they have only part-day sun exposure or filtered light. Hail will do little damage to any of the penstemons except the very large-flowered hybrids that have tender blooms and foliage.

Many penstemons are secund and should be placed so that the flowers will face the sun and the viewer. Although many penstemon flowers are beautiful when backlit, particularly the reds and those that are glandular-hairy, most will be enjoyed where they face the viewer and the sun.

Species that are quite open with medium or small, pale flowers are most effective against a dark background hedge, fence or wall.

## Purchasing Plants

Once you have decided what kind of plants you want to grow and where they will be planted, you are ready to purchase plants! You may prefer to raise most of your plants from seed yourself, but if you have seen some penstemons and are eager to grow them, you will want to purchase a few plants to enjoy while waiting the year or two that seeds take to become plants full of bloom.  (Don't be reluctant to buy a plant that you can't immediately think of a location for; you can enjoy and learn from it even if you don't have a perfect location!)

If you are looking for common ones, there will usually be many hybrid penstemons and a few species in most local independent nurseries.  Look for nurseries that specialize in wildflowers for more species.  You may even find some, such as 'Husker Red', *P. barbatus* hybrids and the 'Mexicali' hybrids in the giant hardware, discount and food store nurseries. **All plants should be carefully examined to be sure they are insect and disease-free before purchase.** Some growers recommend quarantining plants from unknown nurseries, plant sales or acquaintances for a few weeks. Plants should not have roots spiraling around the inner wall of the pot or extending through the drainage holes. Look for deep pots.  Unless you live in one of the unusual and  blessed areas where anything will grow, choose young, small plants as early in the spring as available.  You might call your local nurseryman or contact the many mail order suppliers listed in the appendix in the fall or winter to ask if you can obtain particular species that you want while they are small.  Too often local nurseries cater to those who will only buy plants when they see them in bloom.  This is fine for many plants; annuals particularly, but most perennials need a while to get well established in the garden before it is time for them to bloom, especially where late spring and  summer are hot and dry.  Some nurseries do "up-pot" their plants into soil that is close enough to garden soil that they can be transplanted directly into good garden soil during the late spring and summer without disturbing the roots, but a plant that has had a longer time to become established in the garden will generally perform better.  In areas where fall is long and winter comes gradually, young plants can be set out in late summer or early fall and will be very well established by their bloom time.  Consult other gardeners in your area about fall planting.

Although the many penstemon species grow wild around the country along roadsides, it is not a good idea to dig them from the wild.  Federal and state laws prohibit collection in most parts of the country and full grown plants do not survive digging.

**Planting Out**

**The following directions apply to gardeners in difficult climates such as high altitudes where the sun is strong and where temperatures and climate conditions can vary from mild to freezing any day in the planting seasons.  Those in gentler climates can probably plant young plants directly in the garden and shelter them from direct sun for a week to ten days, water regularly for the first growing season, and have great success.**

When you have small plants from local nurseries or mail order suppliers, prepare a soil mix that is similar to your garden soil but enriched with some compost, loosened with sand and moistened. Remove plants from their containers one at a time and wash the potting soil away by swishing in a bucket of water, or shaking it off if the roots are not too tangled, until the roots are bare.  Separate the roots and spread over some of your soil mix in a larger pot.  Firm additional soil mix among and over the roots and up to where stems break from the crown.  Water with a transplant solution and set the plants in a location where they are protected from strong winds and sun.  If they have just come from a coldframe or greenhouse they may also need protection from cold.  Gradually expose them to outdoor conditions when it is mild.  If they need watering again, set them in a tray of water only until the top of the pot shows moisture. Remove from the water tray. After two or three weeks they will be ready to set into prepared holes in the ground to which a small amount of slow-release fertilizer has been added. Be sure the crown is in the soil but not buried. Firm the soil around the crown and water with transplant solution to settle soil around the roots. Add more soil if the crown is exposed after the plant has been watered in. An up-ended basket or translucent row cover will be needed for several days after plants have been set out in case weather conditions suddenly become harsh.

## Fertilization

Wildflowers can grow very well without fertilizer, and many penstemons will perform well in some types of gardens without fertilizer. This does not mean that they should never be fertilized. Slow release fertilizer granules can be used in the spring when planting or cleaning up and diluted liquid fertilizer sprays may be applied before bloom and again later for long-blooming and reblooming varieties. Generally, the longer a plant blooms, the more often it should be fertilized, but never with heavy applications, and high nitrogen fertilizers should always be avoided.

## Watering

"Drought tolerant" is a vague term and means different things to different people. Penstemons are not as "drought tolerant" as a cactus, but some do grow and bloom in the same deserts as many cacti. Most penstemons have some degree of drought tolerance; even eastern and northern species require less water than do roses or annuals. Plants have many mechanisms to protect them from drying out such as woody stems, small leaves, thick leaves, and hair and other coatings on the leaves. They also have long roots that grow deeply into the soil if the soil is penetrable. These need to be watered deeply and infrequently. Generally, plants with large, thin, bright green leaves require more water than those with small or leathery or hairy leaves. The amount of water you need to apply will depend on the water-holding capacity of your soil, depth of the soil, natural humidity and precipitation and the origin of the varieties you have chosen. If you are growing local species and have improved your soil to some degree so that water sinks through it rapidly, you will rarely have to give them supplementary water after they have become well established. Creating wells around the plants is not necessary in soils that drain well. They can use extra water in the months before blooming and during the bloom period if precipitation is low. Drip irrigation, soaker hoses or hand watering are preferred watering methods. After blooming, watering can be reduced. Many species are surprisingly low in water usage in the west when given suitable light and soil conditions. **Most hybrids bred for garden conditions are not as drought tolerant as species and perform better with regular watering. The large-flowered hybrid species should never be allowed to dry completely.**

## Mulches

Penstemons need to have their crowns dry so a mulch that absorbs and retains water can be very damaging. If you want to mulch a bed that contains penstemons, choose a mulch that protects the soil from the sun but does not hold water. Hard shells, such as pecan, are attractive and are not generally water-holding unless applied to great depth. Shredded bark or ground tree trimmings, pine needles, pine and cedar duff can also be used. They should not be pulled right up to the crown. There are many types of gravel and grit available in most areas and they may be the best choice in arid climates. Look for regional products that do not retain water.

## Pruning

Little pruning is needed on penstemons but removing stems after flowering is completed helps to encourage the formation of new basal shoots and prolong the life of plants. Some species and many hybrids will have a second flush of bloom if cut back, particularly in long-summer areas. Many large-flowered hybrids and bedding types need only dead-heading rather than cutting back to bloom continuously. It is a good idea to leave a few of the lower seed capsules on a couple of stems to dry if you would like more plants of the same appearance. You can allow seeds to fall in place or capture them before the capsules open for growing more plants or sharing with other gardeners. Often birds will find fallen seed and plant it for you in surprising locations!

Large species, such as *P. palmeri* and *P. clutei* form thick, woody stems in their second and third years from which new shoots sprout at many closely spaced nodes. These should be thinned out to maintain the plant for four or more years.

Bushy plants such as *P. ambiguus*, *P. triphyllus* and *P. diphyllus* should be cut back to a few inches in fall or early spring and they will grow new herbaceous blooming stems.

The northwestern Dasanthera species, cultivars and hybrids frequently have leaves turn brown or lose most of their leaves when exposed to winter sun and dry conditions. They need to be cut back, but not until late spring to be sure you are not removing live wood. Sometimes old plants do not produce new growth in the center. This can be remedied by piling a loose, very gritty soil mix on top of the decumbent stems in the open area to encourage new growth. Continue this top-dressing throughout the year to mimic the scree conditions in which they are at home.

## Protection

If you have chosen species from your area, they usually will not need winter protection unless you have placed them in a location unlike that in which they naturally existed. In this case you may want to apply protection such as evergreen boughs for shade from strong sun or wind. Make use of micro-climates around your property when you select locations for plants.

## Pests, Insects and Disease

**Penstemons are generally less susceptible to pests than most plants if given appropriate growing conditions.** Older foliage and stems are bitter and rabbits, deer, quail, slugs, snails etc. generally do not like them if anything else is available. They may nip off stems and leave them, but do not eat the basal leaves unless conditions are extremely dry. The following lists of insects and diseases are seldom seen but have been reported on penstemons.

Although usually not severe, they can be quite damaging and unsightly in some situations. **The best defenses against insects and diseases are well-grown, healthy plants that are not under stress and are in sites where air moves freely, the soil drains well, debris is regularly removed and watering, if necessary, is done when the leaves will dry quickly. Overly fertilized plants with lush growth are more subject to attack than those with normal growth. <u>Integrated Pest Management</u> strategies are recommended as a first choice if you do have problems.** You can read about them in Organic Gardening books and on the Internet. Check with local plant specialists for recommendations if chemical controls are needed. Follow all label directions carefully when using chemicals to control pests on penstemons.

**Insects**

**Aphids** are small, less than 1/16 inch long, soft-bodied insects that suck juices from penstemon foliage. There are many species and they come in various colors and multiply rapidly. Symptoms of aphid feeding include curling leaves and leaf discoloration. They excrete a sticky residue which may attract ants, flies and other insects. They are more apt to occur in crowded borders and where air cannot move about the plants. They can spread diseases as well as distorting leaves, so should be attended to as soon as noticed. A strong spray with 2 tablespoons of liquid soap/gallon once or twice should get rid of them.

**Borers** are larvae that tunnel into flower stalks. Their presence is indicated by a hole with sap or a mealy material near it. Cut off the affected stem and crush it.

**Cutworms** can destroy plants by cutting them off near ground level. Young plants are most susceptible. They are usually not a problem except in gardens that are watered frequently. There are several granular products that can be sprinkled on the soil if they do become a problem.

**False Plant Bugs** are about 1/8 inch long and gray. They feed on young new shoots and can also destroy buds and blooms. Use insecticidal soap spray.

**Flea Beetles** of several species are insects up to ¼ inch long that can be seen jumping off foliage when the plants are disturbed. They may chew holes in the leaves and even devour whole leaves and plants. They usually do not bother healthy plants but may be found when plants are stressed. Many times, just shaking the plants gently will dislodge the beetles and they can be swept up or stomped. If they have laid eggs and the larvae are in the ground you will have to look for and go after them several times until no more appear. If you choose to use insecticides, apply at the first sign of them. Several applications will probably be needed. The plants should then be well-watered to alleviate stress.

**Grasshoppers** are plant feeders that may be a problem to all plants in dry years in the mid-west and west. They usually need to be attacked on a large scale when they first appear as they are very mobile. Most insect sprays do not affect mature grasshoppers.

**Lacebugs** are small insects, 1/8 inch long, that have clear wings with many veins as adults while their immature form is dark, spiny and wingless. They suck sap from plant parts and excrete a sticky fluid. Use insecticidal soap for control.

**Leafhoppers** are small, fast-moving, wedge-shaped insects that also suck sap from plants and are usually found on the underside of the leaves. They can spread some virus infections and if found should be treated immediately with an insecticide.

**Lygus Bugs** are small and brown, about 3/16 inch long, and damage plants by sucking out sap. They kill young growing tips and deform flowers. Use insecticidal soap for control.

**Pittosporum Pit Scale** is probably the most serious problem that can occur on penstemons because the insect is highly mobile, particularly among the Dasanthera and Caespitosi sections of penstemons and many other genera. The scale is flat with a tan to white-colored hard shell, approximately ¼ inch long. The toxin injected into the plant causes a 'pit-forming' response. The stems become swollen, distorted, stunted and discolored. If you see it when it is just getting started, immediately cut out any parts infected and get rid of them. Look for the active insect stage in late winter and early spring and spray all plants in the area with a refined horticultural oil in two applications a week to ten days apart. Systemic insecticide and insecticidal soap can also be used.

**Spider Mites** are minute members of Arachnida, not a true insect. They suck sap from leaves, leaving a whitish stippling on them that can lead to drying and death. They may also form a dense webbing. Often a strong spray of water, being sure to reach the underside of the leaves, will remove them. The plant should be watered well to restore vigor since healthy plants are less likely to be attacked.

**Thrips** are small 1/16 inch long slender insects that scurry around on plant parts. They like to hide in tight areas of the plants. They feed by rasping plant material and sucking the released sap. Nymphs are creamy white but adults come in various colors. All above ground parts of the plants are susceptible, but flowers and buds are particularly attacked. Infested buds, flowers and other parts become stippled and distorted and can have a sand-papered appearance, with small green fecal spots. Gently shake the plant to dislodge them and stomp or sweep up. If this fails to control them, use insecticidal soap spray for control.

**Verbena Bud Moth** larvae have a habit of tying leaves and buds together with a silky web. They may also move into seed capsules and feed on the developing seed. Remove as soon as spotted.

## Diseases

**Leaf Spot** attacks stems and leaves. Fungi are the cause and dark spots develop from which the middle often drops out, leaving a hole. Removal of affected leaves and stems, cleaning up in the fall and, only if it becomes a serious problem, application of an appropriate chemical control, are recommended. Many new varieties of cultivars and hybrids have been selected for disease resistance.

**Powdery Mildew** appears as a whitish, almost velvety growth on the surface of leaves. It can cause leaves to become distorted, discolored and die. Such leaves should be promptly removed. It is more prevalent in damp climates and as summer temperatures cool. Mid-western species are the most susceptible. Keep foliage dry as much as possible. Use a fungicide only for severe cases.

**Stem and Crown Rots** can be caused by a single disease organism or by a complex of diseases. Plants wilt and die quickly. Remove plants and do not replace with anything related. The best protection against this too frequent problem is to be sure soil is not over-watered and drains well.

**Damping Off** is primarily a problem with germinating seeds. Clean, sterile rooting mixtures and containers, good air movement, bright light and temperatures below 60 degrees F. will help avoid the problem.

**Viruses** have occasionally been reported to infect penstemons. Symptoms include stunting and leaf distortion. They are spread by aphids and leafhoppers. Remove and dispose of plants properly as soon as discovered. Never propagate infected plants. No cures have been found.

**Nematodes** can infect penstemon roots in rare cases. Irregular swellings are found on the roots of the plant when it is dug up after it has turned yellow or wilted and died. Plant should be removed and disposed of properly. Replace with other plants that are not susceptible.

**Rust** appears as spots filled with orange to reddish dust-like material which is actually a mass of microscopic spores. Most gardeners tolerate it and only try to control it with a fungicide in severe infections.

## Chapter 5

## Methods of Propagation

## Starting From Seeds

Propagating penstemons from seed can be an exciting and rewarding activity for a gardener. It is a thrill to bring into bloom plants from far away; especially ones that are not found in every garden in your area and ones that offer a challenge. Through the American Penstemon Society and many commercial seed collectors you can obtain seeds and grow varieties that will fill many special places in your garden.

It should be remembered that wild-collected seeds do not germinate as reliably as commercially grown seeds because their quality is dependent on the weather conditions of the area in which they were collected. They will germinate quite well when collected after a normal summer, but in years of drought may have a very low germination percentage. It is a good idea to sow a quantity of seed that is several times the number of plants you desire. The germination times given with the plant descriptions previously apply to seeds started in containers outside and are only to give you an idea of when to look for germination but are not a guaranteed time.

Penstemon seeds often germinate best after being stored dry for 6 months to a year, so do not discard seed that is not fresh. If you can collect seed yourself, store it in paper, not plastic, envelopes in a cool, dry location. You will usually get reasonable germination for about five years after collection, and possibly even longer for some species.

Many penstemon seeds require a long cool, moist **stratification** time before they will germinate. Almost every grower has his or her own method of accomplishing this. Probably the most common is to prepare a mix of new perlite and vermiculite and thoroughly dampen it, pack it into new or washed pots, sow the seed on top, press lightly and place them outside in the winter. The pots need to be protected from birds, rodents, insects and heavy, washing rains, but allowed to undergo variations in temperature in good light. Clean sand may also be used with the perlite and vermiculite, and the proportions of the ingredients should be adjusted so that the seeds of plants that grow in dry conditions are sown on a mix that contains less vermiculite. The seeds can be sown anytime from November through early March in cold climates and germination will begin when the weather warms up. Germination of wild seed often takes place over several months or years as nature's way of insuring that some plants will survive the vagaries of weather.

Another method of providing **stratification** is to place seeds on damp sand or perlite in a plastic fold-over sandwich bag with a plastic tag on which is written in pencil the name, date and seed source. Several of these are folded, bundled and placed in the refrigerator (not the freezer). They should be checked regularly to add a couple of drops of water if it has evaporated and removed from the refrigerator for planting at the first sign of germination. The seeds should immediately be placed on top of the soiless mix in the pots prepared as above and moved to a location where they get very bright light and gradually warming temperatures. A warm sun room will serve for a few days to get them growing, but they should be moved to a cool shed, basement, garage or porch where a bank of fluorescent lights can be hung 3 - 5 inches above them if they are not in daylight. The young seedlings can be fed with dilute solutions of fertilizer once they have true leaves. Growing at a temperature between 40 and 60 degrees F will keep them from drying out rapidly and prevent damping-off disease. The lights can be mounted so that they are parallel and on chains to be raised as the plants grow. It is convenient to have the lights on an automatic timer and set them to be on 14 - 16 hours a day. The plants should be separated into individual pots or containers in soil that is a mix of garden soil with sand, pumice or whatever lightener you prefer as soon as they have two pairs of true leaves. Use a transplant solution or root stimulator on them at this time. Completely soluble fertilizer, highly diluted, can also be added. Move the trays of pots outside when the weather is good and back under cover or under the lights if the temperature drops rapidly. They need gradual exposure to outdoor conditions of all types, including strong sun, wind and dryness. **In temperate climates**, when the seedlings have two or three pairs of leaves they can be planted out in prepared beds and covered with row cover. If you have a cold frame that does not get too hot they can be placed in it, but it is easy to lose small plants if the temperature inside rises too rapidly. In severe climates, plants grown at cool temperatures and exposed gradually to sun and wind are ready to go into the garden in early April while still quite small. When transplanted from pots into the garden, some protection such as an openwork basket or row cover should be used for a week. This method gets plants off to a rapid start, and is especially good for scarce seed and for the impatient gardener who can't stand the long wait through February and March to get growing!

If you have a generous amount of seed, the simplest and easiest way to start it is right in the ground. Choose a location that will be in the shade during the part of the winter when the sun is very low, but that rain and snow can reach. In the late fall, loosen the soil and scatter the seed thinly on top so it is spaced with enough room to move the plants after they have developed. Put a very thin layer of coarse sand or gravel over the seeds. You can then forget them until spring arrives and they begin sprouting as the sun reaches them! They will become sturdy plants, easy to transplant to permanent locations by the end of April.

These suggestions are only to help you get started. You will probably develop your own method that is best for the climate you have after your first year of growing penstemons from seed.

## Vegetative Propagation

There are several methods of vegetative propagation which are used to insure that new plants are identical to their parents. Seed propagation of wild plants does not produce identical plants. Vegetative methods of propagation include division, layering, cuttings and tissue culture. Tissue culture methods will not be covered here because of specialized equipment and facilities needed.

## Division

Many species of penstemons, from little ones to very big ones, and hybrid clumps can be divided to make several clumps after a couple of years. Those that can be divided are usually mentioned in the descriptions. If not, gently loosen the soil around the base to see if all the roots are coming off a single stem or if the crown divides into several rosettes; these are the ones you can divide. You may also want to divide plants that become less floriferous after several years when the clumps have become quite woody.

Sometimes a species grown from seed will produce one or more plants that are especially desirable for height, color or other qualities and you will want to reproduce them by division rather than just hoping that plants from their seed will have the same qualities. Division is a much surer and quicker way to have more of those very desirable plants.

To divide, water the plant well and dig it up the next day. Take it to a cool, shady location, wash off the soil and break it apart into sections so that each has some roots and a rosette of leaves. In temperate climates it may be replanted in the ground immediately. In harsher climates, place each of the sections into a pot of moist soil similar to that in which it was flourishing, water well with a transplant solution and place in a shaded location where it can recover. It is important to water pots of soil from the bottom, because soil may shrink from the sides of the pot and water applied at the top will run down the sides rather than penetrating the mass of soil and roots. Gradually bring it into bright sun and wind and when wilting no longer occurs it can be replanted in the ground. Water transplants regularly until well established.

In some locations, right after blooming is a good time to divide. In many locations it may be desirable to wait until the worst of the summer heat is over before dividing, or even divide plants that bloom long and late in early spring. This will depend on your climate and the plant you want to divide.

**Layering**

This is another form of division that is used to multiply plants that have stems that lay along the ground or spread along the ground before bending upward. You may see that some stems have already sent roots into the ground. These can be cut apart with a sharp knife without disturbing the mother plant. The new sections are then potted up and grown on or planted out immediately if the roots are sufficiently developed for the size of the section. If there are no roots on the spreading stems, remove some leaves and mound good soil around them. Sometimes you can gently bend a stem to the ground, remove leaves where it touches the ground and dust with rooting powder. It may be necessary to pin the stem with a bent wire to maintain close contact with the soil. Mound some good soil over the contact point. After several weeks, new roots and top growth will occur and the section can be removed and treated as a division. The Dasanthera section, Ericopsis section and *Penstemon pinifolius* are usually propagated this way.

A form of layering takes place naturally on *P. ambiguus*, but the new growth begins on underground stems or roots that cannot be seen. The new green stems will be several inches from the mother plant. When they have become firm in late August or September, depending on when the summer rains occured, a sharp, deep cut with a spade will separate the new plant and it can be planted in a new location or potted up to develop more roots if necessary.

## Cuttings

Another form of propagation that preserves the qualities of a specific plant and can produce many plants from one is to cut portions of the stems and force them to develop roots. This is very easy on some species, but not all. Tip cuttings are taken from non-flowering stems, or portions of flowering stems near the base can be used when they are firm but not woody. They may be taken from late spring through fall, depending on what facilities are available for growing and storing them until time to plant out. They should be just a few inches long, with four to six pairs of nodes, depending on the size of the plant and leaves and the spacing of the nodes. Gently remove leaves from the bottom of the stem so that one or two pairs of nodes are exposed. Cut just above the nodes still bearing leaves for the top cut. If leaves are large they may be cut in half. The dry cutting may be dusted with a rooting hormone powder or dipped in a root stimulating liquid, but should be tapped firmly to remove excess before insertion. The rooting medium can be a mix of perlite, vermiculite and/or sand, three to five inches deep. A soil heating cable below the rooting medium is used by many growers but is not absolutely necessary. Again, all materials used should be clean to avoid disease. The rooting medium should be well-dampened before the insertion. Open a hole or slice before the insertion so that rooting powder will not be rubbed off when inserting the cutting. Leaves should be above the rooting medium when the cutting is in place. Once the cuttings are firmed in, they will need warmth, light, but not direct sun, some air movement and humidity. The cuttings must not be allowed to wilt, but they must have some air movement about them to prevent disease. A greenhouse is an ideal location for growing cuttings, but it can be done in cold frames and in pots enclosed in clear plastic bags. The bags should not touch the leaves. A few small holes in the bag will prevent the mini-greenhouse from becoming too humid. Each species being propagated should be separate from others because they do not root at the same rate. When roots are well developed, the new plants are transferred to a soil mix and watered with a dilute liquid fertilizer until conditions are right for planting out.

**Chapter 6**

**Creating Your Own Hybrids**

There are many reasons for hybridizing flowers, not the least of which is delight in creating something entirely new. In addition, hybrids are sometimes more satisfactory garden plants and better adapted to your garden conditions because they have genes for adaptation from different sources. They may also have greater vigor. You may produce hybrids more adapted to your own climate and site by crossing species from mild climates with ones that do well in your garden. Many home gardeners have produced beautiful, hardy hybrids. The techniques are simple.

As mentioned in Chapter 3, hybrids do occur in the wild where species are within the same range and are not unusual within a subgenus such as Dasanthera. The Dasantheras that commonly produce many hybrids are *P. fruticosus, P. davidsonii, P. barrettiae, P. rupicola* and their subspecies. They are closely related and have the same pollinators so the chances are very good that the pollen of one species will be transferred to the pistil of another species. Many wild crosses may be multiple crosses. Less common are hybrids in other sections where the species are not in close proximity. These have been created in most cases by someone deliberately bringing the plants together to achieve crossing.

You should determine which penstemons you want to cross by deciding what results you want to achieve. It may be to create a shorter form, a hardier plant or a more rounded stem of flowers from one that is secund. Hybridization is usually considered easiest with species that belong to the same subsection or section, but not always. Pollen from plants that are hybrids will sometimes be more readily accepted by some species than pollen from other species

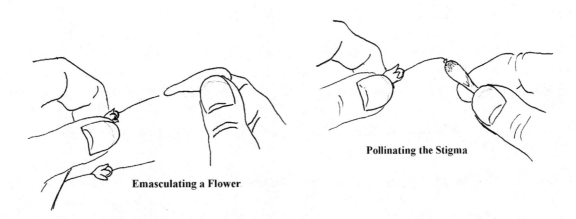

Pollinating the Stigma

Emasculating a Flower

The first step is to collect pollen from species or hybrids that will be used as the male parent. The pollen is collected on a pipe cleaner or Q-tip from flowers that have very recently opened if it is to be used immediately. It may also be collected into a capsule or small vial if it is to be preserved for later use, in which case it should be refrigerated. To be sure that it has not been contaminated with pollen from another species by wind or a visiting insect, some breeders collect the anthers before they open and place them in a warm and protected location until they have shed their pollen, which is then refrigerated.

The flowers to receive pollen are prepared by removing the anthers, staminode and petals, which is usually done just before the flower opens. This is called **emasculation.** To facilitate the pollination, all but one or two flowers are first removed from a cluster. The flowers to be pollinated must have the petals and anthers removed by grasping the sepals with the fingers of one hand and with the fingers of the other hand gently clasping the <u>lower</u> side of the outer end of the bud and pulling it forward. The pistil is in the roof of the bud so it is not damaged if only the lower side of the bud is held and carefully pulled away. What remains is the ovary, enclosed in the sepals, and the style with the stigma. The lobes or petals, staminode and anthers come off together. The stigma is usually not ready to receive pollen when the bud is first removed. It may be hours to days before you can see the small sticky knob develop at the outer end of the style to receive the pollen. Insects will not visit a flower that has been emasculated, but, to protect it from wind pollination, it can be enclosed in a small paper bag. The style will usually bend downward and a tiny sticky knob will be visible when it is receptive. It may be receptive for several days. The pollen, from a nearby plant or that which has been saved previously and refrigerated, is applied generously on the receptive stigma of the female parent. The pollinated stigma should be labelled immediately with a small string tag, giving the name of the female parent or receptor species, followed by an "x" and the name of the male or pollen donor species. With successful pollination, the style withers and the ovary begins to swell. It will take approximately six weeks, depending on species and weather conditions, for the seeds to ripen. The seeds should be collected after the capsule has turned brown, but before the capsule splits. Once the seeds are dried and harvested, the information on the tag can be transferred to the seed envelope. Unsuccessful pollinations should be part of the records you keep also.

When the seeds are grown out, some of the resulting plants will look like one parent and some like the other and some will be intermediate. (Remember Mendel?) Although you may not get the result you desire from the first generation, it is worthwhile to pollinate some of them again and grow future generations of the first cross and later ones since some characteristics may not show in the first generation. This can be a very exciting aspect of growing penstemons if you have patience! For those desiring more details on breeding penstemons, we recommend the book entitled <u>Breeding Ornamental Plants</u>" edited by D. J. and M. B. Callaway, from Timber Press, published in 2000. It has a chapter on penstemons.

You can produce plants that are more adapted to your climate by hybridizing ones that are not well adapted to your conditions and frequently lost with ones that are adapted and live many years. This was done by Bruce Meyers, a member of the American Penstemon Society in producing the Mexicali Hybrid. **Enjoy yourself with this rewarding hobby!**

## Appendix 1

## Some Penstemons Suggested for Beginners by Region

### Northeastern USA
*P. albertinus*
*P. barbatus* hybrids
*P. digitalis*
*P. hirsutus*
*P. ovatus*
*P. smallii*
*P. serrulatus*
American and Canadian hybrids
Meyer's Mexicali Hybrids

### Great Lakes, Ohio Valley, SE Canada
*P. albertinus*
*P. barbatus* hybrids
*P. digitalis*
*P. hirsutus*
*P. ovatus*
*P. smallii*
*P. strictus*
*P. virens*
Subsection Proceri species
American and Canadian hybrids
Meyer's Mexicali Hybrids

### Central USA and Canada
*P. angustifolius*
*P. cobaea*
*P. glaber*
*P. grandiflorus*
*P. mensarum*
*P. nitidus*
*P. secundiflorus*
*P. strictus*
*P. teucrioides*
*P. tubaeflorus*
American and Canadian hybrids

### Southeastern USA
*P. calycosus*
*P. canescens*
*P. digitalis*
*P. smallii*

*P. multiflorus*
*P. pallidus*
*P. tenuis*
*P. tubaeflorus*

### South Central USA
*P. cobaea*
*P. digitalis*
*P. laxiflorus*
*P. murrayanus*
*P. tenuis*
*P. triflorus*
*P. tubaeflorus*

### Desert Southwest
*P. ambiguus*
*P. barbatus*
*P. cardinalis*
*P. eatonii*
*P. linarioides*
*P. palmeri*
*P. parryi*
*P. pinifolius*
*P. pseudospectabilis*
*P. secundiflorus*

### Northwestern Coast, USA
### Southwestern Coast, Canada
### Great Britain and Europe
*P. albertinus*
*P. attenuatus*
*P. canescens*
*P. digitalis*
*P. heterophyllus*
*P. ovatus*
*P. pallidus*
*P. serrulatus*
*P. tenuis*
Subsection Proceri species
Subgenus Dasanthera species
European Large-flowered hybrids

# Appendix 2

## Native Species of Penstemons by Country, State and Province

### Canada

#### Alberta

*P. albertinus*
*P. albidus*
*P. confertus*
*P. ellipticus*
*P. eriantherus*
*P. gracilis*
*P. lyallii*
*P. nitidus*
*P. procerus*

#### British Columbia

*P. albertinus*
*P. attenuatus*
*P. confertus*
*P. davidsonii*
*P. ellipticus*
*P. eriantherus*
*P. fruticosus*
*P. gormanii*
*P. gracilis*
*P. lyallii*
*P. nitidus*
*P. ovatus*
*P. procerus*
*P. pruinosus*
*P. richardsonii*
*P. serrulatus*

#### Manitoba

*P. albidus*
*P. arenicola*
*P. eriantherus*
*P. gracilis*
*P. nitidus*

#### Northwest Territory

*P. gormanii*

#### Nova Scotia

*P. digitalis*

#### Ontario

*P. digitalis*
*P. gracilis*
*P. hirsutus*
*P. tubaeflorus*

#### Quebec

*P. digitalis*
*P. hirsutus*

#### Saskatchewan

*P. albidus*
*P. gracilis*
*P. nitidus*
*P. procerus*

#### Yukon Territory

*P. gormanii*
*P. procerus*

# Appendix 2

**United States    (\* indicates found only in this state)**

## Alabama

P. australis
P. calycosus
P. canescens
P. digitalis
P. laevigatus
P. laxiflorus
P. tenuiflorus

## Alaska

P. gormanii
P. procerus

## Arizona

P. albomarginatus
P. ambiguus
P. ammophilus*
P. angustifolius
P. barbatus
P. bicolor
P. breviculus
P. caespitosus
P. clutei*
P. comarrhenus
P. dasyphyllus
P. deaveri
P. discolor*
P. distans*
P. eatonii
P. fendleri
P. laevis
P. lanceolatus
P. lentus
P. linarioides
P. nudiflorus*
P. oliganthus
P. ophianthus
P. pachyphyllus
P. palmeri

P. parryi
P. petiolatus
P. pinifolius
P. pseudoputus
P. pseudospectabilis
P. ramosus
P. rostriflorus
P. rydbergii
P. stenophyllus
P. strictiformis
P. strictus
P. subulatus*
P. superbus
P. thompsoniae
P. thurberi
P. utahensis
P. virgatus
P. watsonii
P. whippleanus

## Arkansas

P. alluviorum
P. arkansanus
P. cobaea
P. digitalis
P. laevigatus
P. laxiflorus
P. pallidus
P. murrayanus
P. pallidus
P. tenuis
P. tubaeflorus

## California

P. albomarginatus
P. anguineus
P. azureus
P. barnebyi
P. bicolor
P. caesius*
P. calcareus*

P. californicus
P. centranthifolius
P. cinicola
P. clevelandii
P. confusus
P. davidsonii
P. deustus
P. eatonii
P. filiformis*
P. floridus
P. fruticiformis
P. gracilentus
P. grinnellii*
P. heterodoxus
P. heterophyllus
P. humilus
P. incertus*
P. janishiae
P. labrosus
P. laetus
P. miser
P. monoensis*
P. neotericus*
P. newberryi
P. palmeri
P. papillatus*
P. parvulus
P. patens
P. personatus*
P. procerus
P. pseudospectabilis
P. purpusii*
P. rattanii
P. roezlii
P. rostriflorus
P. rupicola
P. rydbergii
P. scapoides*
P. speciosus
P. spectabilis
P. stephensii*
P. sudans
P. thompsoniae

*P. thurberi*
*P. tracyi\**
*P. utahensis*
*P. venustus*

Colorado

*P. acaulis*
*P. albidus*
*P. alpinus*
*P. ambiguus*
*P. angustifolius*
*P. arenicola*
*P. auriberbis*
*P. barbatus*
*P. brandegeei*
*P. breviculus*
*P. buckleyi*
*P. caespitosus*
*P. cobaea*
*P. comarrhenus*
*P. crandallii*
*P. cyanocaulis*
*P. cyathophorus*
*P. debilis\**
*P. degeneri\**
*P. eatonii*
*P. eriantherus*
*P. fremontii*
*P. gibbensii\**
*P. glaber*
*P. glabrescens*
*P. gracilis*
*P. grahamii*
*P. grandiflorus*
*P. griffinii*
*P. hallii\**
*P. harbouri\**
*P. harringtonii\**
*P. humilis*
*P. jamesii*
*P. laricifolius*
*P. lentus*
*P. linarioides*
*P. mensarum\**
*P. moffatii*

*P. oliganthus*
*P. ophianthus*
*P. osterhoutii*
*P. pachyphyllus*
*P. penlandii\**
*P. procerus*
*P. procumbens\**
*P. radicosus*
*P. ramaleyi\**
*P. retrorsus\**
*P. rostriflorus*
*P. rydbergii*
*P. saxosorum*
*P. scariosus*
*P. secundiflorus*
*P. strictiformis*
*P. strictus*
*P. teucrioides\**
*P. utahensis*
*P. versicolor\**
*P. virens*
*P. virgatus asa-grayi*
*P. watsonii*
*P. whippleanus*
*P. yampaensis\**

Connecticut

*P. calycosus*
*P. digitalis*
*P. hirsutus*
*P. pallidus*
*P. tubaeflorus*

Delaware

*P. digitalis*
*P. hirsutus*
*P. pallidus*

Florida

*P. australis*
*P. laevigatus*
*P. laxiflorus*
*P. multiflorus*

*P. pallidus*
*P. tenuis*
*P. tubaeflorus*

Georgia

*P. australis*
*P. calycosus*
*P. canescens*
*P. dissectus\**
*P. laevigatus*
*P. laxiflorus*
*P. multiflorus*
*P. pallidus*
*P. smallii*

Idaho

*P. acuminatus*
*P. albertinus*
*P. aridus*
*P. attenuatus*
*P. compactus*
*P. confertus*
*P. cusickii*
*P. cyananthus*
*P. cyaneus*
*P. davidsonii*
*P. deustus*
*P. diphyllus*
*P. elegantulus*
*P. ellipticus*
*P. eriantherus*
*P. flavescens*
*P. fruticosus*
*P. gairdneri*
*P. glandulosus*
*P. globosus*
*P. humilis*
*P. idahoensis*
*P. janishiae*
*P. laxus\**
*P. lemhiensis*
*P. leonardii*
*P. lyallii*
*P. miser*

*P. montanus*
*P. nitidus*
*P. palmeri*
*P. payettensis*
*P. perpulcher\**
*P. pratensis*
*P. procerus*
*P. pumilis\**
*P. radicosus*
*P. rydbergii*
*P. seorsus*
*P. speciosus*
*P. subglaber*
*P. triphyllus*
*P. venustus*
*P. watsonii*
*P. whippleanus*
*P. wilcoxii*

## Illinois

*P. alluviorum*
*P. calycosus*
*P. deamii*
*P. digitalis*
*P. grandiflorus*
*P. hirsutus*
*P. pallidus*
*P. tubaeflorus*

## Indiana

*P. alluviorum*
*P. calycosus*
*P. canescens*
*P. deamii*
*P. digitalis*
*P. grandiflorus*
*P. hirsutus*
*P. pallidus*
*P. tubaeflorus*

## Iowa

*P. albidus*
*P. digitalis*

*P. gracilis*
*P. grandiflorus*
*P. pallidus*

## Kansas

*P. albidus*
*P. ambiguus*
*P. angustifolius*
*P. buckleyi*
*P. cobaea*
*P. digitalis*
*P. fendleri*
*P. grandiflorus*
*P. jamesii*
*P. pallidus*
*P. tubaeflorus*

## Kentucky

*P. alluviorum*
*P. brevisepalus*
*P. calycosus*
*P. canescens*
*P. digitalis*
*P. hirsutus*
*P. pallidus*
*P. tenuiflorus*

## Louisiana

*P. digitalis*
*P. laxiflorus*
*P. murrayanus*
*P. tenuis*
*P. tubaeflorus*

## Maine

*P. calycosus*
*P. digitalis*
*P. hirsutus*
*P. pallidus*
*P. tubaeflorus*

## Maryland

*P. calycosus*
*P. canescens*
*P. digitalis*
*P. hirsutus*
*P. laevigatus*
*P. pallidus*

## Massachusetts

*P. calycosus*
*P. digitalis*
*P. hirsutus*
*P. pallidus*
*P. tubaeflorus*

## Michigan

*P. calycosus*
*P. digitalis*
*P. hirsutus*
*P. pallidus*

## Minnesota

*P. albidus*
*P. digitalis*
*P. gracilis*
*P. grandiflorus*
*P. pallidus*

## Mississippi

*P. alluviorum*
*P. laevigatus*
*P. laxiflorus*
*P. tenuiflorus*
*P. tubaeflorus*

## Missouri

*P. alluviorum*
*P. arkansanus*
*P. calycosus*
*P. canescens*
*P. cobaea*

*P. digitalis*
*P. grandiflorus*
*P. pallidus*
*P. tubaeflorus*

Montana

*P. albertinus*
*P. albidus*
*P. angustifolius*
*P. arenicola*
*P. aridus*
*P. attenuatus*
*P. caryi*
*P. confertus*
*P. cyananthus*
*P. cyaneus*
*P. davidsonii*
*P. deustus*
*P. diphyllus*
*P. ellipticus*
*P. eriantherus*
*P. flavescens*
*P. fruticosus*
*P. gibbensii*
*P. glaber*
*P. gracilis*
*P. laricifolius*
*P. lemhiensis*
*P. lyallii*
*P. montanus*
*P. nitidus*
*P. payettensis*
*P. procerus*
*P. radicosus*
*P. rydbergii*
*P. whippleanus*
*P. wilcoxii*

Nebraska

*P. albidus*
*P. angustifolius*
*P. cobaea*
*P. digitalis*
*P. eriantherus*

*P. glaber*
*P. gracilis*
*P. grandiflorus*
*P. haydenii*
*P. tubaeflorus*

Nevada

*P. acuminatus*
*P. albomarginatus*
*P. ambiguus*
*P. arenarius**
*P. barnebyi*
*P. bicolor*
*P. comarrhenus*
*P. confusus*
*P. deustus*
*P. dolius*
*P. eatonii*
*P. floribundus**
*P. floridus*
*P. heterodoxus*
*P. humilis*
*P. immanifestus*
*P. janishiae*
*P. kingii*
*P. laetus*
*P. leiophyllus*
*P. leonardii*
*P. linarioides*
*P. miser*
*P. moriahensis**
*P. newberryi*
*P. pachyphyllus*
*P. pahutensis**
*P. palmeri*
*P. patens*
*P. patricus*
*P. petiolatus*
*P. pratensis*
*P. procerus*
*P. pseudospectabilis*
*P. pudicus**
*P. radicosus*
*P. rhizomatosus**
*P. roezlii*

*P. rostriflorus*
*P. rubicundus**
*P. rydbergii*
*P. speciosus*
*P. sudans*
*P. thompsoniae*
*P. tiehmii**
*P. utahensis*
*P. watsonii*

New Hampshire

*P. calycosus*
*P. digitalis*
*P. pallidus*
*P. tubaeflorus*

New Jersey

*P. digitalis*
*P. hirsutus*
*P. laevigatus*
*P. pallidus*
*P. tubaeflorus*

New Mexico

*P. alamosensis**
*P. albidus*
*P. ambiguus*
*P. angustifolius*
*P. auriberbis*
*P. barbatus*
*P. brandegeei*
*P. breviculus*
*P. buckleyi*
*P. cardinalis*
*P. cobaea*
*P. comarrhenus*
*P. crandallii*
*P. dasyphyllus*
*P. deaveri*
*P. eatonii*
*P. fendleri*
*P. gracilis*
*P. griffinii*

P. inflatus
P. jamesii
P. lanceolatus
P. lentus
P. linarioides
P. neomexicanus*
P. oliganthus
P. ophianthus
P. palmeri
P. parviflorus
P. pinifolius
P. pseudoparvus*
P. pseudospectabilis
P. ramosus
P. rostriflorus
P. rydbergii
P. secundiflorus
P. strictiformis
P. strictus
P. superbus
P. thurberi
P. virgatus
P. whippleanus

New York

P. calycosus
P. digitalis
P. hirsutus
P. pallidus

North Carolina

P. australis
P. calycosus
P. canescens
P. digitalis
P. laevigatus
P. pallidus
P. smallii

North Dakota

P. albidus
P. angustifolius
P. digitalis

P. eriantherus
P. glaber
P. gracilis
P. grandiflorus
P. nitidus
P. procerus

Ohio

P. alluviorum
P, brevisepalus
P. calycosus
P. digitalis
P. hirsutus
P. pallidus
P. tubaeflorus

Oklahoma

P. albidus
P. alluviorum
P. ambiguus
P. angustifolius
P. arkansanus
P. buckleyi
P. cobaea
P. digitalis
P. fendleri
P. grandiflorus
P. laxiflorus
P. murrayanus
P. oklahomensis*
P. tenuis
P. tubaeflorus

Oregon

P. acuminatus
P. anguineus
P. attenuatus
P. azureus
P. barrettiae
P. cardwellii
P. cinicola
P. confertus
P. cusickii

P. davidsonii
P. deustus
P. elegantulus
P. eriantherus
P. euglaucus
P. fruticosus
P. gairdneri
P. glandulosus
P. glaucinus*
P. globosus
P. gracilentus
P. heterophyllus
P. humilis
P. janishiae
P. kingii
P. laetus
P. miser
P. newberryi
P. ovatus
P. parvulus
P. payettensis
P. peckii*
P. pennellianus
P. pratensis
P. procerus
P. rattanii
P. richardsonii
P. roezlii
P. rupicola
P. rydbergii
P. seorsus
P. serrulatus
P. spatulatus*
P. speciosus
P. subserratus
P. triphyllus
P. venustus
P. wilcoxii

Pennsylvania

P. calycosus
P. canescens
P. digitalis
P. hirsutus
P. laevigatus

*P. pallidus*
*P. tubaeflorus*

## Rhode Island

*P. calycosus*
*P. digitalis*
*P. hirsutus*
*P. pallidus*
*P. tubaeflorus*

## South Carolina

*P. australis*
*P. canescens*
*P. laevigatus*
*P. smallii*

## South Dakota

*P. albidus*
*P. angustifolius*
*P. digitalis*
*P. eriantherus*
*P. glaber*
*P. gracilis*
*P. grandiflorus*
*P. nitidus*

## Tennessee

*P. alluviorum*
*P. brevisepalis*
*P. calycosus*
*P. canescens*
*P. digitalis*
*P. hirsutus*
*P. laevigatus*
*P. pallidus*
*P. smallii*
*P. tenuiflorus*
*P. tubaeflorus*

## Texas

*P. albidus*

*P. ambiguus*
*P. arkansanus*
*P. baccharifolius*
*P. barbatus*
*P. buckleyi*
*P. cardinalis*
*P. cobaea*
*P. dasyphyllus*
*P. digitalis*
*P. fendleri*
*P. grandiflorus*
*P. guadalupensis**
*P. havardii*
*P. jamesii*
*P. lanceolatus*
*P. laxiflorus*
*P. murrayanus*
*P. superbus*
*P. tenuis*
*P. triflorus**
*P. tubaeflorus*
*P. wrightii**

## Utah

*P. abietinus**
*P. acaulis*
*P. ambiguus*
*P. ammophilus**
*P. angustifolius*
*P. arenicola*
*P. atwoodii**
*P. barbatus*
*P. bracteatus**
*P. breviculus*
*P. caespitosus*
*P. carnosus**
*P. comarrhenus*
*P. compactus*
*P. concinnus*
*P. confusus*
*P. crandallii*
*P. cyananthus*
*P. cyanocaulis*
*P. deustus*
*P. dolius*

*P. duchesnensis**
*P. eatonii*
*P. eriantherus*
*P. flowersii**
*P. franklinii**
*P. fremontii*
*P. goodrichii**
*P. grahamii*
*P. humilis*
*P. immanifestus*
*P. laevis*
*P. leiophyllus*
*P. lentus*
*P. leonardii*
*P. linarioides*
*P. longiflorus**
*P. marcusii**
*P. moffatii*
*P. montanus*
*P. nanus**
*P. navajoa*
*P. ophianthus*
*P. osterhoutii*
*P. pachyphyllus*
*P. palmeri*
*P. parvus**
*P. patricus*
*P. petiolatus*
*P. pinorum*
*P. platyphyllus**
*P. procerus*
*P. pseudoputus*
*P. radicosus*
*P. rostriflorus*
*P. rydbergii*
*P. scariosus*
*P. sepalulus**
*P. speciosus*
*P. strictiformis*
*P. strictus*
*P. subglaber*
*P. thompsoniae*
*P. tidestromii**
*P. tusharensis**
*P. uintahensis**
*P. utahensis*

P. virgatus
P. wardii*
P. watsonii
P. whippleanus
P. yampaensis*

Vermont

P. calycosus
P. digitalis
P. hirsutus
P. pallidus

Virginia

P. australis
P. brevisepalis
P. canescens
P. digitalis
P. hirsutus
P. laevigatus
P. pallidus
P. smallii

Washington

P. acuminatus
P. attenuatus
P. barrettiae
P. cardwellii
P. confertus
P. davidsonii
P. deustus
P. diphyllus
P. ellipticus
P. eriantherus
P. euglaucus
P. fruticosus

P. gairdneri
P. glandulosus
P. humilis
P. ovatus
P. pennellianus
P. procerus
P. pruinosus
P. richardsonii
P. rupicola
P. rydbergii
P. serrulatus
P. speciosus
P. subserratus
P. triphyllus
P. venustus
P. washingtonensis*
P. wilcoxii

West Virginia

P. brevisepalus
P. canescens
P. digitalis
P. hirsutus
P. laevigatus
P. pallidus

Wisconsin

P. digitalis
P. gracilis
P. grandiflorus
P. hirsutus
P. tubaeflorus

Wyoming

P. absarokensis*

P. acaulis
P. albidus
P. alpinus
P. angustifolius
P. arenicola
P. aridus
P. attenuatus
P. caespitosus
P. caryi
P. cyananthus
P. cyaneus
P. cyathophorus
P. deustus
P. ellipticus
P. eriantherus
P. fremontii
P. fruticosus
P. gibbensii
P. glaber
P. gracilis
P. grandiflorus
P. humilis
P. laricifolius
P. montanus
P. nitidus
P. pachyphyllus
P. paysoniorum*
P. procerus
P. radicosus
P. rydbergii
P. saxosorum
P. secundiflorus
P. strictus
P. subglaber
P. virens
P. virgatus
P. watsonii
P. whippleanus

# Appendix 2

## Mexico and Guatemala

### Aguascalientes

P. miniatus
P. hidalgensis
P. imberbis
P. lanceolatus
P. coriaceus

### Baja California

P. angelicus*
P. californicus
P. centranthifolius
P. clevelandii
P. eximeus*
P. labrosus
P. rostriflorus
P. thurberi
P. vizcainensis*

### Cedros Island

P. cerrosensis*

### Chiapas

P. gentianoides

### Chihuahua

P. ambiguus
P. amphorellae
P. barbatus
P. campanulatus
P. dasyphyllus
P. fasciculatus
P. fendleri
P. filisepalis
P. gentryi
P. kunthii
P. lanceolatus
P. miniatus

P. mohinoranus
P. occiduus
P. pinifolius
P. rotundifolius
P. stenophyllus
P. superbus
P. wislizenii

### Coahuila

P. amphorellae
P. barbatus
P. baccharifolius
P. campanulatus
P. dasyphyllus
P. henricksonii
P. lanceolatus

### Durango

P. barbatus
P. campanulatus
P. dasyphyllus
P. lanceolatus
P. miniatus
P. occiduus
P. plagapineus
P. salterius
P. stenophyllus
P. vulcanellus
P. wislizenii

### Guanajuato

P. amphorellae
P. campanulatus
P. coriaceus
P. hidalgensis
P. imberbis
P. kunthii
P. potosinus

### Guerrero

P. hintonii
P. kunthii

### Hidalgo

P. campanulatus
P. hartwegii*
P. hidalgensis
P. kunthii
P. tenuifolius

### Jalisco

P. bolanius*
P. hidalgensis
P. imberbis
P. kunthii
P. lanceolatus
P. miniatus
P. tenuifolius
P. coriaceus

### Mexico & D.F.

P. campanulatus
P. gentianoides
P. hidalgensis
P. kunthii
P. miniatus
P. miniatus

### Michoacan

P. barbatus
P. campanulatus
P. gentianoides
P. kunthii
P. miniatus

Morelos

*P. campanulatus*
*P. kunthii*
*P. miniatus*

Nayarit

*P. kunthii*
*P. miniatus*
*P. plagapineus*
*P. tepicensis*

Nuevo Leon

*P. baccharifolius*
*P. campanulatus*
*P. lanceolatus*
*P. leonensis*

Oaxaca

*P. gentianoides*
*P. isophyllus*
*P. kunthii*
*P. miniatus*
*P. perfoliatus*

Puebla

*P. campanulatus*
*P. gentianoides*
*P. isophyllus*
*P. kunthii*
*P. miniatus*

Queretaro

*P. hidalgensis*
*P. kunthii*

San Luis Potosi

*P. campanulatus*
*P. coriaceus*
*P. hidalgensis*

*P. imberbis*
*P. lanceolatus*

Sinaloa

*P. plagapineus*
*P. wislizenii*

Sonora

*P. barbatus*
*P. campanulatus*
*P. dasyphyllus*
*P. gentryi*
*P. miniatus*
*P. parryi*
*P. pinifolius*
*P. stenophyllus*
*P. superbus*

Tamaulipas

*P. baccharifolius*
*P. campanulatus*
*P. lanceolatus*

Tlaxcala

*P. kunthii*

Vera Cruz

*P. gentianoides*
*P. miniatus*

Zacatecas

*P. coriaceus*
*P. hidalgensis*
*P. imberbis*
*P. lanceolatus*
*P. miniatus*
*P. moronensis*
*P. occiduus*
*P. tenuifolius*

Penstemons have not been reported in the remaining states of Mexico.

**Guatemala**

*P. gentianoides*
*P. skutchii\**

# Appendix 3

## Finding Penstemons in the Wild

Anyone who has travelled any distance in the western states during the spring and summer months has seen penstemons along the roadsides if they are interested in the vegetation. Many species grow best in gravelly roadsides and highway departments are beginning to use penstemons in their seed mixes when they replant after new construction or rebuilding of roads.

In the eastern and central states it is not as easy to find penstemons in the wild. Many are woodland species and do not show along the roadsides. Some are almost endangered species even in the states where they are native, and the traveller seeking them out will need to make inquiry of local Native Plant Societies and Wildflower and Garden Clubs. You can also visit herbaria in universities and botanical gardens to get information on where to look for specific wildflowers.

A few tall white or pale pink or lavender species show in the rough borders of fields as you drive through the states of Arkansas, Missouri, Oklahoma and Kansas in May. Once you become aware of them, you will spot them more easily.

One way to see penstemons is to visit National, State and County Parks. Many have botanists among their staff and have made plant lists for visitors. They can also tell you the best time to plan a trip to see flowers in bloom, as it may vary from March in southern California or Arizona to the middle of July at high elevations of the northern states. A general inquiry early in the year and again when the blooming season has begun will be helpful in planning a trip. When you arrive, you can get specific directions for areas where bloom is peaking.

The following lists will give you some ideas for planning trips. They are by no means all the places to look, but a good start!

**Northwest US**

<u>**Washington**</u>
**Mt. Ranier:** most in late June and early to mid-July
*Penstemons fruticosus, serrulatus, ovatus, confertus, procerus, rupicola, davidsonii*
**Olympic National Park:** late June and July
*Penstemons davidsonii, ovatus, procerus, serrulatus*
**Cascades:** May - August
*Penstemons davidsonii, fruticosus, procerus, serrulatus*

<u>**Oregon**</u>
**Crater Lake:** late June - August
*Penstemons davidsonii, rupicola, rydbergii, speciosus*

## Idaho
**Craters of the Moon:** mid-June - late July
*Penstemons cusickii, cyaneus, deustus, laxus, speciosus*
**City of Rocks National Reserve:** June - August
*Penstemons attenuatus ssp. militaris, cyananthus ssp. subglaber, humilis, procerus*

## Wyoming
**Grand Teton National Park:** late June through August
*Penstemons attenuatus, cyananthus ssp. subglaber, cyaneus, deustus, ellipticus, montanus, procerus, radicosus, rydbergii, subglaber, whippleanus*
**Yellowstone National Park:** mid-June through August
*Penstemons arenicola, attenuatus, cyaneus, deustus, eriantherus, fruticosus, humilis, montanus, procerus, radicosus, rydbergii, whippleanus*
**Devils Tower:** May through June
*Penstemons albidus, eriantherus, glaber, gracilis, grandiflorus*

## Montana
**Glacier National Park:** late June and July
*Penstemons albertinus, albertinus x wilcoxii, attenuatus, confertus, ellipticus, eriantherus, lyallii, nitidus, procerus, rydbergii, wilcoxii*
**Bighorn Canyon National Recreation Area:** May, June and July
*Penstemons aridus, caryi, eriantherus, glaber, humilis, laricifolius, nitidus, radicosus*

## Southwestern US

## California
**Lassen Volcanic National Park:** June and July
*Penstemons cinicola, davidsonii, deustus* var. *pedicillatus, neotericus, newberryi, rydbergii* var. *oreocharis, speciosus* and *newberryi* x *davidsonii*
**Death Valley National Park:** June
*Penstemons calcareus, floridus* var. *austinii, fruticiformis, palmeri, rostriflorus, scapoides, speciosus*
**Pinnacles National Monument:** April to July
*Penstemons centranthifolius, heterophyllus*
**Lava Beds National Monument:** late May through early July
*Penstemons humilis, deustus, laetus, speciosus*
**Joshua Tree National Monument:** mid-April through June
*Penstemons centranthifolius, clevelandii, eatonii, fruticiformis, incertus, stephensii, thurberi*
**Yosemite National Park:** June to August
*Penstemons azureus, davidsonii, heterodoxus, laetus, newberryi, procerus, rostriflorus, rydbergii, speciosus*
**Sequoia and Kings Canyon National Parks:** May to August
*Penstemons azureus, caesius, davidsonii, grinnellii, heterodoxus, laetus, newberryi, papillatus, parvulus, procerus, rostriflorus, rydbergii, speciosus*

## Nevada
**Great Basin National Park:**  June and July

*Penstemons confusus, eatonii, humilis, leiophyllus* var. *francisci-pennellii, miser, pachyphyllus, palmeri, rostriflorus, speciosus, watsonii*


## Utah
**Zion National Park:**  early April to August

*Penstemons ambiguus, barbatus, caespitosus, comarrhenus, confusus, eatonii, humilis, "x jonesii", a natural cross of laevis and eatonii* var. *undosus, laevis, leiophyllus, leonardii* var. *higginsii, linarioides* var. *sileri, pachyphyllus* var. *congestus, palmeri, rostriflorus, utahensis*

**Bryce Canyon National Park:**  May - July

*Penstemons bracteatus, caespitosus, comarrhenus, eatonii, leiophyllus, rostriflorus, rydbergii*

**Cedar Breaks National Monument:**  July and August

*Penstemons eatonii, leiophyllus, rydbergii, whippleanus*

**Rainbow Bridge National Monument:**  May and June

*Penstemon ambiguus*

**Arches National Park:**  April - June

*Penstemons cyanocaulis, eatonii, utahensis*

**Canyonlands National Park:**  April - August

*Penstemons barbatus, cyanocaulis, eatonii, fremontii, palmeri, utahensis*

**Natural Bridges National Monument:**  April - August

*Penstemons angustifolius, comarrhenus, cyanocaulis, eatonii, fremontii, lentus* var. *albiflorus, pachyphyllus, palmeri, rostriflorus, strictiformis, strictus*

**Capitol Reef National Park:**  April - September

*Penstemons ambiguus, angustifolius, barbatus, caespitosus, carnosus, comarrhenus, eatonii, leiophyllus, ophianthus, pachyphyllus, palmeri, rostriflorus, strictiformis, strictus, utahensis*

**Hovenweep National Monument:**  May - July

*Penstemons angustifolius, barbatus, palmeri, strictus, virgatus*

**Grand Staircase- Escalante National Monument:**  April - September

*Penstemons atwoodii, barbatus, carnosus, comarrhenus, confusus, eatonii, laevis, leiophyllus, linarioides, ophianthus, pachyphyllus, palmeri, rostriflorus,  thompsoniae, utahensis, watsonii,* x *jonesii*


## Arizona
**Chiricahua National Park:**  May - November

*Penstemons barbatus, linarioides, pinifolius, pseudospectabilis* ssp. *connatifolius*

**Sunset Crater Volcano National Monument:**  June - September

*Penstemons barbatus, clutei, jamesii, linarioides, virgatus*

**Organ Pipe Cactus National Monument:**  Februray - May

*Penstemons parryi, pseudospectabilis*

**Grand Canyon National Park:**  February - June

*Penstemons barbatus, caespitosus, eatonii, lentus, linarioides, ophianthus, pachyphyllus, palmeri, pseudoputus, pseudospectabilis, rostriflorus, rydbergii, utahensis, virgatus*

**Saguaro National Park:** March - October
*Penstemons barbatus, linarioides, parryi, pseudospectabilis*

## Colorado
**Mesa Verde National Park:** May - October
*Penstemons angustifolius, barbatus, comarrhenus, eatonii, jamesii, linarioides, ophianthus rostriflorus, strictiformis, strictus*
**Colorado National Monument:** May - July
*Penstemons comarrhenus, crandallii, cyanocaulis, moffatii*
**Black Canyon of the Gunnison National Park** April - July
*Penstemons eatonii, strictus, teucrioides, virgatus, watsonii*
**Rocky Mountain National Park:** late May - August
*Penstemons confertus, glaber, hallii, harbourii, rydbergii, secundiflorus, virens, virgatus* ssp. *asa-grayi, whippleanus*
**Great Sand Dunes National Monument:** May - July
*Penstemons angustifolius, barbatus, crandallii, secundiflorus, virgatus* ssp. *asa-grayi*
**Dinosaur National Monument:** May - July
*Penstemons angustifolius, angustifolius* ssp. *vernalensis, arenicola, caespitosus, fremontii, humilis, pachyphyllus* var. *mucronatus, radicosus, scariosus* var. *cyanomontanus, scariosus, strictus, watsonii*

## New Mexico
**Chaco Culture National Historic Park:** May - July
*Penstemons angustifolius, angustifolius* ssp. *caudatus, barbatus, barbatus* ssp. *trichander*
**Capulin Volcano National Monument:** June, July and August
*Penstemons, angustifolius, barbatus, jamesii*

**Central US**

## North Dakota
**Theodore Roosevelt National Park:** late May - mid-July
*Penstemons albidus, angustifolius, eriantherus, gracilis, nitidus*

## South Dakota
**Badlands National Park:** May - July
*Penstemons albidus, angustifolius, eriantherus, glaber, gracilis, grandiflorus*
**Wind Cave National Park:** May - late July
*Penstemons albidus, angustifolius, glaber, gracilis, grandiflorus*

## Nebraska
**Scotts Bluff National Monument:** May - September
*Penstemons angustifolius, angustifolius* var. *caudatus, glaber*

## Arkansas
**Hot Springs National Park:** April - July
*Penstemons arkansanus, digitalis, laxiflorus, tubaeflorus*

**Texas**
**Big Thicket National Preserve:** April - June
*Penstemons murrayanus, tenuis, laxiflorus*
**Guadalupe Mountains National Park:** April - August
*Penstemons ambiguus, barbatus, cardinalis, dasyphyllus, fendleri, triflorus* ssp. *integrifolius*
**Big Bend National Park:** April - October
*Penstemons baccharifolius, barbatus* ssp. *torreyi, dasyphyllus, fendleri, havardii, lanceolatus,*
    *wrightii*

**Eastern US**

**Virginia**
**Shenandoah National Park:** June
*Penstemons canescens, laevigatus*
**Tennessee**
**Great Smoky Mountains National Park:** May - July
*Penstemons canescens, brevisepalus, smallii*

## Appendix 4

**Penstemons in Nurseries, Botanical Gardens and City Parks**

Serious gardeners know that there is much to be learned by visiting gardens across the world. Gardens that are open to the public have a mission to show a wide variety of plants that can be grown in their region. It is in the interest of nurserymen also to present new and different plants. Many have display gardens. Some are already growing a variety of penstemons and will be happy to point them out to you and talk about other varieties. By letting them know of your interest you can encourage them to experiment with new species, cultivars and hybrids. Check the phone books wherever you go for nurseries that have display gardens.

Some public gardens that almost always have a selection of penstemons on display in season are:

**United States**
National Wildflower Research Center, 4801 La Crosse Ave., Austin, TX
San Antonio Botanic Gardens, 555 Funston Pl., San Antonio, TX,
Rio Grand Botanic Garden, 2601 Central Ave, NW, Albuquerque, NM
Tucson Botanical Gardens, 2150 N. Alvernon Way, Tucson, AZ
Tohono Chul Park, 7366 North Paseo del Norte, Tucson, AZ
Arizona-Sonora Desert Museum, 2021 North Kinney Rd., Tucson AZ
Boyce Thompson Southwestern Arboretum, Superior, AZ
Desert Botanical Garden, 120 North Galvin Parkway, Phoenix, AZ
University of California at Riverside, CA
Rancho Santa Ana Botanic Gardens, 1500 N. College Ave, Claremont, CA
Theodore Payne Foundation, 10459 Tuxford Street, Sun Valley, CA
Berry Botanic Garden, 11505 SW Summerville Ave, Portland, OR
Leach Botanical Garden, 6704 SE 122nd Ave., Portland, OR
Bellevue Botanical Garden, 12001 Main Street, Bellevue, WA
Red Butte Garden and Arboretum, 300 Wakara Way, Salt Lake City, UT
Denver Botanic Garden, 1005 York Street, Denver, CO
Hudson Gardens, 2888 West Maplewood Ave., Littleton, CO
Betty Ford Alpine Garden, Vail, CO
Missouri Botanical Garden at Gray's Summit, MO
Chicago Botanic Garden, 1000 Lake Cook Rd., Glencoe, IL
University of Nebraska, West Central Center, North Platte, NE

**Canada**
Butchart Gardens, 800 Benvento Ave., Brentwood Bay, Victoria, British Columbia
Devonian Botanic Garden, University of Alberta, Edmonton, Alberta
Montreal Botanic Garden, Montreal, Quebec
**Great Britain**
Royal Botanic Garden, Edinburgh, Scotland
Royal Horticultural Society Garden at Wisley, England

# Appendix 5

## The Classification of the Genus Penstemon

   To call up mental pictures of nearly 300 penstemon species is an impossibility. By placing them into a classification system based on the appearance of the opened anthers of the flowers, they do fall into six subgenera that have different characteristics.

   Two species are so different from each other and all other penstemon species that they are placed in their own subgenera. Another subgenus, Dasanthera, includes nine similar species. The remaining three subgenera are further divided into sections and some of these are divided into subsections.

| The Subgenera | Sections | Subsections |
|---|---|---|
| Cryptostemon | | |
| Dissecti | | |
| Dasanthera | | |
| Saccanthera | Bridgesiani | |
| | Saccanthera | Serrulati |
| | | Heterophylli |
| Habroanthus | Glabri | |
| | Elmigera | |
| Penstemon | Ambigui | |
| | Baccharifolii | |
| | Chamaeleon | |
| | Coerulei | |
| | Cristati | |
| | Ericopsis | Caespitosi |
| | | Ericopsis |
| | | Linarioides |
| | Fasciculus | Campanulati |
| | | Fasciculi |
| | | Perfoliati |
| | | Racemosi |
| | Peltanthera | Centranthifolii |
| | | Havardiani |
| | | Peltanthera |
| | | Petiolati |
| | Penstemon | Arenarii |
| | | Deusti |
| | | Gairdneri |
| | | Harbouriani |
| | | Humiles |
| | | Multiflori |
| | | Penstemon |
| | | Proceri |
| | | Tubaeflori |

**Subgenus Cryptostemon**
*Penstemon personatus*

**Subgenus Dissecti**
*P. dissectus*

**Subgenus Dasanthera**
*P. barrettiae*
*P. cardwellii*
*P. davidsonii*
*P. ellipticus*
*P. fruticosus*
*P. lyallii*
*P. montanus*
*P. newberryi*
*P. rupicola*

**Subgenus Saccanthera**
**Section Bridgesiani**
*P. rostriflorus*
**Section  Saccanthera**
Subsection  Serrulati
*P. diphyllus*
*P. glandulosus*
*P. richardsonii*
*P. serrulatus*
*P. triphyllus*
*P. venustus*
Subsection  Heterophylli
*P. azureus*
*P. caesius*
*P. cusickii*
*P. filiformis*
*P. floribundus*
*P. gracilentus*
*P. heterophyllus*
*P. kingii*
*P. laetus*
*P. leonardii*
*P. neotericus*
*P. papillatus*
*P. parvulus*
*P. patricus*
*P. platyphyllus*
*P. pudicus*

*P. purpusii*
*P. rhizomatosus*
*P. roezlii*
*P. scapoides*
*P. sepalulus*
*P. tiehmii*

**Subgenus Habroanthus**
**Section Glabri**
*P. absarokensis*
*P. alpinus*
*P. ammophilus*
*P. brandegeei*
*P. caryi*
*P. comarrhenus*
*P. compactus*
*P. cyananthus*
*P. cyaneus*
*P. cyanocaulis*
*P. deaveri*
*P. debilis*
*P. fremontii*
*P. gibbensii*
*P. glaber*
*P. hallii*
*P. idahoensis*
*P. laevis*
*P. leiophyllus*
*P. lemhiensis*
*P. longiflorus*
*P. mensarum*
*P. moriahensis*
*P. navajoa*
*P. neomexicanus*
*P. nudiflorus*
*P. pahutensis*
*P. parvus*
*P. payettensis*
*P. paysoniorum*
*P. penlandii*
*P. pennellianus*
*P. perpulcher*
*P. pseudoputus*
*P. saxosorum*
*P. scariosus*
*P. speciosus*

*P. strictiformis*
*P. strictus*
*P. subglaber*
*P. tidestromii*
*P. uintahensis*
*P. virgatus*
*P. wardii*
**Section Elmigera**
*P. barbatus*
*P. cardinalis*
*P. eatonii*
*P. henricksonii*
*P. imberbis*
*P. labrosus*
*P. wislizenii*

**Subgenus Penstemon**
**Section Ambigui**
*P. ambiguus*
*P. thurberi*
**Section Baccharifolii**
*P. baccharifolius*
**Section Chamaeleon**
*P. dasyphyllus*
*P. lanceolatus*
*P. ramosus*
*P. stenophyllus*
**Section Coerulei**
*P. acuminatus*
*P. angustifolius*
*P. arenicola*
*P. bracteatus*
*P. buckleyi*
*P. carnosus*
*P. cyathophorus*
*P. fendleri*
*P. flowersii*
*P. grandiflorus*
*P. harringtonii*
*P. haydenii*
*P. immanifestus*
*P. lentus*
*P. nitidus*
*P. osterhoutii*
*P. pachyphyllus*
*P. secundiflorus*

*P. versicolor*
**Section Cristati**
*P. albidus*
*P. atwoodii*
*P. auriberbis*
*P. barnebyi*
*P. breviculus*
*P. calcareus*
*P. cobaea*
*P. concinnus*
*P. distans*
*P. dolius*
*P. duchesnensis*
*P. eriantherus*
*P. franklinii*
*P. goodrichii*
*P. gormanii*
*P. grahamii*
*P. guadalupensis*
*P. jamesii*
*P. janishiae*
*P. marcusii*
*P. miser*
*P. moffatii*
*P. monoensis*
*P. nanus*
*P. ophianthus*
*P. pinorum*
*P. pumilus*
*P. triflorus*
**Section Ericopsis**
<u>Subsection Caespitosi</u>
*P. abietinus*
*P. acaulis*
*P. caespitosus*
*P. crandallii*
*P. glabrescens*
*P. procumbens*
*P. ramaleyi*
*P. retrorsus*
*P. teucrioides*
*P. thompsoniae*
*P. tusharensis*
*P. yampaensis*
<u>Subsection Ericopsis</u>
*P. laricifolius*

<u>Subsection Linarioides</u>
*P. californicus*
*P. discolor*
*P. linarioides*
**Section Fasciculus**
<u>Subsection Campanulati</u>
*P. bolanius*
*P. campanulatus*
*P. coriaceus*
*P. gentryi*
*P. hintonii*
*P. kunthii*
*P. potosinus*
*P. tepicensis*
<u>Subsection Fasciculi</u>
*P. fasciculatus*
*P. filisepalis*
*P. gentianoides*
*P. hartwegii*
*P. isophyllus*
*P. leonensis*
*P. miniatus*
*P. mohinoranus*
*P. occiduus*
*P. pinifolius*
*P. plagapineus*
*P. skutchii*
<u>Subsection Perfoliati</u>
*P. hidalgensis*
*P. moronensis*
*P. perfoliatus*
<u>Subsection Racemosi</u>
*P. amphorellae*
*P. salterius*
*P. tenuifolius*
*P. vulcanellus*
**Section Peltanthera**
<u>Subsection Centranthifolii</u>
*P. alamosensis*
*P. centranthifolius*
*P. cerrosensis*
*P. confusus*
*P. parryi*
*P. patens*
*P. subulatus*
*P. superbus*

*P. utahensis*
*P. wrightii*
<u>Subsection  Havardiani</u>
*P. havardii*
*P. murrayanus*
*P. rotundifolius*
<u>Subsection Peltanthera</u>
*P. angelicus*
*P. bicolor*
*P. clevelandii*
*P. clutei*
*P. eximeus*
*P. floridus*
*P. fruticiformis*
*P. grinnellii*
*P. incertus*
*P. palmeri*
*P. pseudospectabilis*
*P. rubicundus*
*P. spectabilis*
*P. stephensii*
*P. vizcainensis*
<u>Subsection Petiolati</u>
*P. petiolatus*
**Section Penstemon**
<u>Subsection Arenarii</u>
*P. albomarginatus*
*P. arenarius*
<u>Subsection Deusti</u>
*P. deustus*
*P. sudans*
*P. tracyi*
<u>Subsection Gairdneriani</u>
*P. gairdneri*
*P. seorsus*
<u>Subsection Harbouriani</u>
*P. harbouri*
<u>Subsection Humiles</u>
*P. albertinus*
*P. anguineus*
*P. aridus*
*P. degeneri*
*P. elegantulus*
*P. griffinii*
*P. humilis*
*P. inflatus*

*P. metcalfei*
*P. oliganthus*
*P. ovatus*
*P. pruinosus*
*P. pseudoparvus*
*P. radicosus*
*P. rattanii*
*P. subserratus*
*P. virens*
*P. whippleanus*
*P. wilcoxii*

Subsection Multiflori

*P. multiflorus*

Subsection Penstemon

*P. alluviorum*
*P. arkansanus*
*P. australis*
*P. brevisepalis*
*P. calycosus*
*P. canescens*
*P. deamii*
*P. digitalis*
*P. gracilis*
*P. hirsutus*
*P. laevigatus*
*P. laxiflorus*
*P. oklahomensis*
*P. pallidus*
*P. smallii*
*P. tenuiflorus*
*P. tenuis*

Subsection Proceri

*P. attenuatus*
*P. cinicola*
*P. confertus*
*P. euglaucus*
*P. flavescens*
*P. glaucinus*
*P. globosus*
*P. heterodoxus*
*P. laxus*
*P. peckii*
*P. pratensis*
*P. procerus*
*P. rydbergii*
*P. spatulatus*

*P. washingtonensis*
*P. watsonii*

Subsection Tubaeflori

*P. tubaeflorus*

# Appendix 6

## Sources of Seeds, Plants and other Supplies

### Seed Sources

American Penstemon Society ($10.00 Membership required)
1569 South Holland Court
Lakewood, Colorado 80232

North American Rock Garden Society ($25.00 Membership required)
P.O. Box 67
Millwood, NY 10546

### Commercial Seed Sources

Northwest Native Seed
17595 Vierra Canyon Rd. #172
Prunedale, CA 93907 3352
E- mail oreonana@mbay.com

Plants of the Southwest
3095 Agua Fria
Santa Fe, NM 87507
Website: www.plantsofthesouthwest.com

Rocky Mountain Rare Plants
1706 Deerpath Rd.
Franktown, CO 80116-9462
Website: www.rmrp.com

Southwestern Native Seed
Box 3727
Show Low, AZ 85902

Thompson and Morgan, Inc.
P. O. Box 1308
Jackson, NJ 08527
Website: www.thompson-morgan.com

Western Native Seed
P. O. Box 188
Coaldale, CO 81222
719-942-3935
info@westernnativeseed.com

## Plant Sources that Ship

Agua Fria Nursery
1409 Agua Fria
Santa Fe, NM 87501
Call 505- 983-4831 or write for catalog

Arrowhead Alpines
P. O. Box 857
Flowerville, MI 48836
Call 517-223-3581
Website: www.arrowheadalpines.com

Bluestone Perennials
7211 Middle Ridge Rd.
Madison, OH 44057
800 - 852 - 5243
Website: www.bluestoneperennials.com

Digging Dog Nursery
P. O. Box 471
Albion, CA 95410
Phone 707-937-1130
e-mail business@diggingdog.com
Website: www.diggingdog.com

Forestfarm
990 Tetherow Rd.
Williams, OR 97544
Website: www.forestfarm.com

Goodwin Creek Gardens
P. O. Box 83
Williams, OR 97544
800 - 846-7359
Website: www.goodwincreekgardens.com

Heronswood Nursery
7530 N. E. 288th St.
Kingston, WA 98346
Website: www.heronswood.com

High Country Gardens   (Santa Fe Greenhouses)
2904 Rufina Street
Santa Fe, NM 87505
800 - 925-9387
Website: www.highcountrygardens.com

Joy Creek Nursery
20300 NW Watson Rd.
Scappoose, OR 97056
Website: www.joycreek.com

Pacific Rim Native Plants(75+ species of penstemons are shipped from WA;
44305 Old Orchard Road  others can be custom grown if seed is available)
Chilliwack, BC V2R 1A9
Canada
e-mail  plants @ hillkeep.ca
Website:  www.hillkeep.ca

Paradise Gardens Rare Plant Nursery
Rt. 1 Box2630, Bonners Ferry, ID 83805
Website  www.paradisegds.homestead.com

Pine Ridge Gardens
P. O. Box 200
832 Sycamore Rd.
London, AR  72847
Website:  www.pineridgegardens.com

Plants of the Southwest
3905 Agua Fria
Santa Fe, NM 87507
Website:  www. plantsofthesouthwest.com

Siskiyou Rare Plant Nursery
2825 Cummings Rd.
Medford, OR 97501
Website:  www. siskiyourareplantnursery.com

Sunscapes Rare Plant Nursery
330 Carlile Avenue
Pueblo, CO 81004
Website:  www.sunscapes.net

## Other Supplies:

**We highly recommend that you obtain a 10x hand lens for the pleasure it will bring you.**

Science Kit & Boreal Laboratories    Offers several from  $5.95 - $9.50
777East Park Drive
P. O. Box 5003
Tonawanda, NY 14151
(800) 828 3299
www.sciencekit.com

Edmund Scientific Offers several from $24.95
60 Pearce Ave.
Tonawanda, NY 14150
(800 728 6999
www.scientificsonline.com

**For the gardener who would like to experiment with many varieties of penstemons, deep and narrow conetainers are most convenient. They can be obtained with a rack that holds 98 of them from:**

Green Valley Garden Supply, P. O. Box 2209, Grass Valley, CA 95945  www.groworganic.com

## Appendix 7

**Judging Penstemons in Flower Shows**

When penstemons are submitted for display in the horticultural section of flower shows, some guidelines for judging them can be useful. The following scale of points for judging specimen penstemons was prepared by Leslie Schroader, a certified judge for the National Council of Garden Clubs.

*Individual cut specimens are usually placed in a clear glass container with water for display. If the schedule calls for more than one stem of the same cultivar, hybrid or species, uniformity must also be considered.*

| | | |
|---|---|---|
| **Color:** | True to variety, consistent, clear, intense | 25 |
| **Florets:** | Typical of variety, consistency of placement, uniformity of placement, sturdy attachment | 15 |
| **Form:** | Open florets, buds showing color, total inflorescence | 15 |
| **Stem:** | Robust, proportioned to foliage and floriferousness | 10 |
| **Foliage:** | Consistent with variety, uniform size and attachment; rich, uniform color patterns | 10 |
| **Substance and Texture:** | Firmness, thickness and durability | 10 |
| **Conditioning And Grooming:** | Free of spray residue, mechanical injury, insects, diseases, yellowing foliage, dead or dying florets, etc. | 10 |
| **Correct and Legible Label:** | Genus, species and cultivar names | 5 |
| **Total** | | 100 |

*Collections are a group of specimens, with a minimum of five specimens, judged for cultural perfection, with artistic effect secondary. All must be grown by the exhibitor and each displayed in a separate container, but exhibited as a group. Each specimen is judged as above and the group judged with the following criteria.*

| | | |
|---|---|---|
| **Cultural Perfection:** | Accurate to the cultivar description | 35 |
| **Color:** | Clear, bright, harmonious | 20 |
| **Number, Size, Form:** | | 15 |
| **Typical Habit:** | | 15 |
| **Conditioning and Grooming:** | | 10 |
| **Naming:** | | 5 |
| **Total** | | 100 |

## Appendix 8

## Other Books on Penstemons

There are many books which contain information about penstemons. When you have become a 'Penstemaniac', you will want to consult some of them. Because penstemons are found in all the states except Hawaii, you can consult local and regional Floras in your library or, if you don't find them there, in Botanical Garden and University Libraries. Particularly recommended because of the large number of species they include are <u>Intermountain Flora,</u> Volume Four from the New York Botanical Garden and <u>The Jepson Manual</u> for California.

These books are written by botanists usually and will require you to become familiar with the vocabulary of botany. A most useful book for that purpose is <u>Plant Identification Terminology</u> <u>An Illustrated Glossary</u> by James G. and Melissa Woolf Harris. Spring Lake Publishing, P. O. Box 266, Payson, UT 84651. Copyright 1994

Other books:

Heflin, Jean. Copyright 1997. <u>Penstemons, The Beautiful Beardtongues of New Mexico</u>
    Available from the New Mexico Native Plant Society c/o Lisa Johnson 505-748-1046
    \<cityhall@artesia.net

Lodewick, Robin and Kenneth. <u>Key to the Genus Penstemon,</u> 1999 and
    Penstemon Nomenclature 3rd Edition 2002.
    Available from Kenneth Lodewick, 2526 University Street, Eugene, Oregon 97403

Nold, Robert. <u>Penstemons</u> 1999 Timber Press 1333 S. W. Second Avenue, Suite 450, Portland, OR 97204

Strickler, Dee. <u>Northwest Penstemons</u> 1997
    Available from The Flower Press, 192 Larch Lane, Columbia Falls, MT 59912

Way, David and James, Peter. <u>The Gardener's Guide to Growing Penstemons</u> 1998
    Timber Press 1333 S. W. Second Avenue, Suite 450, Portland, OR 97204

## Application for Registration of New Cultivar or Hybrid

Proposed Name_____

Applicant_____

Address_____

City_____State_____Zip_____

Telephone_____E-mail_____Business?_____

Describe the origin of the new cultivar or hybrid, giving where found, parentage if known, how it differs from typical species, or other cultivars or hybrids, whether it comes true from seed, how long it has been grown, how long it lives, best means of propagation. Include photo, slide or CD if possible.

Plant size:  Height_____; Width of plant in bloom_____

Do stems grow_____upright, _____ascending,_____prostrate?

Stem leaves: Length_____Width_____Shape_____Attachment_____

Basal leaves: Length_____Width_____Petioled?_____Persistent through winter?_____

Type of

Inflorescence_____Secund?_____Length_____Width_____

Approximate duration of bloom_____

Recurrent bloom?_____Continuous?_____

Individual Flower Description:  Shape_____Length_____Width at throat_____

Pressed width including lobes_____

Description:  Color(s), Guidelines?_____Other markings_____

Anthers after opening:_____

Staminode_____

.............................................................................................................................

**Number assigned by Registrar_____Date_____**

**Signature of Registrar_____**

This form may be duplicated.

Mail to:  Dr. Dale T. Lindgren
West Central Research and Extension Center
        461 West University Drive
        North Platte, NE 69101-7756

## Membership in the American Penstemon Society

The American Penstemon Society is dedicated to the advancement of knowledge about penstemons, their introduction into cultivation and the development of new and improved cultivars. The society was formed in 1946 by a group of gardeners who had been collecting and growing penstemons in many different parts of the country. Their purpose is to grow and study all species possible, to promote the use and enjoyment of penstemons in gardens, to study penstemons in the wild and promote their conservation, to aid in the identification of penstemons, and to acquaint penstemon enthusiasts with each other. Members are also active in hybridizing and selecting superior forms for gardens. We invite you to join us in studying, growing and enjoying North America's loveliest wildflowers.

The **Seed Exchange** is an invaluable service of the Society. Members send in seed from their gardens and from the wild and it is redistributed to other members once a year on request at very modest cost.

**Round Robins** or correspondence circles are an important part of the society's program. They are the means through which members share their experiences and their knowledge of penstemons. Through them the members become acquainted with each other and they often lead to visits to other parts of the country and life-long friendships.

The **Bulletin of the American Penstemon Society** is published twice yearly and mailed to every member and a number of libraries. Articles cover all aspects of penstemons, from cultivation and germination to announcements of new species and cultivars, reports of new findings, excerpts from Round Robins of particular interest, and announcements and reports of trips.

An **Annual Meeting** takes place somewhere in the country each year to which all members are invited. It usually consists of planned field trips to see penstemons in the wild, visits to gardens and a program and business meeting.

**The Slide Collection and Library** are available for borrowing by members for the cost of postage.

Membership in the American Penstemon Society is $10.00 a year for US and Canadian Memberships. Overseas membership is $15.00, which includes 10 free selections from the Seed Exchange. US Life membership is $200.00. Dues are payable in January of each year. Checks or money orders in US funds only, please, should be made payable to the American Penstemon Society and may be sent to Ann Bartlett, Membership Secretary, 1569 South Holland Ct., Lakewood, CO 80232 USA together with your name and address and a few words about your interests.

## Ordering Information for Book, CD and Photo Portfolio

All orders for this book from the US, Canada and Mexico should be sent to

Infinity Publishing.com
519 West Lancaster Avenue
Haverford, PA 19041-1413

or
www.buybooksontheweb.com

or for additional information,
(877)289-2665

It will not be available from other sources for about a year.

Orders from overseas may be sent with payment in US funds to
APS Books and CDs
in care of
Ellen Wilde, 110 Calle Pinonero, Santa Fe, NM 87505

Overseas airmail shipping will be $9.00

The CD will be $25.00 plus $3.00 shipping. It will have photos of 220 species
in several aspects plus information and maps and photos of cultivars and hybrids.
It can be used on Windows or Mac equipment.
You will be able to transfer photos from it to your hard drive.

The Portfolio of Penstemon Species will have whole plant portraits of over
100 species, not including those used on the book cover, in alphabetical order,
so that the pages can be removed and slipped into the book.
It will sell for $12.00 plus $3.00 shipping.

All orders for the CD and Photo Portfolio should be sent to
APS Books and CDs as above.

All photographs are copyrighted by the photographers and APS

# NOTES

# NOTES

# NOTES

**NOTES**

# NOTES

# NOTES